WHEN PRINCIPLES PAY

WHEN PRINCIPLES PAY

Corporate Social Responsibility
and the Bottom Line

Geoffrey Heal

Columbia University Press

Publishers Since 1893

New York   Chichester, West Sussex

Copyright © 2008 Columbia University Press

Library of Congress Cataloging-in-Publication Data

Heal, G. M.

When principles pay : corporate social responsibility and the bottom

line / Geoffrey Heal.

p.   cm.

Includes bibliographical references and index.

ISBN 978-0-231-14400-1 (cloth : alk. paper)—ISBN 978-0-231-51293-0 (e-book)

1.   Social responsibility of business—Economic aspects. 2.   Profit—Moral

and ethical aspects. 3.   Industrial management–Social aspects. 4.   Social justice.

5.   Business ethics—Case studies. I.   Title. II.   Title: Corporate social

responsibility and the bottom line.

HD60.H398   2008

658.4'08—dc22   2008002767

∞

Columbia University Press books are printed on permanent and durable

acid-free paper.

Printed in the United States of America

c 10 9 8 7 6 5 4 3 2 1

To my wife and daughters

> We have always known that heedless self-interest was bad
> morals; we know now that it is bad economics.
>
> —Franklin Delano Roosevelt, January 20, 1937

Are principled behavior and profitable behavior intrinsically in conflict, or can corporations do well and also do good? Newspaper headlines suggest a conflict—we see stories of mortgage companies enriching themselves by predatory lending to poor families, defense contractors entering into improper relationships with defense department officials, coal companies and automobile companies lobbying aggressively to allow continued emissions of greenhouse gases, and investment banks and rating agencies packaging junk bonds as high-quality debt. These examples all suggest that businesses have found it necessary to behave in an unprincipled fashion to make money. The headlines, however, give only part of the story: what you can easily miss is that some of the worst predatory lenders are now bankrupt, the defense contractor executives responsible for improper relationships with the defense department have been fired and the company fined, and many of the investment bankers responsible for the excesses of the structured finance binge of 2006 and 2007 will have lost their jobs by the time this book is in print. True, the auto companies and coal companies are still lobbying aggressively—but almost as if to spite them the world's most valuable and profitable car company is Toyota, which has positioned itself as the green car company par excellence. Perhaps the headlines are misleading; perhaps there is a cost to antisocial corporate behavior that is felt on a slightly longer timescale than the apparent gains. And of course headlines are notoriously biased—they only tell us what is deemed newsworthy, and good behavior is rarely as newsworthy as bad. So we don't see headlines telling us that for the last decade BP has been reducing its greenhouse gas emissions voluntarily, that Starbucks works to reduce the environmental impact of coffee production, or that Nike and other footwear and textile makers are working to monitor and improve labor conditions at their subcontractors. Nor do we see headlines telling us that stock markets penalize companies for poor environmental behavior or that socially responsible investment (SRI) funds shun the "sin stocks" of companies with poor social or environmental records. Yet all of these things are true.

There is indeed a temptation to cut social and environmental corners in pursuit of short-term profits, but there are widespread and increasingly powerful forces that penalize those who transgress and reward those who do not. This book is about these two sets of forces and the balance between them. In fact, as most of us are only too aware of why it is tempting to cut corners, most of the book is about the countervailing forces, the forces that reward those who behave well and penalize the corner-cutters. These forces are not so obvious, and some will probably surprise you, especially the role of capital markets.

The main point that I want to make is that our market-based economy and its political environment are evolving fast, particularly with respect to the treatment of behavior that is socially or environmentally damaging. What is "acceptable behavior" is changing; furthermore, penalties are routinely associated with unacceptable behavior, as are rewards with acceptable behavior. These incentives operate outside of the marketplace in the strict and narrow sense and involve interactions between corporations, regulatory bodies, consumers, and civil society in the form of nongovernmental organizations (NGOs) and activist groups. Taken together, these interactions can significantly change the attractions of the alternatives facing a corporation. They can make antisocial behavior much less attractive than it might have been only a decade or so ago. Consumers or regulatory bodies, spurred on in many cases by NGOs or other activist groups acting through the Internet, can react quickly to behavior that they disapprove of, in the process damaging a company's prospects.

The chapters that follow give many examples. Stock markets have come to anticipate some of these consequences and mark down the shares of companies opening themselves up to such damages. In part, this is due to the activities of SRI funds, but the effect seems to go beyond anything that can be explained by the scale of these funds. Chapters 2 and 3 explore these issues.

Subsequent chapters study how these issues play out in particular industries and companies—the financial sector and Citibank, pharmaceuticals and Merck, Wal-Mart, Starbucks, Monsanto, and Interface. We then switch to a global perspective, looking at globalization, child labor, and marketing goods and financial services to the very poor. Then we try to bring all this together from the perspective of corporate executives.

This is an optimistic book. It starts from the premise that capitalism—as we knew it from the 1950s to the end of the last century—was massively successful at generating income and economic growth but often at the expense of the natural environment and sometimes at the expense of the underprivileged. The growing environmental and social costs of economic activity were daunting and seemed to some to call into question the whole enterprise of economic growth. Now things are changing: they have not yet changed enough, but we can see where they are going; we can see the outline of a new system in which we can enjoy the undoubted benefits of a competitive market economy without the social or environmental costs. It is a system in which the forces that I describe in this book have grown stronger and become more clearly articulated—a system where consumers and civil society groups, together with activist shareholders and SRI funds, play an increasing role in shaping the incentives faced by the corporate world. It is a system in which principles pay.

WHEN PRINCIPLES PAY

1

Introduction

Goodness is the only investment that never fails.

—Henry David Thoreau

Companies face choices on environmental and social issues. They can worry about pollution or greenhouse gas emissions, or ignore them. Likewise, they can be concerned about employment conditions in third-world subcontractors, or neglect them. This book is about the incentives that they face in making these choices. Are there incentives that lead a corporation to minimize its environmental impact, or to take a stance that is supportive of minorities and of the less privileged members of society? Or are the forces that they face neutral on these issues or even oriented in the opposite directions? These questions matter. Corporations have profound impacts on society in many ways over and above the obvious one of producing goods and services for us. They can generate pollution, drive globalization, employ low-paid labor in poor countries, and contribute to climate change, to name only a few. Their actions in these areas are controversial. So it matters whether they face incentives to direct these impacts in a manner consistent with the social good. I am going to argue that in many cases they do. But an important part of the argument is that this does not happen automatically: it happens as the result of the interaction of a range of non-market forces involving the legal system, the regulatory framework, and, increasingly, civil society. The theme of this book is therefore the interactions between corporate behavior and civil and legal society, and how these interactions structure the company's incentives on social and environmental issues.

It is not just the actions of corporations that are controversial: there is controversy over a more basis set of issues, namely the responsibilities of corporations on social and environmental matters. There are diverse opinions on this, ranging from a sense that a corporation has open-ended obligations to most of society and is a vehicle for correcting many social ills to the contrary position that its obligations go no further than making profits for its shareholders. Corporations themselves differ on these issues: the Business Roundtable, for example, believes that corporations have wide-ranging responsibilities to a variety of "stakeholders." The Roundtable identifies stakeholders as customers, employees, suppliers, communities, society at large, stating that "responsibility to all these constituencies constitutes responsibility to society, making the corporation both an economically and socially viable entity."[1] In practice, many companies define their obligations in a much more limited way. Closely associated with debates about the role of the corporation in society are debates about the roles of organizations that are state-appointed or self-appointed policemen of the corporation, including regulatory bodies such as the U.S. Federal Trade Commission, and nongovernmental organizations (NGOs) that critique and try to influence corporate behavior.

I am not going to take a position on corporate responsibilities, on what corporations should do on social and environmental issues. I am instead going to investigate the forces that drive their behavior in these areas and argue that, perhaps surprisingly to some, there are growing forces that make it in a company's financial interest to be concerned about its social and environmental footprint. There is evidence that capital markets penalize companies for what is perceived as antisocial behavior, and that consumers are increasingly willing to do the same. To the extent that this is true, companies can gain financially from concern about environmental and social impacts of their activities. In these cases, there need be no conflict between being profitable and doing what is seen as good for society.

One of the factors that matters in this discussion is the practice of socially responsible investment, known as SRI. This is the practice of structuring investment funds to avoid investing in corporations that are seen as transgressing in some manner. One of the earliest such funds was the Pioneer Fund, founded in 1928 by evangelical Protestants who opposed the consumption of alcohol and tobacco. Pioneer Fund avoided investing in any company involved in the production of alcohol, cigars, or cigarettes. A further movement in this direction occurred in 1971 when a group of churches and religious orders formed the Interfaith Center on Corporate Responsibility (ICCR) with the aim of filing shareholder resolutions and presenting religious challenges to corporate practices with which they disagreed. Today SRI is a significant business: about 10 percent of all institutionally managed funds in the United States are SRI funds, implying that trillions of dollars are invested in this way.

SRI has evolved considerably since the Pioneer Fund. Some is still screened investment, that is, investment in funds that screen out companies with certain characteristics, such as involvement in alcohol, gambling, or weapons production. Others use a more nuanced approach to SRI, rating companies according to their social responsibility and then investing preferentially in companies with higher ratings. The performance of SRI funds relative to non-SRI funds can provide insights into the effect of social and environmental responsibility on financial performance. The relative returns of SRI and non-SRI funds provide evidence on the relationship between social and environmental responsibility and profitability, a central question from a managerial or investor perspective. If being responsible leads to superior financial performance, then investing in companies that have superior social and environmental performance should lead to a superior return.

This brief discussion has touched on all the main themes of the following chapters. The remainder of this chapter addresses a basic question: what is a corporation's role in society? I will start from Adam Smith's vision of the invisible hand, updated to allow for a more refined understanding of economics and for changes in the issues on society's agenda since the eighteenth century. Chapter 2 develops a theme stated earlier in this chapter, the relationship between social, environmental, and financial performance. How and when does social or environmental performance affect profitability? How does it affect share prices and how does the stock market react to information about these aspects of a firm's behavior? Chapter 3 develops the socially responsible investment theme, looking at how the SRI industry has evolved, what we know about the returns to SRI funds, and what they tell us about the returns to responsible behavior. Chapters 4–7 present a number of industry studies, showing how these issues play out in a wide range of industries, from financials and pharmaceuticals to Wal-Mart and

Starbucks and Monsanto. Chapters 8–10 look at what has been the most controversial aspect of social responsibility, the role of corporations in poor countries. Is it responsible to outsource production to low-wage countries? Can big companies make money by selling to the very poor? The remaining chapters pull the earlier ideas together into an analysis of how social and environmental performance fit into accounting and into corporate strategy, and develops an executive perspective on social responsibility. The chapter on accounting (Chapter 11) discusses how we can quantify social and environmental performance and incorporate data on this into financial statements, giving a more complete perspective on a company's overall performance—a "triple bottom line," in the words of a phrase that is widely used but rarely defined. In discussing social and environmental issues in the context of corporate strategy, I present a managerial perspective on how and when to develop these aspects of a corporation's behavior.

Adam Smith and Corporate Responsibility

Adam Smith glimpsed some of the eternal verities of economics, propositions that are central to how economic systems work, and though his successors have refined and modified our understanding, his ideas remain an excellent starting point. Smith, of course, never spoke directly of social or environmental responsibility. In 1776 the underlying concept would not have been understood. Corporations as we know them today barely existed, and their role in economic life was limited. Nevertheless, the Scottish moral philosopher, thinking at a time when North America was a British colony and the industrial revolution mainly a thing of the future, set out a framework that is still productive in the vastly different world of today.

Adam Smith is most widely known for the phrase "the invisible hand." He argues that in a competitive market economy

> every individual...neither intends to promote the public interest, nor knows how much he is promoting it. He intends only his own security, his own gain. And he is in this led by an invisible hand to promote an end which was no part of his intention. By pursuing his own interest he frequently promotes that of society more effectively than when he really intends to promote it.

Smith was saying something revolutionary and counterintuitive here. He was arguing against do-gooders and in favor of self-interested behavior, at first sight a strange position for a moral philosopher. What is counterintuitive is the claim that self-interested behavior by each individual in society is good for society as a whole—"By pursuing his own interest he frequently promotes that of society." In the eighteenth century, this idea was amazing, and even today after many years of familiarity we can still find the concept surprising. Might not self-interested behavior by millions of people lead to chaos and conflict? This scenario certainly seems plausible.

How did Smith reconcile self-interested behavior with an idea of the social good? The answer lies in another much-quoted sentence: "It is not from the benevolence of the butcher, the brewer, or the baker that we expect our dinner, but from their regard to their own interest." In other words, firms and traders do not provide us with what we want and need because they love us. Rather, they do it because they love themselves and their families. They can make money in doing so. If we want or need something, then we are willing to pay for it, and so in principle someone else can make a living by providing it. Our demand gives others an incentive to provide what we need, and incentives are central to the operation of economic systems.

This argument breaks down for the very poor, who may need food or medicines but are unable to pay for them and so unable to stimulate others to meet their needs. The failure of the pharmaceutical industry to produce a malaria vaccine is a perfect illustration: malaria sufferers desperately need treatment, but are too poor to pay a price that would make its development profitable. I will return to this later.

So from Smith's perspective the market economy is good for society because business can make a living by meeting other people's unmet needs. Smith goes on to argue that in the absence of markets and trade, every household would have to meet all of its own needs; in a market system, in contrast, all can benefit from the division of labor. Some specialize in baking, others in brewing, and so on. As a result, each trade is conducted by specialists with a gain in efficiency relative to a world where everyone is a jack-of-all-trades.

What can Smith's world view tell us about a corporation's responsibilities? In a nutshell, this is a redundant question. After all, if self-interested behavior by corporations leads to the social good, what more can we ask of the corporate sector? Why would we worry about this whole set of issues? There is no need to press for responsible behavior by corporations: in such a Smithian world, the conflicts that give rise to an apparent need for corporate responsibility as something over and above profit orientation would be absent, and all that society would ask of its corporations is that they seek to profit by meeting citizens' needs.

This is precisely the line taken by a prominent contemporary conservative economist, Milton Friedman, who saw himself as a direct intellectual descendent of Adam Smith. In a widely cited article in the Sunday *New York Times* in 1970,[2] Friedman remarked that

> there is one and only one social responsibility of business—to use its resources and engage in activities designed to increase its profits so long as it stays within the rules of the game, which is to say, engages in open and free competition without deception or fraud.

His argument is Smithian: to make profits, corporations have to meet people's needs, and in a competitive world they have to do so at reasonable prices. In the process, they provide income and employment, and pay taxes. So corporations meet our needs, provide income and employment, and produce tax revenues, making it churlish to expect more of them.

In addition, Friedman adds an argument that was not relevant in Smith's time, an argument that derives from the separation of ownership and control typical of modern corporations that are owned by shareholders, usually institutional investors such as pension and mutual funds, but managed by professional managers. Managers owe responsibility to their employers, the shareholders, and not to society as a whole, Friedman argues. In fact, he claims that the only responsibility managers have to society as a whole is to follow the law and act within the generally accepted ethical conventions. Friedman has scathing comments on business people who talk of the need to preserve the environment, maintain diversity, or meet other social goals, remarking that "businessmen who talk this way are unwitting puppets of the intellectual forces that have been undermining the basis of a free society these past decades." Friedman then articulates clearly what is implicit in Smith on the issue of corporate obligations to society: that a discussion of this is redundant because a well-functioning market will ensure that corporations operate fully in the public interest.

If corporations do well financially by doing good for society, then the panoply of regulatory institutions that characterize a modern economy is largely redundant. In Adam Smith's world we would need a competitive authority to ensure that firms compete rather than collude, but most of the rest of our contemporary regulatory framework would be redundant, including the nongovernmental groups that concern themselves about firms' actions with respect to the environment and with respect to the less fortunate members of society.

External Costs

Is this an accurate picture, or is something missing here? Much of what Smith said is correct, and for someone writing in 1776 his insights were extraordinary. What's more, he expressed himself clearly and memorably, which has helped keep his words in front of us. There is a lesson there for some of today's economics writers! But there are two crucial points missing from the Smith and Friedman arguments. Smith was unaware of them, but Friedman was not: indeed he mentions one of them only to sweep it under the carpet when he refers to "governments having the responsibility to impose taxes and determine expenditures for such 'social' purposes as controlling pollution or training the hard-core unemployed." Governments do indeed have such a responsibility, which arises naturally from issues that Adam Smith missed. They were not as relevant back in the colonial era as they are today. Central to understanding governmental roles is the recognition of when corporate interests are fully aligned with those of society and when they are not. In 1952 in an immortal and overly assertive phrase, Charles E. Wilson ("Engine Charley"), president of General Motors, asserted that "what's good for General Motors is good for America." Mr. Wilson was claiming, more prosaically, that corporate and social interests are fully aligned. To understand what this claim involves, let us start with some interesting examples.

Consider Apple, Intel, and Microsoft: in twenty years they created the personal computer industry, an industry affecting everyone in the developed world and many in developing countries, changing lives and businesses, and creating billions of dollars in value for shareholders and tens of thousands of jobs for new employees. They contributed massively to society and did so for the cause of making money for their shareholders. They made money for their shareholders by developing goods that consumers wanted, paid taxes to the government, and illustrate well Adam Smith's view of capitalism as a system in which self-interest leads to the common good.

But sadly not all firms are like them: a dramatic contrast is provided by the tobacco companies, who sell a poison that is slow-acting and addictive, so that they can actually make money while killing their customers. It is true that they pay taxes and provide employment, but even so many people will have difficulty in seeing them as a positive force in society. What about the auto and oil companies, which help us experience freedom by means of personal mobility, while polluting the environment and changing the climate? They seem to be intermediate between the two cases. What differentiates high-tech firms like Microsoft, Apple, and Intel from the tobacco, oil, and auto companies?

To understand this we have to go beyond Adam Smith, to the concepts of private and social costs, a distinction attributable to Cambridge economist Arthur Pigou, who wrote in the first half of the twentieth century. When a firm's private and social costs are the same, which is more or less the case with the tech sector, markets work well for society, aligning corporate and social interests. But when corporate and social interests are not aligned, markets don't do such a good job, as is the case with tobacco and, to a lesser degree, oil and autos. This explains the conflict between corporations and society in these sectors, and the differences between these sectors and the others.

The private costs of an action are those paid by the person carrying it out. A car user pays fuel bills, maintenance bills, and insurance bills, among others. These then are some of the private costs. There are other costs of auto use that do not fall on the user, examples being the costs of pollution, of contributions to climate change, and of adding to congestion. Driving an auto imposes costs in each of these categories on everyone in the community; indeed, in the case of climate change the costs are imposed on everyone in the world. These are the external costs of using a car, and the total cost of auto use is the sum of the private costs and the external costs: this sum is called the social cost. External costs are the costs of an activity that are paid by other people, people who are not responsible for the activity and possibly gain no benefit from it. When there are no external costs, the invisible hand does a great job of running the economy and ensures that the outcome is efficient, that the economy's resources are well used, and that none of the resources are wasted.[3]

Economists make this precise in a proposition called "The First Theorem of Welfare Economics," which asserts that under certain conditions, among them no external costs, competitive markets lead to economic efficiency. External costs are an important characteristic of some of the industries where there are conflicts between corporations and society: the tobacco industry imposes external costs on its consumers, their families, and on the health-care system, and the oil industry, like the auto industry, is a driving force behind pollution and greenhouse gas emissions. So when these industries grow, some of the costs of their growth are paid by citizens who have no connection with them, because of the externalization of costs. These citizens naturally ask why they should shoulder these extra costs, which are neither of their choosing nor associated with any benefit to them. Not surprisingly, there can be opposition to the growth of firms with external costs. High-tech firms, in contrast, externalize few of their costs, which is why the growth of Apple, Intel, and Microsoft was unambiguously positive for the economy and for society as a whole, and was well received.

This discussion of external costs gives us some intuition into when, to quote "Engine Charley" once again, "what's good for General Motors is good for America." A precondition for the alignment of corporate and social interests is that no costs are externalized. This is a requirement if what is good for General Motors, or any other corporation, is to be good for America too. Adam Smith did not think of this point—pollution was probably not a serious problem in his day, and climate change certainly was not—and Milton Friedman implicitly and perhaps disingenuously assumed in his *New York Times* article that the government was taking care of the problem. The most straightforward way for a government to address this issue is to tax the activity that externalizes costs by an amount equal to the externalized costs. So if the external costs of using a gallon of gasoline are $1.50, this means a $1.50 tax on gasoline. Then the cost to the user of using gasoline reflects all the costs of its use, private as well as external. In the absence of a corrective policy of this type, external-cost-generating activities tend to be carried out on too great a scale for the good of society, implying that their operation generates conflicts between those carrying out the activities and those bearing the external costs.

Conflicts between corporations and society over environmental issues almost always derive from external costs associated with pollution, pollution being the classic example of an external cost. Some of the costs of an activity are externalized to the population as a whole through the spread of pollutants. Deforestation is another source of environmental conflict, again driven by differences between costs and benefits. To a landowner, forests typically have economic value only as lumber and farmland, whereas to society at large they have recreational value, existence value,[4] value in biodiversity support, and value in carbon sequestration. Deforestation imposes external costs on the community by withdrawing many benefits that it has been receiving from the forest and is another source of environmental conflict, again driven by externalization of costs. The significant external costs associated with the environmental impacts of corporations are the main reason we have agencies such as the U.S. Environmental Protection Agency, and a range of legislation designed for environmental protection. They also explain the growth of the environmental NGO sector, with groups such as Environmental Defense, Natural Resources Defense Council, Greenpeace, Friends of the Earth, The Nature Conservancy, the Union of Concerned Scientists, and many others, several of whom will feature in later chapters. Without external costs, there would be no rationale for any of this.

A review of firms and industries where social and environmental issues have arisen provides many more examples of externalization of costs—in fact, it will be a common theme of many examples in the chapters that follow. BP provides an illustration: in 1997 it took a stand on climate change, accepting very early on the scientific evidence behind Intergovernmental Panel on Climate Change (IPCC) forecasts and acknowledging the appropriateness of reducing greenhouse gas emissions. BP imposed a firm-wide cap on greenhouse gas emissions and began a corporate emissions trading system.[5] Emissions have been reduced significantly, ahead of schedule, and BP claims that this has not only cost nothing, but has also in fact increased net income by about $600 million. Viewed from an economic perspective, what BP has done is to acknowledge that its operating costs—private costs—are less than the social costs of its activities and take measures to bring the two into line. In economic jargon, it has internalized some external costs. It has moved to reduce greenhouse gas emissions, something indicated to be appropriate by social costs but not by private. Dow Chemical presents a similar case: it responded to pressures to reduce pollution by systematically cutting back on all sources by which it could lose chemicals to the environment, and in the process claims to have saved tens of millions of dollars of valuable solvents.[6] Dow, like BP, has acted as if a social cost were a private cost. These companies have moved to avoid conflicts with society over environmental issues, conflicts that could have cost them greatly in terms of goodwill and brand equity, and in the process have also saved themselves significant amounts of money. Their investments paid them what in other contexts has been termed a "double dividend."

So BP and Dow were able to make money by reducing pollution, which suggests that in fact they had miscalculated their private costs initially, and that pollution was surprisingly not the least expensive way of disposing of their wastes. How could this be? One contributing factor is that in some cases the costs of polluting, costs that were saved by ending pollution, were opportunity costs.[7] BP was flaring natural gas from some of its oil wells. There was no cash cost for this and so no line item in the accounts showing it as a cost, but there were revenues forgone as this gas could be collected and sold. Likewise with Dow, the loss of expensive reagents and products into the environment reduced the yield of its production processes in a way that was hard to see, and this was not visible in its accounting data. So in these examples social costs did to some degree have private counterparts, but these were noncash costs that were not visible from standard accounting perspectives. Many corporations may be missing noncash private costs like these, and in the process overstating the differences between private and social costs and between the corporate and public interests, an accounting shortcoming that good social and environmental policies can remedy.

Heinz provides another example of a company that profited from careful response to an environmental conflict, in this case over the killing of dolphins while fishing for tuna, a side effect causing the social costs of tuna fishing to exceed the private costs. The problem was that catching tuna often involved killing dolphins, and Heinz, a major seller of canned tuna, was held responsible for this.[8] Environmental NGOs organized a boycott of Heinz, and in response Heinz chose to change their tuna sources from the eastern to the western Pacific, where the dolphin bycatch is much less, thereby becoming the dolphin-friendly tuna source. They incurred extra costs in doing this, but enhanced their brand and earned the congratulations of prominent politicians and environmentalists, avoiding what would almost surely have been a costly and bruising confrontation with environmental groups. In terms of our economic model, they did what BP and Dow did: they brought their private costs into line with the greater social costs and internalized external costs.

Growing coffee on plantations destroys tropical forests and biodiversity, again externalizing some of the costs of coffee production. Starbucks, working in conjunction with the NGO Conservation International, has invested in environmentally friendly sourcing of coffee, to some degree offsetting these external costs. Similarly with bananas, plantation production can have profoundly negative environmental and social impacts, and recently in conjunction with the NGO Rainforest Alliance, Chiquita has reorganized its plantations to minimize these negative impacts and cut back on the externalization of costs.[9] McDonald's packaging produces waste, externalizing collection and disposal costs, hence McDonald's moves, in conjunction with the NGO Environmental Defense, to produce less bulky packaging. Shell's proposal to dispose of the Brent Spar oil buoy in the North Sea was seen, incorrectly in retrospect, as externalizing substantial disposal costs and was opposed by Greenpeace and others on these grounds.

Monsanto provides a complex example of a company damaged by its failure to anticipate conflicts over possible external costs associated with its products. Monsanto invested billions of dollars genetically modifying crops to make them more productive and to require less use of insecticides, rendering the growing process less environmentally harmful.[10] Their aim was to make agriculture sustainable while improving crop yields in poor countries.[11] With this aim and with proprietary technologies to implement it, Monsanto should have been a poster child for corporate environmental responsibility; they were instead destroyed by opposition from environmental groups. Consumer opposition to genetically modified crops led to their being abandoned by farmers, financially weakening Monsanto, which was then taken over. Monsanto's problem was that it focused on one private–social cost gap—that associated with the use of insecticides on growing crops—but in the process missed another more serious one—that associated with people's fears of genetically modified foods. From the consumer perspective, Monsanto was seeking to raise farm productivity and lower farm pollution by passing to consumers new and unknown risks, the risks of foodstuffs that had never been extensively tested. Monsanto's failure was not a failure to take its environmental responsibilities seriously, but a failure to implement this thoroughly and follow through on all of its implications.

Many of the cases and examples that are central to a discussion and evaluation of corporate social and environmental responsibilities hinge on the externalization of some aspect of a product's costs. One interpretation of several nonmarket systems that impinge on corporate behavior is that their role is to force corporations to internalize the external costs associated with their activities. Legal systems, regulators, and NGOs can all be seen in this light as systems that raise the firms' awareness of the full social costs of their activities and pressure them to treat external costs as private costs. They can also pressure society to sanction firms that do not respond. To the extent that they do this well, these institutions correct a shortcoming in the market mechanism and serve a real economic purpose.

Fairness

There is another important limitation of the invisible hand. Market economies are efficient provided costs are not externalized, but they need not be fair. Markets are important in determining the distribution of income and wealth, but nothing in the way they operate implies that the ways in which income and wealth are distributed within the population will seem fair or reasonable. People who have scarce and highly valued skills, such as opera singers or rock stars or football players, will be rich, while those with more abundant but socially valuable skills, such as teachers or social workers or police officers, may be poor. Inheritances may transmit fortunes from a productive and successful generation to its less valued successors.

Contemporary debates about outsourcing are in part about fairness and illustrate this class of conflict. What is the fair wage for unskilled labor in the garment industry in poor countries? Competitive markets will set this low, because they reflect the balance of supply and demand, with an abundance of labor driving the price down to little more than a dollar a day. Is this socially acceptable? Is it consistent with generally accepted ideas of justice and fairness? The question seems especially sharp when people earning a dollar a day for a long and arduous day's work are making goods that are sold for a hundred dollars or more to consumers earning tens of thousands annually. For some, this seems clearly unjust; for others, it is just a reflection of how the world operates. The underlying point here is that the efficiency of markets does not imply that their distributional outcomes are socially acceptable: this is a matter on which opinions can legitimately differ widely, and do so. It is a classic source of social conflict. Many of the debates concerning social responsibilities arise from this.

Some of these debates have implicitly been mentioned already: the sweat-shop issue is a source of much debate about social responsibilities. This is a debate about the acceptability of market outcomes in terms of fairness and equity. Is it reasonable that the people who make our shoes or clothes should work ten hours or more daily for one or two dollars? Is it reasonable that children should work in these conditions? If not, whom should we charge with responsibility for remedying this situation and how should they go about it? What are the responsibilities of Western companies out-sourcing some of their production processes to low-wage areas—should they pay the local wages, U.S. wages, or somewhere in between? These are core issues in discussions of social responsibilities, and they reflect the fact that the invisible hand is dexterous at using resources efficiently, but not at ensuring outcomes that most people think fair.

Such debates inevitably arise in a market economy. They arise not only in an international context, though they are perhaps at their sharpest there, but also in domestic issues. Current debates about Wal-Mart's wage and benefit levels are a reflection of this same syndrome within the U.S. econ-omy. In a very different disguise, this issue also arises in the financial sector: debates about insider trading, favoritism in the allocation of initial pub-lic offerings, or hidden commissions in insurance policies are all debates about what is a fair and proper distribution of the gains from market par-ticipation. In the United States, the recent failures of several large corporate pension funds, even as senior corporate executives earn millions of dollars a year with huge guaranteed pensions, raise similar questions.[12] As in the environmental case, conflicts and debates about fairness involve government agencies and citizen groups, with participants including regulators such as the state attorneys general and the Food and Drug Administration in the United States, consumer protection agencies in other countries, and NGOs concerned about poverty in developing countries.

Shareholders

Many twentieth-century economists have stressed the fact that shareholders are the owners of a company and those to whom executives have a duty. Furthermore, that duty, as was clear in the discussions of Friedman's views, is to maximize profits. Profits go to shareholders and are the returns to the capital that they invest in the company. So, maximizing profits is maximizing the return to shareholders. The legal system in the United States (but not in all other advanced industrial countries) has determined that profits are one of the primary goals of the corporation, though not the exclusive goal, and have explicitly permitted the use of some of a corporations' resources in the promotion of the interests of nonshareholders. The famous case of *Dodge v. Ford* affords some insight into this. It arose from Henry Ford's decision to stop paying extra dividends to shareholders in order to raise wages and investment. Ford declared that his aim was to "Do as much good as we can, everywhere, for everybody concerned..." He went on to say:

> My ambition is to employ still more men, to spread the benefits of this industrial system to the greatest possible number, to help them build up their lives and their homes. To do this we are putting the greatest share of our profits back in the business.

The Dodge brothers, shareholders, sued him on the grounds that his primary obligation was to their welfare and that he was failing in his duty to shareholders. They won, with the court in Michigan ruling that

> The difference between an incidental humanitarian expenditure of corporate funds for the benefit of the employees, like the building of a hospital for their use and the employment of agencies for the betterment of their condition, and a general purpose and plan to benefit mankind at the expense of others, is obvious.

There should be no confusion (of which there is evidence) of the duties which Mr. Ford conceives that he and the stockholders owe to the general public and the duties which in law he and his co-directors owe to protesting, minority stockholders. A business corporation is organized and carried on primarily for the profit of the stockholders. The powers of the directors are to be employed for that end. The discretion of directors is to be exercised in the choice of means to attain that end, and does not extend to a change in the end itself, to the reduction of profits, or to the nondistribution of profits among shareholders in order to devote them to other purposes.[13]

The Court's statement that "a business corporation is organized and carried on primarily for the profit of the shareholders. The powers of the directors are to be employed for that end" is a very stark summary of the shareholder-centered perspective on corporate responsibility, though this was softened by the statement elsewhere that

We do not draw in question, nor do counsel for the plaintiffs do so, the validity of the general proposition stated by counsel that ... although a manufacturing corporation cannot engage in humanitarian works as its principal business, the fact that it is organized for profits does not prevent the existence of implied powers to carry on with humanitarian motives such charitable works as are incidental to the main business of the corporation.[14]

U.S. law does not recognize a legally enforceable duty to maximize profits: in fact, as the Dodge case suggests, it specifically permits firms to sacrifice profits to public interest goals whose attainment is not required by law.[15] Over thirty states have "corporate constituency" statutes that allow companies to consider the interests not only of shareholders but also of customers, suppliers, employees and the community at large. The American Law Institute's Principles of Corporate Governance state that

Even if corporate profits and shareholder gain are not thereby enhanced, the corporation, in the conduct of its business ... (2) May take into account ethical considerations that are reasonably regarded as appropriate to the responsible conduct of business; and (3) May devote a reasonable amount of resources to public welfare, humanitarian, educational, and philanthropic purposes.[16]

Another important legal issue here is the "business judgment rule," which states that if the executives of a corporation believe that a policy is in the best interests of shareholders, then shareholders who disagree with the policy have no grounds for legal redress. The essence of this rule is that courts will not argue with the business judgment of a corporation's executives: they judge legal issues and not business ones. This gives considerable discretion to executives to promote social and philanthropic ends on the grounds that they will contribute to the company's long-term profitability.

In contrast to the shareholder-centered perspective, the late Sumantra Ghoshal, a management guru from the London Business School, developed an apparently persuasive argument that employees rather than shareholders deserve to be treated as the primary concern of managers. He argued that employees carry more risk than shareholders.[17] If a company fails, the employees lose their jobs and the investments they have made in knowing the company's business. Finding another job is difficult and usually involves a pay cut. Often employees lose their pensions too. Shareholders, he argued, are less exposed: they have diversified portfolios and can readily find other investments, standing to loose less from failure. Indeed, if the company appears to be doing badly, they can sell their shares and move on much more easily than employees. So employees are more at risk in a company's failure than the shareholders and perhaps, Ghoshal argued, deserve more consideration than they receive in the shareholder-centric model that dominates economists' thinking.

There are two fallacies here. First, it is not accidental that economists see profit maximization as the proper objective of the corporation. The invisible hand works well only if corporations do maximize profits. The first theorem of welfare economics, to which I alluded before, states that efficiency in the use of society's resources emerges from competitive profit-maximizing behavior on the part of firms, provided that there are no external costs and certain other conditions are met. So from an economic perspective it is not shareholders who have primacy, it is profits. Profits represent value added by a company, the difference between the cost of its inputs and the value of its outputs, and for a well-run economy we generally want this value added by the corporate sector to be as large as possible. But profits normally go to shareholders, so shareholders seem to have primacy. But, a propos of Ghoshal's observations, employees can be shareholders too. Indeed, in many of the most successful new corporations in the United States, employees are significant shareholders.

Second, it is also a fallacy that shareholders are less committed to the company than employees. While some shareholders such as hedge funds undoubtedly are, and move into and out of a company's shares at short notice, there are many large pension funds that take long-term positions in corporations and expect to hold them through all the vicissitudes of corporate life. Large pension funds are so big that they have to focus their investments mainly on large-cap companies, and the sizes of their stakes in these are such that they cannot quickly sell and move to another firm: doing so would move prices too sharply against them.

Conclusions

In the ideal world of Adam Smith, companies do well by society just by making profits—they do well and do good at the same time. This is the point of Milton Friedman's 1970 piece in *The New York Times*. But the eighteenth century and the Enlightenment are behind us, and the world in which we live is a world of external costs and of disputes about what is a fair distribution of the benefits from economic activity. In this world, the invisible hand needs some help to reach an efficient outcome. Here, corporate interests are not automatically aligned with the social interest. Society gains from realigning corporate interests with social interests, and corporations also gain from this realignment as it reduces conflicts between them and society. Conflicts between social and corporate interests in general hurt both parties: they hurt society because the outcome of economic activity is not what we collectively want, and they hurt corporations because the corporation is generally the loser in the long run. So if corporations behave as if they have obligations on the social and environmental fronts as well as in the area of profits, then both sides can gain. Society can gain from a fairer or more efficient allocation of resources and the corporation from a less conflictual relationship with the environment in which it operates. In the next chapter we shall see some of the reasons why a corporation might voluntarily choose to assume social and environmental obligations that are not legally mandated. Ultimately, I will argue, this is a matter of self-interest. Primarily, this self-interest arises from considerations of liability and of brand enhancement, though there are other dimensions in which this can prove rewarding.

2

Social, Environmental, and Financial Performance

A firm's social and environmental performance can certainly affect its financial outcomes: the question is how. What is the mechanism at work here? Do social and environmental concerns reduce profits by diverting cash and attention from other more strategic issues, or do they help profits through other mechanisms? Responsible behavior can certainly be profitable. At the opposite extreme, seriously unethical behavior can decimate profits, or even lead to bankruptcy, as evidenced by Enron, Worldcom, Arthur Anderson, and many others. A more interesting and less obvious observation is that, within limits, more ethical behavior can add to profits, and that a company's social and environmental reputation affects its stock-market valuation. Two distinct strands of research have focused on these relationships.

The first strand tries to understand the mechanisms by which social and environmental behavior can affect a company's internal operations and its position in the marketplace. It looks at the connection between these aspects of performance and labor turnover, between these and brand image, and the role of social and environmental behavior in what is known as "enterprise risk management"—the management of risks of a nonfinancial type. Such risks include loss of reputation, consumer boycott, and loss of brand value. The second strand of research is based on statistical analysis of the relationships between the rating of a company's social and environmental performance and various measures of financial success, such as profits and stock-market value. Social and environmental ratings are provided by several vendors, including Innovest Strategic Value Advisors and KLD Research and Analytics. Both sell evaluations of publicly traded companies' performances in the social and environmental areas, just as firms such as Moodys and Dow Jones sell ratings of financial performance and Morningstar rates mutual funds. The buyers are the same as for corporate ratings—fund managers who need the information for investment decisions.

Chapter 1 suggested that corporations voluntarily assume certain social and environmental obligations to anticipate and minimize conflicts between corporations and society and its representatives, internalizing external costs or minimizing distributional conflicts. A review of cases studying the impact of corporate social and environmental behavior suggests that reduction of conflicts is indeed a major contribution of positive programs in these areas. A comprehensive list of the benefits that commentators have linked to social and environmental programs goes further and includes, in addition to reducing the risk of conflicts, the reduction of waste, improving relations with regulators, generating brand equity, improved human relations and employee productivity, and a lower cost of capital. Each of these bears examination in more detail.

Risk Management   One of the most important payoffs to social and environmental responsibility comes in the field of enterprise risk management. High-profile companies in potentially controversial areas—and this includes most areas nowadays—run a risk of bad press or, even worse, NGO actions, consumer boycotts, or lawsuits as a result of their actions. Examples abound: Nike suffered from damaging press and a loss of image as a result of allegations that employees in its overseas suppliers operated in sweatshop conditions, with low wages, long hours and unacceptable health and safety conditions. No company with a valuable retail brand image would want to be subject to the accusations that came Nike's way, or to the revelation that some of these accusations were correct. They are bound to have an impact on consumer loyalty and the company's market position. Other clothing companies have been subject to similar accusations, including The GAP and Kathie Lee Gifford's line of clothing. In a very different industry, Shell Oil suffered from a consumer boycott led by the NGO Greenpeace as a result of its attempt to dispose of the oil buoy Brent Spar in the North Sea at the end of its useful life. Greenpeace alleged, incorrectly we now know, that this would damage the marine environment and that it was preferable to tow the buoy ashore and dispose of it there. Greenpeace launched a boycott of Shell's products in Europe, with a significant impact on its sales in several major markets.

Another company with a high profile and a potentially vulnerable brand, Starbucks, has deliberately pursued a policy of trying to compensate for some of the environmental and social harm that its coffee-sourcing policies might inflict by promoting environmentally friendly coffee sources, in cooperation with a large environmental NGO, Conservation International. Starbucks has made a substantial investment in buying coffee from growers with an environmentally friendly profile, and they recently agreed to purchase coffee through the Fair Trade NGO, which guarantees that the prices paid to growers are in excess of world prices and provide a reasonable living standard.[1] Starbucks is therefore taking preemptive action on both the possible sources of conflict with society—environmental degradation and fair treatment of the low paid.[2] As we shall see, consumers in certain market segments are sensitive to a companies' social and environmental behavior and react to these in their purchasing decisions. Starbucks' hope is that consumers will discriminate in favor of the responsible trader, or at least against those who do not make their credentials in this area clear. To date, this policy has stood them well and they have stayed out of the eye of the storm. BP's proactive policy on climate change, discussed in Chapter 1, has played a similar role for them.

In the United States, in particular, most companies live in fear of law suits. They fear being sued for pollution, for inflicting harm on consumers, for misrepresenting their financial prospects, and a myriad of other reasons. There are good reasons for these fears. Merck, a pharmaceutical company with a history of financial and medical success, now faces an avalanche of lawsuits arising from the performance of its painkiller Vioxx. Jones Manville and most other asbestos companies were driven to bankruptcy by lawsuits arising from the possible carcinogenic effects of asbestos. Tobacco companies have paid billions in the settlement of health-related suits. Ford and the tire manufacturer Firestone paid tens of millions in the settlement of damages arising from crashes of Ford Explorer SUVs equipped with Firestone tires. The insurance giant AIG faces shareholder suits arising from the need to restate its accounts for several recent years. All in all, the risk of litigation is very real and is something that actively concerns senior executives. Managing social and environmental performance risks is part of a strategy for minimizing this litigation risk.

We will see later in this chapter that the stock market penalizes companies that are known to emit toxic pollutants, presumably in part because of the risk of litigation. Freshfields Bruckhaus Deringer, a major European corporate law firm, discusses reasons for adopting social and environmental obligations in its review of Corporate Social Responsibility[3] and notes that "[a] more remote, but not inconceivable, incentive (*for adopting social and environmental obligations*) lies in the possibility that a company which can arguably be held not to have complied adequately with some CSR norms at least may find itself the target of civil action in plaintiff-friendly jurisdictions." They also mention the widespread adoption of the "polluter pays principle" in many countries, and its general acceptance by international bodies such as the Organization for Economic Cooperation and Development (OECD). Commenting on this, they note that

> It is a long established principle of environmental liability that the "polluter pays" to put right any harm, or detriment it causes to the environment. Increasingly, legislation looks to impose liability for harm caused regardless of how long ago it occurred. Prime examples of this are: the introduction of the UK contaminated land regime, which imposes primary liability for the clean-up of contaminated land on the person who caused or knowingly permitted the presence of the contamination where they can be traced; and the recently adopted environmental liability directive (*of the European Union*), which establishes a framework of environmental liability to prevent and remedy environmental and biodiversity damage based entirely on this principle.

Much the same has been true in the United States for almost thirty years now. The key legislation here is the 1980 Comprehensive Environmental Response, Compensation and Liability Act (CERCLA), commonly known as the Superfund Act. This act holds companies liable for the costs of pollution and the costs of restoring polluted areas to a clean state, even if the pollution complied with all relevant laws at the time that it occurred. This is a particularly strongly worded law, which imposes strict, joint and several liability on companies. Strict means that negligence does not have to be proven in order to prove liability, while joint and several liability means that any one company can be liable for the entire cost of cleanup, even if it only contributed to a small part of the pollution: there is no attempt to prorate liability to the contributions to pollution. These provisions are in contrast to those under common law, which allows an aggrieved party to sue for damage from pollution but with much higher standards for establishing liability.[4]

The Union Bank of Switzerland (UBS) also comments on the connection between social and environmental behavior and the reduction of liabilities in its recent report on corporate social responsibility, commenting that

> If a firm or industry "externalises" costs, the affected stakeholder is very rarely given the opportunity to agree the transfer of costs, and so the "price" (perhaps very small in the eyes of the firm but very large in the eyes of other stakeholders) is not negotiated at the time when costs are externalised. The danger to firms is that, if the balance of power between stakeholders changes, the price of the exchange may be renegotiated at a future date, and sometimes, but not always, in a court of law.[5]

They are arguing here that the externalization of costs will generally produce a potential liability to the externalizing company, implying that reducing external costs is a mechanism for reducing potential liabilities. Developing this point further, UBS goes on to comment that

> The US Environmental Protection Agency (EPA) has devised a useful definition of a potential environmental liability, which we have adapted here to cover the broader concept of corporate social liability:

> - A corporate social liability is an obligation to make a future expenditure due to past or ongoing manufacturing or other commercial activity, which adversely affects any aspect of the environment, the economy, or society.
> - A *potential* corporate social liability is a potential obligation to make a future expenditure due to past or ongoing manufacturing or other commercial activity, which adversely affects any aspect of the environment, the economy, or society.
> - A "potential corporate social liability" differs from a "corporate social liability" because an organisation may have an opportunity to prevent the liability from occurring by altering its own practices or adopting new practices in order to avoid or reduce adverse environmental, economic or social impacts.

UBS goes on to argue that corporate balance sheets should carry warnings about potential corporate social liabilities and that valuation exercises by stock-market analysts should take these liabilities into account. In this, they are close to a recommendation of the U.K. government, which in a white paper "Modernising Company Law" published in July 2001 proposed that each company publish every year an Operating and Financial Review (OFR) that analyzes and discusses the main factors and trends that affect the company's performance. These would include any social and environmental factors that might affect the shareholders' evaluation of the company's prospects.

The examples above make it clear that socially or environmentally irresponsible behavior can be costly. There are three mechanisms driving these costs: one based in the courts, one based on the actions of civil society and NGOs, and the final one based on consumer responses to perceived corporate misbehavior. We will encounter these mechanisms again and again: they provide important disciplines to the corporate world and go a long way toward reconciling corporate and social interests in situations where they might otherwise differ. The last two—actions by civil society and consumers— have only recently become an important part of the economic landscape and are still evolving. Probably this reflects people's increasing ability to link different parts of the economic system, understanding that their buying decisions affect poor people in the third world, or the status of tropical rainforests. These connections are important and powerful but far from obvious. If awareness continues to grow, we can expect to see more "conscientious consumerism" and more pressure on companies to consider the full implications of their actions.

Waste Reduction   BP and Dow Chemicals, both mentioned in the previous chapter, illustrate well how environmentally responsible policies can cut costs and raise profits by reducing waste. Oil fields usually have natural gas at high pressure over them, called associated gas, and BP had traditionally burned this, as did most oil producers, producing greenhouse gases on a large scale. BP discovered that capturing associated gas to prevent its release facilitated its transportation and sale, thus providing a new source of revenue that exceeded the costs of capture. The latest BP reports claim that their greenhouse gas reduction program has netted them $630 million in savings and extra revenues. The chemical company Du Pont has reported similar experiences in its program to reduce chemical leakage into the environment. Indeed, its in-house program proved so profitable that it has profited from the expertise gained from tackling its own problems by forming a unit to sell cleanup services to other companies. It expects annual revenues of more than $1 billion from this business. In a similar vein, Dow Chemical's U.S. operations in Louisiana averaged a return of 204 percent on investments in energy-saving projects between 1981 and 1993. Stories like these are a recurring theme in studies of the benefits from improved environmental performance, and they suggest that many companies are just not seeing the savings available from better management of materials and processes until they focus on their environmental impact.[6]

Regulatory Protection   A corporation's relationships with officialdom can be of real significance in heavily regulated industries. BP appears to have influenced the greenhouse gas reduction policies adopted by the European Union, playing a role in persuading the EU to meet its obligations under the Kyoto Protocol by an emission trading system similar to that which BP has adopted for its own internal use. It is likely that its reputation for being proactive with respect to greenhouse gas management was important in establishing BP's credentials to the European Union regulators. A reputation for being "green" can also be of use to an oil company in negotiations for access to potential oil reserves in environmentally sensitive areas, such as the forests of central and South America or the area around the Caspian Sea. Applications for exploration permits in such areas are generally contested by environmental groups, and a reputation for environmental sensitivity may be an asset in overcoming the reservations raised. In general, a regulatory decision in favor of a company with a strong reputation for socially responsible behavior will be greeted more positively than one in favor of a company seen as antisocial in its conduct, and this must influence regulators in their decisions.[7]

Brand Equity   An elusive but nevertheless critical concept for many modern corporations is "branding." With strong competition and little in terms of technology differentiating the available products, a product's "buzz" or image can be critical in tipping customers' decisions, and this is often the product of ephemeral fads and fashions that are easily destabilized. Nike's market momentum dropped off when the low wages paid to its developing country employees were publicized, and Shell suffered a loss of sales in Europe at the time of the dispute over its disposal of the Brent Spar oil buoy. Starbucks, as noted, has found it worthwhile to invest in avoiding conflicts that could damage its reputation and in publicizing its links with Conservation International. All of these effects testify to the fact that social and environmental policies affect the value of a company's brand.

Employee Productivity   There are several aspects to the impact of social and environmental behavior on a firm's relationship with its employees. People seek to work for "good" companies, companies they can be proud of. They do not like having to justify or excuse their companies to their friends and families, and as a result companies with a good record have more success recruiting, maintaining, and motivating employees than companies with a poor record. A survey of MBA attitudes toward potential employers emphasizes this point, noting that they are willing to take lower pay in order to work for companies that have a more positive social image.[8] Roy Vagelos, ex–chief executive and chairman of Merck, tells a story that reinforces this point.[9] In the late 1980s and 1990s, Merck developed a drug that cured river blindness, a painful disease that afflicted millions in tropical Africa, eventually leaving them blind. None of the victims could afford to pay for the drug, and after failing to get the U.S. government and the World Health Organization to pay for the medicine at cost, Merck eventually made the decision to supply and to distribute it to all affected populations free of charge. By 2003 it had treated about thirty million people through this program. The cash cost to Merck was considerable, but Vagelos believes that Merck's River Blindness program enabled it to recruit able scientists, who would not otherwise have been available, and thus contributed to its human and intellectual capital, its main asset.

Another aspect of the relationship between social responsibility and employee management works through what economists have called the "efficiency wage theory." The central premise here is that employees work harder and more effectively if they are paid more, so productivity can be raised by paying more than the minimum needed to fill jobs, and consequently paying more than the market wage may help profits by boosting output by more than it boosts costs. This insight is not a new one but goes back to the nineteenth century, as *The Economist* has noted:[10]

> The notorious "robber barons" built much of America's educational and health infrastructure. Company towns, such as Pullman, were constructed, the argument being that well-housed, well-educated workers would be more productive than their feckless, slum-dwelling contemporaries.

> Companies introduced pensions and health-care benefits long before governments told them to do so. Procter & Gamble pioneered disability and retirement pensions (in 1915), the eight-hour day (in 1918) and, most important of all, guaranteed work for at least 48 weeks a year (in the 1920s). Henry Ford became a cult figure by paying his workers $5 an hour—twice the market rate. Henry Heinz paid for education in citizenship for his employees, and Tom Watson's IBM gave its workers everything from subsidised education to country-club membership.

So it can be in a company's interest to pay more than is strictly necessary to retain its labor force, contributing both to its bottom line and to developing a reputation for being a good employer and being socially responsible. Even the "robber barons" of the era of unfettered capitalism knew this.

Cost of Capital   The right choices on social and environmental issues may reduce a company's cost of capital through the impact of Socially Responsible Investment (SRI). A growing movement, SRI now accounts for 10 percent of funds under professional management in the United States and a smaller but growing fraction in European countries. SRI funds are invested with restriction on the shares that can be purchased. These may be simple bans on alcohol and tobacco or more sophisticated rules that invest preferentially in firms receiving high ratings for their social and environmental performance. A sophisticated SRI fund allocates its investments by sector in much the same way as a conventional fund, but within each sector it is guided by social and environmental ratings as well as by the financial characteristics of companies. If significant sums of money are invested preferentially in companies with good CSR records, their cost of capital may fall.

What the Data Tell Us

There are clearly a number of plausible mechanisms by which social and environmental performance could affect profits and case studies to suggest that on occasions they have done so. But is this of significance for most firms? Does it represent an important phenomenon for the economy as a whole, or are these cases merely cute anecdotes with little generality? The only way to determine this is to look at some aggregate data, and to let the numbers speak. Many studies have tried to tease some statements from the data on this topic, and while there is not one that is unambiguous, the studies taken as a whole indicate that a good CSR record is correlated with superior financial performance. There are gaps in the data and there is room for more research to reinforce the conclusions, but the overall implication is clear and unmistakable. Of course, one needs to think carefully what this correlation means: anyone with even a modest background in statistics will be aware that a correlation between two things does not mean that one causes the other. Fortunately, some of the studies make it possible to resolve questions of causation and conclude that some aspects of social and environmental behavior drive stock-market valuation, rather than valuation driving social and environmental behavior or both being caused by a third factor such as managerial skills.

A great majority of relevant studies measure a company's social and environmental performance by some aspect of its environmental record. Data on companies' environmental records are easy to obtain and also rather easy to interpret: the U.S. Environmental Protection Agency (EPA) makes much of this publicly available. Data on other aspects of social and environmental performance are in contrast the proprietary information of rating agencies such as Innovest and KLD, and although these agencies are willing to make the data available to researchers, the data is nevertheless less accessible. This data also reflects a number of judgments by the raters about what are significant aspects of social and environmental behavior and what are not, judgments that researchers may not wish to have embedded in their work. So in over 90 percent of the studies about the connection between social, environmental, and financial performance, the first two are measured by some set of readily available environmental performance data. This gives a limited perspective of the general relationship between social responsibility and financial performance.

Measuring financial performance requires careful thought. Profit is probably what comes to mind at first, but there are limitations here. If a firm raises its investment, then as investment is a cost its profits drop, and vice versa. Yet its underlying financial performance is unchanged. Similarly, profits can be influenced by acquisitions, write-offs, and a variety of irregular events. For these reasons and others, most researchers have worked with the *market-to-book ratio* as a measure of financial performance. This is a firm's stock-market valuation divided by the book value of its assets, which should represent the cost of acquiring those assets today. So this ratio represents the difference between what it would cost to buy the firm's assets, its buildings, machines, equipment, and so on, and the value that the stock market puts on the firm. If the cost of acquiring a firm's assets is $1 million and its market value is $2 million, with a market-to-book of 2, this tells us that the firm's managers have made its assets worth far more than they cost and are adding value to the corporation. If, on the other hand, the market value were only $1.1 million, with a market-to-book of 1.1, it is clear that the managers are adding far less. In the limit, a market-to-book of 1 tells us that the firm is only worth what its assets sell for individually: the corporation in which they are embedded adds nothing to them.

There are other points we need to be aware of when testing for a connection between environmental performance and market-to-book. For example, in most industries large firms have higher market-to-book ratios than small firms. If large firms also rate higher for environmental performance, then there will appear to be a connection between market-to-book and environmental rating, but only because the most successful firms are large and also rate well on environmental matters. Both market-to-book and environmental rating are correlated with size, so there is a correlation between them. This, however, does not imply that environmental performance helps valuation or vice versa. In cases like this, we have to correct for firm size in our statistical studies, which means asking whether among firms of a given size those with higher environmental performance also have higher market-to-book ratios. There are other factors for which researchers have to correct, one being the industry in which a firm operates. Some industries just have higher rates of profit than others—for example, pharmaceuticals— and if they also rate high environmentally, then they will give the appearance of a connection between environmental performance and valuation, even though environmental performance may be neither a cause nor an effect of the high valuations. High valuations could be caused by the lack of competition for blockbuster drugs, and the impression of superior environmental performance may come from the fact that researching and manufacturing pharmaceuticals has little environmental impact. Again, we allow for this by asking whether within the pharmaceutical industry the firms with higher valuations have better environmental records.

Another approach to detecting the connection, if any, between social, environmental, and financial performance lies in studying the performance of SRI funds. They invest preferentially in firms with a high social and environmental ratings, and if indeed such firms have superior performance, then SRI funds might exhibit superior returns. Of course, the returns to SRI funds depend not only on the extent to which they select the stock of firms showing high social ratings but also on the general investment management skills of the fund managers and the sectors of the market in which they invest. So deducing a relationship between social, environmental, and financial returns from the performance of SRI funds is complex, but nonetheless possible, and is the subject of Chapter 3.

Pollution and Stock-Market Value   Every year since 1989 the U.S. EPA has published the Toxics Release Inventory (TRI), a listing of the amounts of over six hundred toxic pollutants released by certain manufacturing corporations in the United States employing over ten people. The criterion for inclusion on the list is that the firm either manufactures over 25,000 lb. of one of the specified chemicals or uses over 10,000 lb. It is worth noting that the data on toxics releases in the TRI is self-reported by firms to the EPA and not subject to outside verification and so may contain errors, presumably in the direction of underreporting. This action was initiated by EPA under powers given by the Emergency Planning and Community Right-to-Know Act of 1986. One of the first papers to illuminate the connection between CSR and capital markets was Hamilton's 1995 study using this data. Hamilton looked at the treatment of the TRI announcement for 1989 by the press and also at its impact on share prices.[11] He used what is called event study methodology to identify how the announcement of toxic releases affected the stock-market values of the releasing firms relative to the market as a whole. What this means is that Hamilton first studied how the share prices of companies featuring in the TRI moved relative to the rest of the stock market over the year prior to the release of the TRI data. This gave an idea of the normal relationship of TRI company share movement to the movement of the rest of the market. He then studied the movement of TRI shares on the day of the release of TRI data and for a week afterward, and compared this movement with that of the rest of the market. The pattern after the release of TRI data was very different from that established over the previous year. From this, he was able to show that the release of TRI data caused the shares of TRI firms to drop relative to what would have been expected of them on the basis of the previous year's movement. Hamilton found a significant negative impact of the release of TRI data on stock prices, with an average impact on releasing firms' stock-market values of $4.1 million. The size of the impact depends on the number of chemicals released by the firm, increasing by $236,000 for each additional chemical.

An interesting aspect of these results is that the release of toxic chemicals is a negative external cost imposed on the rest of society, clear evidence of social costs in excess of private costs, and the study shows that capital markets are penalizing this. There is therefore a reason to believe that reducing the excess of social over private costs—as in the cases of BP and Dow—may raise stock-market value and reward shareholders. This is in keeping with the perspective stated in the UBS report cited earlier to the effect that externalization of costs generates a contingent liability for a firm.

Several subsequent studies have found results similar to Hamilton's for other countries. Dasgupta, Laplante, and Mamingi (2001) studied the way in which capital markets in Argentina, Chile, Mexico, and the Philippines reacted to information about a firm's environmental performance.[12] Their raw data were public recognitions of firms' superior or inferior environmental performances, drawn from articles in major business newspapers addressing corporate environmental performance. They defined superior environmental performance as recognition by a regulator or other government authority that a firm met or exceeded expected standards, and inferior performance as the filing of a complaint against a firm by a regulator or by a member of the public. The authors analyzed all cases of superior or inferior performance using event study methods. In the case of recognition of superior performance, the average rise in stock-market value was 20 percent, and in cases of poor performance, the drop in value ranged from 5 to 15 percent.

A later study by Dasgupta, Hong, Laplante, and Mamingi (2004) found similar results for The Republic of Korea.[13] The Korean Ministry of the Environment has for many years published monthly a list of firms that fail to comply with the country's environmental laws; this monthly list is called the Monthly Violations Report. Using the event study methodology again, these authors showed that featuring on this list on average caused a company's stock price to drop by 9.7 percent.

What is interesting about all of these event studies is that they find a link between the release of information that a firm is externalizing some of its costs and a change in the stock-market value of the firm. Capital markets clearly penalize firms with external costs. Precisely why they do this is not clear from the studies, but there are several possible explanations. Presumably, capital markets are anticipating that firms will at some point be forced to pay for the external costs, or at least for part of them. They are therefore treating the external cost, or part of it, as a liability to the firm. This is reasonable: there are a number of ways in which external costs can turn into a liability. In the United States the most obvious one is a law suit, with the person or entity on whom the costs are imposed suing to obtain redress. Given the flexibility and ubiquity of the U.S. legal system, such law suits are a real possibility, and with astronomical damage awards also possible, the incentive to avoid this liability is very real. The stock market seems sensible in factoring this risk into a corporation's market value. There are other mechanisms through which external costs imposed on others can be brought back to the originator. A consumer boycott is one: we have already seen the boycott of Shell products in Europe as a result of its decision to dispose of the Brent Spar oil buoy at sea. Regulatory intervention is another real possibility, and in the United States this has often been costly to the regulated corporations, with provisions such as backdating liabilities to a date prior to the introduction of the legislation. As the UBS report cited earlier noted, the risk of provisions like this makes cutting back external costs seem a cost-effective policy, and such risks also make the stock market nervous about significant externalization of costs. All told, it is not surprising that the stock market sees externalized costs, particularly from emissions of toxic chemicals, as a financial liability. In the cases that are the subject of these event studies, the release of toxic pollutants is not shown to reduce profits but to reduce stock-market value. Stock-market value reflects a company's expected future profitability, so the market expects that the liabilities associated with external costs will at some future date reduce profits, but none of the studies cited gives evidence that this has happened so far.

Another salient aspect of these studies of environmental performance is that it is rather clear which way causation runs: it is clear that the release of information about pollution causes stock prices to change rather than vice versa. This may seem so obvious as to be barely worth mentioning but assumes significance, given that many other studies also find correlations between environmental ratings and financial performance but are unable to determine the direction of causation. Indeed, as remarked earlier, using statistical analysis to determine causation is usually fraught with complexity, so it is noteworthy that in these event studies there is an unambiguous implication.

Environmental and Financial Performance   A rather different class of studies of the connection between social, environmental, and financial performance is represented by that of Dowell, Hart, and Yeung (DHY).[14] Measuring the market-to-book ratio, the ratio of the stock-market value of the company to the cost of its tangible assets, they found a positive correlation between market-to-book and environmental performance. Their study is restricted to U.S. manufacturing companies that are in the S&P 500 and that operate both in the United States and in middle-income developing countries.[15] For the study, the authors divided the firms into three categories according their environmental policies. In the first category were those operating a uniform worldwide standard above that required in the United States. In the second category were those operating at U.S. environmental standards world wide, even if this involves exceeding legally required standards outside the United States. In the third category were those adopting standards lower than that of the United States in countries where this is permitted. Clearly, the first group has the highest environmental standards and sets its own worldwide standards above those of the United States, which in areas other than greenhouse gas and vehicle emissions are generally the highest. The second group, operating globally at U.S. standards, has the next highest performance, and the third group, which takes advantage of lax local laws in some countries, has the lowest. It is this measure of environmental performance—membership in one of these three groups—that DHY find to be correlated with the ratio of stock-market value to the cost of tangible assets. Firms in the first group have higher market-to-book ratios than those in the second, whose market-to-book ratios are in turn on average higher than those of firms in the third group.

The DHY study was pioneering and has justly been the focus of much attention. One possible limitation is that their measure of environmental performance is self-reported and is not independently audited: companies were asked to state which of the three categories they fell into and this statement was not checked. And, of course, there is the standard comment that correlation does not imply causation, so that the correlation between market-to-book and environmental performance could arise from one or more other factors that are causing both. This is why the event studies of the relationship between stock-price movement and the release of information about environmental performance are significant: they can cut through this ambiguity. One particularly thought-provoking comment by the authors is that capital market valuations internalize externalities—that is, the capital markets recognize the difference between private and social costs and treat the excess of social over private as a liability that the corporation will have to meet at some point.[16] This is completely consistent with the findings from the event studies and with the interpretation of assuming social and environmental obligations suggested here.

King and Lenox[17] conducted a related study. They work with a larger sample of firms and use data from the EPA's toxics release inventory to construct a measure of emissions for each of them. In fact, they use two measures of emissions: one, the quantity of emissions[18] adjusted for the size of the firm; and the other, a measure of emissions relative to other firms in the same industry. The second is the more natural, as there are certain industries where pollution is almost unavoidable, as, for example, power generation. The question to ask of a power producer is not "Does it pollute?" but rather "Does it pollute more or less than other firms in the same business?" The relative emissions measure speaks to this and shows whether a firm's environmental performance is above or below expectations for its industry. King and Lenox conclude that

> We find evidence of a real association between lower pollution and higher financial performance. We also show that a firm's environmental performance

relative to its industry is associated with higher financial performance. We cannot show conclusively, however, that a firm's choice to operate in cleaner industries is associated with better financial performance, nor can we prove the causal direction of the observed relationships. Thus, our research provides support for a connection between some means of pollution reduction and financial performance, but it also suggests that the reason for this connection remains to be established.

There is, in other words, a clear relationship between financial performance and the relative pollution measure, but the authors are not able to infer a direction of causation. On this issue, they state that "[i]nnovative firms may have lower emissions levels and greater profits. Alternatively managers may choose to improve a firm's environmental performance when they have an especially profitable year." So the causation could go from profits to environmental performance, or there could be no causation between these two, with both resulting from a characteristic such as being innovative. King and Lenox's findings are consistent with those of DHY, indicating from a different and larger sample of firms that there is a correlation between environmental performance (now measured by the quantity of emissions) and market-to-book, but again failing to clarify unambiguously the nature of the causation at work and the reasons for this correlation. We can take it from these two studies that the correlation is well established but not well explained. Hence, the importance of the event studies by Hamilton and his successors, which as emphasized earlier do give an unambiguous statement, which is that causation runs from environmental performance to stock prices.[19]

Social Performance and Market-to-Book

Finally, we turn to some current research being undertaken by my colleagues Ray Fisman and Vinay Nair and me. We too are looking at the relationship between social and financial performance, and in addition we try to see what kinds of firms are investing in superior social performance: what are the characteristics of firms whose social performance is rated high? Answering this question brings in issues of corporate governance, the number of independent directors, and the nature of the shareholdings in the company. We use a measure different from all of the earlier studies. Rather than an aspect of environmental performance, our social performance indicators are derived from the corporate ratings provided by the rating firms Innovest and KLD. These are comprehensive evaluations of the firms' social and environmental performance in many dimensions, extending beyond those purely related to pollution. Market-to-book is again used as a measure of financial performance.

As Innovest and KLD are the main sources of data on integrated CSR evaluations, it is worth reviewing briefly their methodologies. Innovest sets out on its Web site (www.innovestgroup.com) its procedures for evaluating a company. These involve an overview of the sector in which it operates, to assess the social and environmental issues that are germane to that sector, and the collection of data on the company's performance from a wide range of sources, including corporate documents such as filings with the Securities and Exchange Commission, the Environmental Protection Agency and other environmental bodies, industry sources such as trade journals, and NGOs that follow the company's activities. This is followed up by an interview with the company, and finally Innovest gives a rating in the format of AAA, ABB, and so on. The following are some examples of how Innovest defines its final ratings:

AAA: A company with minimal, well-identified environmental/social risks and liabilities, and with a strong ability to meet any losses which might materialize. Extremely well positioned to handle any foreseeable tightening of regulatory requirements, and strongly positioned strategically to capitalize on environmentally/socially-driven profit opportunities.

BBB: A company with strong managerial capability, but one where environmental/social risks and liabilities are a potential source of loss, though not on any material scale. Average level of positioning vis a vis profit opportunities.

CCC: A company where there are significant doubts about management's ability to handle its environmental/social risks and liabilities, and where these are likely to create a serious loss. Well below-average ability to capitalize on environmentally/socially-driven profit opportunities.

KLD rates corporations on the following criteria: community, corporate governance, diversity, employee relations, environment, human rights, and product. Each of these seven criteria is subdivided into five to ten categories. For example, within the community category a company is rated for its giving policies, its support of education, its treatment of indigenous people, the existence of controversies about its investment policies, and any negative economic impacts its actions may have on the community. Within the environment category, KLD looks at issues such as, Are the company's products and services beneficial to the environment? How much pollution does it produce, and how much of toxic chemicals and hazardous wastes does it emit? What is its recycling policy? Does it use alternative fuels? What is its impact on climate change? Within each category, the company's performance is rated either as a strength, a weakness, or as neutral for the company, indicated by ratings of 0/1 in a strengths column or as 0/1 in a weaknesses column. The final output here is a profile of zeros and ones evaluating the company's strengths and weaknesses in each category.

Using data from KLD, Fisman, Heal, and Nair construct three different measures of social performance, one environmental, one related to the treatment of employees, and one based on relationships with the community in which the company operates. The environmental measure reflects pollution, energy use, waste generated, and a range of other activities with environmental impacts. The employee-oriented measure reflects relations with unions, gender and race diversity in the labor force, employee law suits, wage levels, and other measures of the treatment of employees. The community measures are based on various measures of giving to the community, support of low-cost housing, and support of educational and cultural objectives. One interesting fact to emerge from this distinction between the different measures of social performance is that the firms that rate highly for one type do not necessarily rate highly for others and, indeed, in general do not. As we look across different firms, we see little correlation between their three scores. Some firms are rated highly on the environmental measure, others on the community measure, and still others provide superior treatment to their employees. Few are good at all, and some are good at none.

We focus mainly on the community measure, as prior studies have dealt comprehensively with the environmental dimension. We find a correlation between community-oriented performance and market-to-book ratios, even after allowing for differences between firm sizes and for differences between industries. We also conclude that this is more important financially for companies that advertise heavily, suggesting that social performance matters financially most to companies to whom image and visibility are important. We also infer tentatively that the level of social performance relative to other firms in the same industry is more important than the level on its own. This, like the result on advertising and social performance, suggests that consumers evaluate firms according to their social performance and choose those with stronger positions. Our finding here is similar to King and Lenox's conclusion that a firm's environmental performance relative to the rest of its industry matters for its financial performance. This result is tentative but is important, as an understanding of how consumers react is of critical importance to firms considering their social policies. When asking what kinds of firms tend to rate highly for social performance, we again find that advertising expenditure is an important variable: firms that spend more on marketing tend to rate higher. This is consistent with the idea that social performance matters for firms for which image and brand reputation are important variables.

The idea that consumers react positively to the firms' social positions is backed by data on the effects of cause marketing, that is, sales campaigns in which the sale of a product is linked to contributions to a popular cause. The following are examples of the impact of cause marketing:

Coca-Cola: In 1997, Coca-Cola donated $0.15 to Mothers Against Drunk Driving for every case of Coca-Cola bought during a six-week promotion in more than four hundred Wal-Mart stores. Coke sales in these stores increased 490 percent during the promotion.

American Express: In 1983, after American Express pledged to donate a penny to the restoration of the Statue of Liberty for every transaction made by its cardholders, use of American Express cards increased by 28 percent and new users increased by 17 percent.

Calphalon Corporation: The Calphalon Corporation co-branded several of its poorly selling pans with the Share Our Strength name and logo and donated $5 to the nonprofit for every such pan sold. Sales of these pans increased 250 percent.

Evian Natural Spring Water: Evian supported Share Our Strength through the "Quench Hunger" program, donating proceeds from sales of cases of one-liter glass bottles to the nonprofit. Case sales of this product increased 20 percent during the promotion.

BT Group: BT Group, a major British telecommunications services company, offered a donation to ChildLine, a twenty-four-hour helpline in the United Kingdom for children in danger, for every customer who signed up for its voicemail service. Sign-ups increased 25 percent during the promotion, and BT saw a direct mail response rate three times the normal rate.

Red: In January 2006, the *Financial Times*[20] reported that the rock singer Bono had agreed to a global cause–marketing campaign with American Express, Emporio Armani, Converse, and GAP. Each of these brands will sell products under the additional Red brand (Amex will launch a Red card) and donate about 1 percent of the proceeds to support The Global Fund to fight AIDS, tuberculosis, and malaria. All of these major brands stated that they expect the link with good causes to bring extra business and provide word-of-mouth marketing that will substitute for conventional promotion costs.

These examples, drawn from a long list of similar cases, do again suggest that consumers are conscious of the social implications of their buying decisions and are willing to let these social implications influence their choices, which is quite consistent with the findings that social and environmental performance affects stock-market values positively. The appendix to this chapter reprints a report by a Whirlpool executive of the effect of cause-related marketing on Whirlpool's sales, indicating a significant impact on consumer loyalty to the company as a result of its sponsorship of Habitat for Humanity.

A very elegant illustration of how consumer responses to a company's environmental and social stances can affect their purchasing choices was provided by an experiment organized by Hiscock and Smyth at the ABC Department Store in Manhattan. ABC is a rather upmarket department store in Manhattan, which is itself an upscale location, so that this experiment does not necessarily speak for the behavior of the general consuming public. Nevertheless, it is thought-provoking. The experimenters found two competing ranges of towels, both made in developing countries of organic cotton and under fair trade conditions. Both were therefore exemplary from the social and environmental perspectives, but neither was initially labeled so in the store. The experimenters first labeled one set of towels to indicate its social and environmental credentials and noted the effects on sales. The effects were dramatic: sales of the labeled brand rose over those of their competitors. Relative sales of the labeled brand were even higher when the prices of the labeled items were increased by 10 percent, and higher again when prices were raised as much as 20 percent. Clearly, consumers were voting with their dollars for products with a positive social and environmental angle. This conclusion is reinforced by a subsequent rerun of the experiment: after the first round all labels were removed and the towels were left unlabeled as initially. After a few months, the experiment was reversed—the previously unlabeled towels were now labeled as organic and fair trade while the others remained in anonymity. Again sales of the labeled towels took off. A similar experiment was conducted for candles, with very similar results.

So there clearly are consumers who judge products partly by their social and environmental credentials, which can therefore be an aid in marketing these products. The experience of the outdoor clothing brand Patagonia in introducing organic cotton, which necessitated a price rise, confirms this: they found no loss of sales in response to a carefully explained replacement of regular cotton by organic cotton and a simultaneous price rise of about 10 percent.[21] These findings are consistent with the Fisman-Heal-Nair findings mentioned earlier, which indicate that socially responsible behavior can help the valuation of companies that spend heavily on promotion and for which image presumably matters. Indeed, it may be behind some of the findings that environmentally responsible behavior is correlated with high market-to-book ratios.

Given that responsible social and environmental performance seems to predispose to superior financial performance, it is natural to ask whether there are aspects of how a firm is run that predispose it to a strong CSR record. The work by Fisman, Nair, and me gives some preliminary ideas. CSR performance seems to be linked to corporate governance and in particular to the composition of the board of directors. A larger fraction of independent directors is associated with higher CSR scores. Independent director here means a member of the company's board of directors who is not related to the senior executives of the company and who does not run a business or nonprofit that trades with or benefits from the company. Independence of the board of directors is generally taken to be a sign of a well-run company, as it indicates a board that can provide some independent checks on the actions of a company's senior executives and is not beholden to those executives. This finding leaves open the question of causation, Does an independent board direct a company to policies that rate higher on CSR, or do independent directors prefer to join boards of companies that have good reputations for CSR, or is there some third factor that is driving both, such as the nature of the senior management in the company? Maybe good managers want independent boards and also want to run companies that are well rated for CSR.

Conclusions

Superior social and environmental performance does appear to improve a company's stock-market valuation, suggesting that those who trade in the market expect that this will in the long run improve profitability. This is particularly true of the environmental aspects but also holds for more general measures. There are good reasons for this: superior social and environmental performance can improve a company's financial performance in many ways, from reducing exposure to risks to improving brand value and employee morale, and the externalization of costs is viewed by the stock market as a liability, and is indeed a liability. Imposing external costs on others is likely to lead to law suits, actions by nongovernmental organizations, and ultimately to regulatory intervention and changes in the legal framework. There are many examples of societies taking punitive actions toward corporations that transgress.

Appendix: Whirlpool and Corporate Social Responsibility

Below are excerpted remarks from the keynote presentation at IEG's *Sponsorship at Light Speed* conference delivered by John Alexander, the company's vice president and general manager, Whirlpool and value brands, North American region. These remarks illustrate in a very concrete context how a company's CSR policies can affect its brand image and consumer loyalty. They are reproduced with the permission of Whirlpool.

To understand how Whirlpool analyzes sponsorship, it's important to understand our industry and business. The major home-appliance category has been in a stalemate for years. It has tended to be a commodity business, which means that it has been characterized primarily by cost and quality parity, with competitors quickly following any new product features.

The industry also has been marked by high fixed costs, slow growth, little customer loyalty to brands, and concentrated trade distribution power.

One of the serious implications of that situation is that price becomes a major element of the consumer's decision process, leading ultimately to marginal shareholder return.

Thus, Whirlpool had two paths we could go down. We could strip all the cost out of our company and play the commodity game, or we could choose the path that we call brand-focused value creation. The second option, which we chose, meant finding ways to build strong brands that consumers would pay a premium for, and then innovating around those brands.

We needed to become much more than a world-class manufacturer. We needed to move from an organization that builds great products, does well at distributing them through the trade, and then hopes to make a great margin on them, to a company that builds brands that people will walk into a store and request, or better yet, demand.

Our mission became "the passionate creation of lifelong relationships with our customers by being their most trusted, desired, and selected brand."

As we started on that path, we did a great deal of work to define what each of our brands' position is, and we developed a clear description of who our target consumer is for each brand. But we also realized that as important as positioning the brand and understanding the target is, unless we understood how to drive value from that consumer, we were going to go nowhere.

The key to success would be understanding those things that make consumers loyal to a brand. This is different than being loyal to a product—"I love my washer, so I would go back and buy the same washer." We want people to be loyal to the Whirlpool brand, so whatever Whirlpool comes out with, they will want to buy.

More than two years ago, we started to build a customer loyalty model. It starts with a list of seven behaviors that we use to gauge consumer loyalty:

- Ask for brand
- Repurchase same brand
- Recommend brand
- Use other products by brand
- Overrule salesperson
- Only buy brand
- Switch store for brand

We define passionately loyal customers as those who answer absolutely yes to four of those seven.

We then define the brand's CLI—customer loyalty index—as the percentage of all customers who are passionately loyal. We believe that the higher a brand's or company's CLI, the better its future growth will be.

But again, the key questions for us to answer were, "What are the touchpoints and drivers of loyalty to the brand in our business and how can we capitalize on them to build our CLI?" We developed an incredibly complex survey model to answer those questions.

The big "aha" for Whirlpool that resulted from this consumer research was that in determining brand loyalty, emotional motivations were twice as important as rational motivations.

This was very scary to a manufacturing company with lots of engineers; we only became a truly brand-focused organization about five years ago. The actions we needed to take to drive growth and profitability were not where our competencies were inside the company.

Certainly one group that needed to be persuaded that this uncharted direction was a good one were our financial people. They needed to know the real impact that increasing our CLI would have on the bottom line.

Our model had a very compelling answer (). Looking at four levels of loyalty, it showed significant increases in ownership as you moved up from level to level. Overall, every one-point increase in our CLI translates into a nearly five percent increase in sales.

Giving the Tin Man a Heart

Once the numbers had persuaded everyone in the company to become interested in driving loyalty, it then became a matter of how to do it.

Our loyalty model showed us what our key drivers of loyalty were. In our survey, we tested about 50 touchpoints of what was important to consumers in terms of loyalty. Product was number one, but we knew that loyalty to the product would not drive us high enough.

What popped out at us was that social responsibility was among the top five loyalty drivers. To be honest, we had added it to the survey at the last minute, not really knowing if it was important to consumers or not.

Up to that point, Whirlpool had not really understood the impact of social responsibility. We were doing a lot of great things in that area, but we viewed them simply as something a $13 billion company should do. We had never connected such activity with business results.

So knowing from one part of our model that we needed to make an emotional connection with consumers and then understanding that social responsibility was very important to that audience, it became clear that a cause was the way to tie those two together.

We didn't have to look any further than inside the company, because we were already supporting Habitat for Humanity Int'l. We had partnered with Habitat since 1999 at a level of $25 million over five years, donating a refrigerator and range to every Habitat home built in the U.S. But we had never leveraged it for our business; it was the best-kept secret Whirlpool had.

When we first started to discuss leveraging the relationship a little more than a year ago, we really wrestled with the idea. We didn't want to be selfish and appear to be exploiting this cause that is dear to our heart.

It is still something we struggle with, but one of our realizations was that leveraging the partnership not only would help Whirlpool, but also would shine a spotlight on Habitat and benefit it by potentially raising interest from other businesses that could offer support.

So our challenge was: How do we go out and let people know what we are doing with Habitat without raising our hand and saying, "Look at us, we're a great company, give us credit for it."

We put that challenge to our PR and advertising agencies, Zeno Group and Publicis, respectively. And they came back with the big idea of linking Habitat with our target audience's passion for music.

And so we launched a program last year working with Reba McEntire. We sponsored the 30-stop Reba Habitat for Humanity Concert Tour presented by Whirlpool. Reba was already working with Habitat, so she was a natural fit.

The most important thing to understand about this program is that it is done to raise awareness and support for Habitat and to establish an emotional connection with consumers by publicizing Whirlpool's commitment to the cause. It is not about product promotion.

Reba is not our brand icon, our corporate spokesperson, or our target consumer. She is a voice. In my first meeting with her, I said, "Our measure of success will be if you can get more people involved in helping this cause by making them aware of Habitat and all the good things about it. I don't want you to sell product. The worst thing you could do is become our spokesperson."

The program, which we are repeating for '05, has many elements. At each concert venue, there is a Habitat tent to get people involved. We support the program with national TV, radio and print advertising and a PR campaign.

In addition to reaching consumers, the program's other key piece is employee engagement. Since we started the relationship with Habitat, we had had thousands of employees who donated their time to the organization. When we told employees that we were now going to tell the whole country how they supported this cause, it made an unbelievable difference.

Results from our annual survey that measures employee engagement rose 25 percent last year, all attributed to the company's social responsibility. Employee engagement is one of the key factors in driving profitability of the company, so this is a powerful argument in favor of supporting worthy causes.

Among the specific elements we put in place for employees were contests in which the winners were able to take trips to see our TV spot with Reba being filmed in Los Angeles and to watch her appearance on *Today* in New York City.

Habitat for Humanity Relationship's Impact on Loyalty and Sales

The initial response from consumers and employees to the Reba/Habitat program was overwhelmingly encouraging; we started receiving emails the day we announced the partnership last spring.

But did the program pass the test in moving the loyalty numbers? Yes it did. Comparing loyalty figures for consumers who were exposed to our Reba/Habitat TV commercial versus those in our initial loyalty study, there was an increase for each of our seven critical behaviors (2).

Overall, the CLI rose from the baseline study's 15 percent to 28 percent.

Looking at visitors to our Web site, we saw a similar increase. Our average Web site visitors had a CLI of 22 percent; consumers who saw the TV ad and then went to the Web site had a CLI of 37 percent.

What is most encouraging is that the behaviors that scored the highest increase were the ones most closely tied to emotional motivations: only buy Whirlpool; ask for Whirlpool; overrule the salesperson and switch stores to buy Whirlpool.

We have had the greatest impact on the emotional piece of the puzzle, the piece we previously did not know how to move.

3

Socially Responsible Investment

According to the Socially Responsible Investment forum, "socially responsible investing (SRI) is an investment process that considers the social and environmental consequences of investments, both positive and negative, within the context of rigorous financial analysis." Mutual funds in their present form go back to 1924 when three Boston securities executives pooled their money to form the Massachusetts Investors Trust. As I noted before, the first SRI fund followed only four years later, when in 1928 evangelical Protestants founded the Pioneer Fund, which avoided investments in companies that made liquors, cigars, or cigarettes, with the idea of using investments as a vehicle for pursuing an ethical or political goal, receiving a boost during the campaigns against apartheid in South Africa. One of the main themes of the anti-Apartheid movement was to encourage divestment from companies doing business in South Africa and to bring pressure for political change in that country.[1] Figure 3.1 shows the growth of SRI funds in the last decade.

SRI investors are now widespread and include nonprofit organizations, religious groups, universities, hospitals, pension funds, and some individuals and corporations, all linked by the idea of using their influence as investors to promote social and environmental goals. They are, of course, interested in returns to their investments, but seek to attain additional nonfinancial goals over and above the standard financial goals. There are three elements to the SRI movement: first, and the most visible, is screened funds, funds that direct their investments to companies meeting certain ethical criteria; the second is shareholder advocacy, the use of the rights of shareholder to lobby a company's management for policies conforming more closely to ethical goals; finally, there is community investment, making funds available to groups with poor access to credit.

FIGURE 3.1 The Growth of SRI Funds

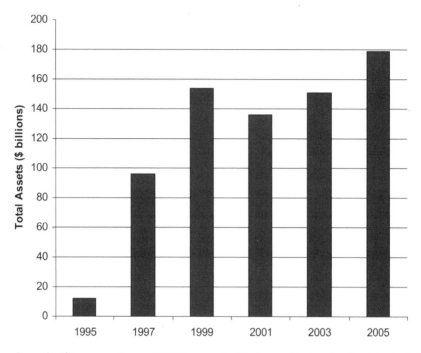

Source: Social Investment Forum, 2005 Report on Socially Responsible Investing Trends in the United States (http://www.socialinvest.org/pdf/research/Trends/2005%20Trends%20Report.pdf).

Screened funds are investment funds that choose their portfolio according to a combination of financial and social or environmental criteria: they seek profitable companies that will provide income and capital gains, but in addition seek to avoid investing in companies that act in ways they disapprove of. The evangelical fund mentioned earlier, the Pioneer Fund that avoided investing in companies making liquor or tobacco products, illustrates this idea. The use of social or environmental criteria need not always involve screening out companies that violate certain norms: recently, we have seen the growth of funds embodying a positive rather than negative approach and seeking to invest preferentially in companies that are highly rated for their performance in social or environmental areas. Figure 3.2 shows the numbers of SRI funds according to the issues that concern them, and gives a picture of the diversity of this area.

FIGURE 3.2 Mutual Fund Assets by Screen Type

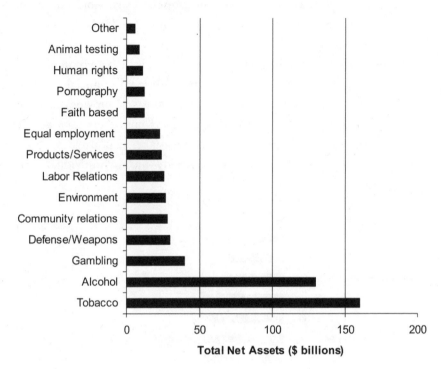

Source: Social Investment Forum, 2005 Report on Socially Responsible Investing Trends in the United States (http://www.socialinvest.org/pdf/research/Trends/2005%20Trends%20Report.pdf).

Shareholder advocacy is different: the idea here is to use shareholdings in a company as an entry to file shareholder resolutions at annual meetings and to start a dialogue with the management on issues that concern the shareholder. Religious groups have increasingly been using this route as a way of influencing corporate policies on matters of concern to them. Some environmental groups have followed this route and are using their shareholdings as a way of opening conversations on their issues. Large institutional investors have long used the influence that shareholdings give them to press management for policy changes, so this is not a new development. What is new is its use in the social and environmental areas. It is in a sense the exact opposite of SRI: SRI funds avoid investing in companies of which they disapprove, whereas activists may buy shares in a company precisely because they disagree with its policies and want to argue with the management. Figure 3.4 gives an indication of the growth of shareholder activism in the early years of the present century, and Figure 3.3 shows the issues of concern to the activists.

Community investing, the final element of SRI, is the provision of capital to communities that are underserved by traditional financial services, typically poor or minority communities. The aim is to provide access to credit, equity capital, and basic banking products not otherwise available to these communities. Community investing makes it possible for local organizations to provide financial services to low-income individuals and

FIGURE 3.3 Shareholder Resolution Activity 2003–05

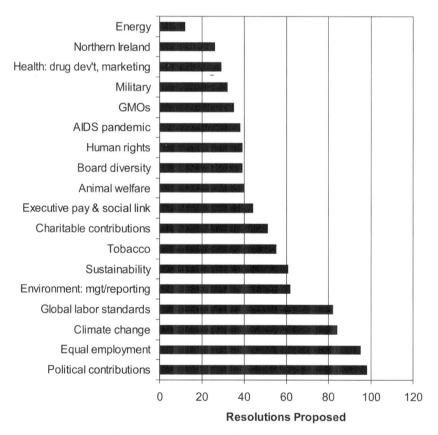

Source: Social Investment Forum, 2005 Report on Socially Responsible Investing Trends in the United States (http://www.socialinvest.org/pdf/research/Trends/2005%20Trends%20Report.pdf).

FIGURE 3.4 Leading Social Issues for Resolutions 2003–05

	2003	2004	2005
Resolutions filed	299	350	348
Resolutions voted on	145	200	177
Resolutions withdrawn	105	87	98
Average votes received	11.9%	11.4%	10.3%

Source: Social Investment Forum, 2005 Report on Socially Responsible Investing Trends in the United States (http://www.socialinvest.org/pdf/research/Trends/2005%20Trends%20Report.pdf).

to supply capital for small businesses and community services, such as child care, affordable housing, and health care. In the United States, the Community Reinvestment Act mandates some level of community investment by financial institutions that operate in minority communities.

The scale of SRI is now sufficient for it to be a significant factor in capital markets: in 2003, a total of $2.16 trillion in assets was invested in professionally managed portfolios using one or more of the three socially responsible investing strategies—screening, shareholder advocacy, and community investing. This represented more than one out of every nine dollars under professional management in the United States. The figure of $2.16 trillion managed by major investing institutions—including pension funds, mutual fund families, foundations, religious organizations, and community development financial institutions—has remained stable for several years, accounting for 10 percent of the total in investment assets under professional management in the United States. According to the Social Investment Forum, from 1995 to 2003, since the inception of the forum's publication of the biennial *Trends Reports,* assets involved in social investing have grown 40 percent faster than all professionally managed investment assets in the United States. Investment portfolios involved in SRI grew by more than 240 percent from 1995 to 2003, compared with the 174 percent growth of the overall universe of assets under professional management over the same time period. As the scale of SRI has grown, so its aims have become more diverse. These numbers probably underestimate the importance of funds that are motivated in part by social and environmental concerns, as many major pension funds such as CalPERS (California Public Employees Retirement System) and the New York State Pension Fund are activists on several social and environmental issues, climate change included. They are among the largest of all funds, but would not be listed as SRI funds in any conventional listing of such funds. Likewise, the endowment funds of rich private universities typically operate within social and environmental guidelines, but again are not formally classified as SRI funds.

Originally confined to avoidance of the "sin stocks" involving alcohol, gambling, and tobacco, there is now an SRI fund to cater for almost every social, ethical, or environmental perspective. Indeed, it is safe to say that each ethical viewpoint championed by an active nongovernmental organization has an investment fund to support its aims. This is a new and growing source of business and competitive advantage for fund managers: an investment management company without an SRI fund is at a competitive disadvantage. The best employers offer their employees a choice of methods for investing defined contribution pension funds and understand that many value the ability to choose an SRI fund, which has led to a proliferation of SRI offerings. In many cases, this is purely a business move and does not imply that the management companies sympathize with the social aims of the funds. Most see social goals as just constraints placed on their portfolio choices. Indeed, a management company may run several funds with contradictory goals.

These developments have led to the growth of a closely linked industry that provides the data on which socially responsible funds base their choices. Until recently a manager could not look up a company's environmental or human rights record online in the same way as its credit rating, accounting data, or earnings forecasts. Now, as noted in the previous chapter, this is possible through companies that specialize in providing the data for managers to screen investments and assess their consistency with a fund's goals. Some go beyond this and compile lists of companies rated by financial and environmental performance, for example, the Innovest group and KLD. Dow Jones, the doyen of financial indices, joined this trend several years ago by introducing its Sustainability Index. This ranks companies according to criteria believed to assess the sustainability of their contributions to society. *The Financial Times* has recently introduced a range of indices covering corporate performance on environmental issues, human rights, social issues, and relations with stakeholders. Even for managers not running SRI funds, this extra information adds value, providing a broader picture of a company and its relationship to the outside world than what is available through conventional financial indices.

The growth of SRI is a natural extension of a phenomenon already well established in retail and capital markets—the use of consumer buying power to attain social goals. Anita Roddick popularized this trend in the United Kingdom with the Body Shop and the U.S. outdoor clothing brand Patagonia has had similar success. McDonald's and Nike have suffered from it and learned to come to terms with it. As we have noted before, this movement is particularly influential in the human rights and environmental fields, where major clothing and shoe brands have been boycotted for their use of sweatshop labor and oil companies such as Shell have been punished for their alleged environmental transgressions. In 1994, *The Economist* spoke of "the era of the corporate image, in which consumers will increasingly make purchases on the basis of a firm's role in society: how it treats its employees, shareholders, and local neighbourhoods…" In many respects, SRI is simply an extension of this process to capital markets: cautious investors are looking at all dimensions of their choices.

The Performance of SRI Funds

Given that a high rating for social and environmental performance is associated with a superior stock-market valuation, it may seem obvious that investing in firms with high social and environmental ratings will lead to a portfolio that performs well. Sadly, matters are more complex than that, and there is controversy about the relative performances of SRI and regular funds. What complicates this issue is that many factors affect the performance of a portfolio, among them the skill of the manager in picking stocks and sectors and in deciding when to be in cash and when in securities. If the best managers go into running conventional funds—and this is just a hypothetical, as there is no evidence that this is true—then conventional funds are likely to perform better, even if the underlying investment methodology favors SRI funds. Some idea of the complexity of deciding whether SRI funds provide superior performance is provided by the performance of SRI funds in the United States over the period 1995–2000; in this period, several SRI funds clearly outperformed the standard benchmark indices. To be thorough, however, we have to ask whether this was because they were SRI funds whether there was another reason. Because of the SRI managers' emphases on avoiding companies that pollute, or are involved in arms manufacture, tobacco or alcohol, the portfolios of SRI funds were overweighted, relative to the standard indices, in stocks such as Microsoft, Intel, and Cisco, all of which are relatively untainted by environmental or social ills.[2] These are precisely the stocks that showed spectacular growth from the mid-nineties to the end of the century, so that the outperformance of SRI funds could be explained by their being overweight in technology stocks. This clearly does not provide a basis for expecting continued superior performance by these funds.

An example in the opposite direction is provided by the data for 2004: in that year, the rise in oil prices led to greatly increased profits for oil companies and huge increases in their share prices. Many SRI funds avoided or were underweight in oil stocks because of their association with pollution and climate change and, as a consequence, missed out on the capital gains from that sector of the economy, this time underperforming conventional funds. Again, this is not a source of underperformance that might be expected to continue in the long term. These two examples make clear the complexity of this issue, and go some way to explaining the ambiguity of statistical studies in this area. The example of the oil sector in 2004 shows that any restriction on portfolio choice can be costly, and the example of concentration in the tech sector in the late 1990s shows that restrictions can serendipitously act to the manager's advantage.

What one might call the received model of portfolio management, when applied to SRI, emphasizes the cost of restrictions on the set of shares in which a manager can invest and is very consistent with the example of the oil sector in 2004. Here is the basic framework. SRI funds must restrict the set of stocks that they can consider as investments, shunning for example, tobacco companies, gambling companies, defense contactors, and many others. As any of these sectors may in some years show exceptional performance—think of oil in 2004 or tech stocks in the late 1990s—these restrictions on a manager's choices must in the long run reduce the return that can be earned. One of the classic illustrations of this perspective is a study by Geczy, Stambaugh, and Levin[3] that looks at the performance of SRI mutual funds. In keeping with the positions taken by many in the finance profession, they argued that SRI funds must always underperform funds that are not constrained by ethical considerations and that the only open question is the extent of the underperformance. Their claim is that for index funds—funds that replicate the performance of an index such as the S&P 500—this underperformance is marginal, whereas for funds with a particular investment style—such as small-cap growth—it may be as high as 3.7 percent per year.

The argument that SRI funds must underperform does not in any way depend on the financial performance of companies with active social and environmental programs and indeed ignores the possibility that social, environmental, and stock-market performance may be related and is rooted in some very basic aspects of one of the widely used models of financial markets, the capital asset pricing model or CAPM. The main argument here is that all information that is relevant to investment decisions is contained in a firm's financial data—its current and past earnings and share prices, data about its equity and debt, and the volatility of its share price and earnings and the correlations between these and the market as a whole. Within this perspective, there is no role for information on social and environmental performance as an input to investment decisions: it is irrelevant. If this affects share price movements, then the relevant information about these effects is already incorporated in what we can see about volatility and correlations with other shares and the market. From this perspective, the argument of Geczy et al. is incontrovertible. Information about social and environmental profiles can add nothing and restricting a manager's choice of stocks can in the long run only lower the average return earned. There may be the occasional exception, such as SRI funds in the late 1990s, but over the long run years like 2004 will outweigh the years when stock restrictions help portfolio performance.

There are, however, alternative perspectives on the investment process. Rather than believing that all information relevant to investment choices is summarized in available financial data, one can take the view that there are aspects of a how a company is run that are not captured by this data and are, however, to some degree reflected in data on its SRI performance. Such data tells investors, for example, that management in a clothing company is well prepared to handle questions about their employees in poor countries, making them less likely to be the subject of a consumer boycott. If they have never been subject to such a boycott in the past, then the risk of a boycott is not one that appears naturally and may not be factored into stock prices. If there has never been a boycott, then historical data will not reflect this risk and may be an inadequate guide to the stock's riskiness. Yet data on social and environmental performance can address this risk. This data also tells us that the executives of an oil company understand and have thought about the environmental impacts of their operation and will be able to deal with criticism from NGOs, and indeed have taken steps to minimize any criticism to which they may be liable. More generally, social and environmental ratings can tell us that management has taken steps to avoid or minimize all liabilities arising from external costs or distributional conflicts. Investors will not be unpleasantly surprised by seeing their company featuring prominently on the U.S. E.P.A.'s *Toxics Release Inventory,* or as the target of activist groups, or as the defendant in a law suit. High social and environmental ratings also tell investors that any benefits from cleaner production, as reaped by B.P. and Dow, are already being harvested. This is all valuable information for investors, relevant to their evaluation of a company and not duplicated by standard historical data about financial characteristics and market performance. From this perspective, attention to social and environmental policies gives an additional dimension of information to analysts, potentially allowing them a different perspective on corporate prospects. Consistent with this is a recent statement by Standard & Poor's, which states that it now recognizes "the growing importance of non-financial disclosure in the overall assessment of a company's risk profile."[4]

There are two different ways of using social and environmental information in managing a portfolio. The first way is the more traditional approach: using this information to exclude certain types of stocks—this is called working with exclusionary screens. Different groups seek to exclude different types of stock: common to most is a desire not to invest in the so-called sin stocks, which include those of tobacco, alcoholic drinks, gambling, and weapons companies. Other groups may seek to exclude stocks of companies with poor environmental performance, poor labor relations, poor human rights records, subcontracting operations in low-wage countries, or one or more of a host of other characteristics. Exclusionary screens clearly do limit a fund-manager's choices and are in principle subject to the criticisms of Geczy and his coauthors.

The second way of using social and environmental information is more sophisticated and less widely practiced. The essence of this is that a manager makes portfolio choices along whatever are his or her conventional lines, using it to narrow down a short list of companies that are candidates for investment. A value-oriented manager, for example, will select short lists of shares in companies that he or she believes to be fundamentally strong but, nonetheless, undervalued, and then within this short list he or she will let social and environmental ratings influence the final choice. Innovest takes an approach to the evaluation of SRI portfolios that illustrates this idea. They look at standard portfolios for specific investment styles, and then ask the following question: What would happen, or would have happened, if the stocks in a particular portfolio had been replaced by similar stock (same sector, same financial characteristics) but with higher social and environmental ratings? They then track both portfolios and find almost universally that the modified portfolio beats the original. Their idea is not to construct an "SRI portfolio," but rather to modify an existing portfolio—be it growth or value or tech—to mimic many characteristics of the original and at the same time achieve a higher rating overall. They then compare the performance of the two. Neither is an SRI portfolio—one is, for example, a small-cap portfolio and the other is a small-cap portfolio modified to retain most of its statistical characteristics but attain higher social and environmental ratings. Consistent with the findings that the portfolios with higher ratings outperform the other is the observation that when firms in a sector are divided into high- and low-ranked on environmental criteria, those in the high-ranked group usually perform better financially than those that are low-ranked.[5]

Unfortunately, the data on the performance of SRI funds relative to the rest of the fund universe is ambiguous. Some SRI funds have outperformed the market consistently—but perhaps this just reflects the skill of the managers and not the merits of their investment philosophy. A recent study by Bauer, Koedijk, and Otten[6] suggests that in the United Kingdom, SRI funds have slightly outperformed their non-SRI competitors, whereas in the United States, the opposite was true in the first five of ten years studied, with a slight outperformance again emerging in the last half of the decade 1990–2001.

What conclusions can we reach from the literature on social and environmental performance, SRI, and capital markets? One robust result seems to be that superior environmental performance is correlated with high values for the market-to-book ratio. This suggests that good social and environmental performance pays, but does not prove it. Another robust conclusion seems to be that SRI funds do not systematically underperform with respect to their non-SRI competitors, suggesting that if there are costs—as opposed to benefits—from social and environmental programs, then they must be small. A more tentative result is that SRI funds may have a small performance edge over their competitors, but this is a more speculative statement, particularly as the performance data is dominated by the 1990s and SRI funds were heavily overweight in high-performing growth stocks over this period. Also tentative is the conclusion that taking into account CSR information can improve the performance of a portfolio of any type, SRI or not.

The Impact of SRI Funds

The aim of SRI investors is, in some general sense, to do good. And they hope to do well financially in the process. We have looked at whether they do well: next, we ask whether they do good. What has their impact been, and have they in fact had a positive influence for the causes that they support? The answers are rather different for the three strands of SRI—screened investment, shareholder activism, and community investment. Puzzlingly, although there is a plethora of studies of the return to screened SRI funds, there is a paucity of studies of their impact. Researchers have either not been interested in whether they have attained their social and environmental goals or have not seen how to check this. In fact, the latter is likely to be the case: it is not easy to see how to check for the impact of SRI funds. By avoiding the shares of certain companies, they shift demand away from these, and to the extent that share prices depend on supply and demand this may lead to lower prices. Lower share prices will concern managers, partly because they are themselves shareholders, partly because other shareholders will be disturbed and may press for changes, and partly because lower share prices raise the cost of capital to a company. Lower share prices mean that more shares have to be sold to raise any given amount of capital, so that more of the company has to be sold to reach given capital goals. It is, however, not obvious that by avoiding certain companies SRI funds will in fact reduce their stock prices. If stock prices depend on expected future earnings, a widely accepted theory of stock prices in the long run, then the fact that SRI funds avoid a company will not affect its stock price, as expected future earnings will not be affected by the funds' behavior. A drop in the price to below-expected future earnings because of selling by an SRI fund will just provide an attractive buying opportunity for others in the market. This is not to deny that information about its CSR performance may affect the market's expectations of a company's future earnings.

The studies discussed in the previous chapter have some bearing on this issue. There we noted that a company's market-to-book ratio is correlated with its social and environmental ratings. We discussed various explanations of why this might be, including the effects of positive environmental and social behavior on a company's performance. In fact, there is another explanation: if a company's market value is correlated with its social and environmental ratings, this could reflect the fact that SRI funds, guided by the SRI ratings, are demanding its shares and inflating its market value. Rather than social and environmental performance raising valuations, it may be that CSR rating acts as a buy signal for SRI funds and raises valuations. So the results we have already seen are consistent with the idea that SRI funds lower the cost of capital to highly rated companies, although they certainly do not prove this. In fact, if this were the case, it would imply that SRI funds are paying above average for their shares and would probably imply lower returns for them in the long run, which as we have noted does not seem to be the case. If we accept the suggestions of the last chapter that superior social and environmental performance lead to higher stock-market valuations, then none of this greater valuation may be attributable to the actions of SRI funds.

The behavior of companies with respect to social and environmental indices such as the Dow-Jones Sustainability Index (http://www.sustainability-indexes.com/) and the *Financial Times'* FTSE4GOOD (http://www.ftse.com/ftse4good/index.jsp) provides interesting but rather casual data on this point from a different perspective. Both indices are claiming to rate companies according to their attainments in the social and environmental area, broadly interpreted, and both are widely known and very visible, given the families of which they are part. In my experience, many large corporations have been willing to incur significant costs to ensure that they are well placed on these indices. Presumably, this implies that their senior executives see benefits in a clear public recognition of their stature in the social and environmental fields, and when I have spoken with them they have generally explained this in terms of a better position in capital markets and better access to capital, though none have cited hard evidence to support this idea.

There is an interesting recent study that bears directly on the issue of whether SRI funds have an impact on stock prices, suggesting that they do. This paper, appropriately named "The Price of Sin: The Effects of Social Norms on Markets," studies the prices of the "sin stocks" that almost every SRI fund avoids.[7] These are stocks in companies that produce alcoholic drinks or tobacco products, or are active in gambling. Alcohol, tobacco, and gambling are activities that most SRI funds screen against, so if SRI funds have an impact on share prices, then it is likely to be visible in the prices of these stocks. A particularly interesting hypothesis is that if SRI funds are influential, then they will tend to depress the prices of sin stocks, so the prices of such stocks will be less than that expected on the basis of the company's financial performance.

An alternative hypothesis is that their boycotting these stocks will have no effect: If the SRI funds depress the prices of sin stocks, then other funds that do not operate ethical screens will find sin stocks attractive buys and will buy enough to bring the price up to the level that their profitability indicates. In other words, the boycotting of these stocks by SRI funds will create arbitrage opportunities for other funds.

Yet another possibility is that the market sees sin stocks as more risky than the average because of the risk of litigation: this has certainly been a factor for tobacco firms in the last two decades. Perceived riskiness will lower a stock's price. The authors, Hong and Kacperczyk (HK), check all of these ideas carefully. Specifically, HK test the following hypotheses: that fewer institutional investors hold sin stocks than other comparable stocks, fewer analysts cover such stocks than comparable stocks, the market values of sin stocks are lower than what should be expected from their financial characteristics, and that companies whose stocks are sin stocks rely more on debt financing than comparable companies. Their data set supports all of these suggestions.

The number of institutional investors holding sin stocks is less than the average, as is the number of analysts who report on such stocks. So they form a relatively neglected part of the market. HK's findings on the pricing of sin stocks are particularly interesting. Sin stocks behave like value stocks—that is, stocks that are underappreciated and undervalued by the stock market. Stocks that are undervalued often perform well as they tend to catch up to the rest of the market, and this is what HK find for sin stocks. Their prices are low, but the total return to holding them is above average. This is good for investors but, of course, bad for the issuers, and as a consequence companies in the sin businesses tend to raise less money on the stock market and more on the debt market than comparable companies: they are in financial terms more highly leveraged with a higher debt-to-equity ratio. (SRI funds do not currently operate in markets for corporate debt, so there is no undervaluation of securities issued by "sin corporations" in these markets.) The authors also try to understand why sin stocks offer a higher return than others. One possible explanation is that they are seen as more risky, because of the chance of product liability litigation. Stocks more risky than the average have to offer a higher return than the average to find buyers. Another explanation is that sin stocks are undervalued just because they are overlooked: some investors are not interested and relatively few analysts cover them. HK decide in favor of the latter explanation. In this they are guided by the fact that after the tobacco settlements of the late 1990s tobacco companies were not at risk for further litigation, as claims against them were settled, yet this did not change their market behavior.

The HK study is the first to give a clear answer to the question: do SRI funds matter? The answer is a limited yes. We still do not know if the prices of "good" stocks are helped by the activities of SRI funds, though we do know that being green helps a company's stock prices—but not necessarily because of the actions of SRI funds. But we do now know that SRI funds have a far-reaching effect on the issuers of sin stocks, affecting their stock prices, who owns them, who follows them, and the companies' financial structures. So even if they do not help firms that "do good," SRI funds may punish the sinners.

When it comes to shareholder activism, matters are much clearer. Corporate law in the United States, and indeed in most countries, allows shareholders with a minimal stake in a company ($2,000 in the United States) to place items on the agenda of a shareholder meeting, to place a five-hundred-word supporting statement in proxy statements distributed before the meeting, and requires that a vote be taken on these matters at the meeting (the vote is not binding on the company). This is a powerful mechanism for embarrassing management about alleged ethical failures. The annual meetings of large corporations receive wide press coverage and these critical resolutions produce negative publicity, possibly leading to boycotts and diminished retail sales. Shareholder advocacy has been used by large institutional investors, such as the CaLPERS and the College Retirement Equities Fund (CREF) in the United States, as a route to more open corporate governance. Large investors have tried to influence corporate policies on such matters as chief executive succession, board membership, and poison pills, although their success rate is not clear.[8] A small fraction of the resolutions submitted lead to the adoption of the recommended policy by the target corporation, although this statistic could be misleading because in some cases, whose number is not known, the institutional investor will approach the corporation before submitting a resolution to see if an agreement can be reached without public debate. There is evidence that the largest institutions have a higher success rate in these nonconfrontational approaches than they do through formal resolutions, perhaps not surprising given the fact that formal resolutions will often be submitted only after lower-key approaches have been tried and have failed. Two informational intermediaries play an interesting role in the process of voting on shareholder resolutions, Institutional Shareholder Services (ISS) and the Investor Responsibility Research Center (IRRC).[9] These groups research the issues that arise in shareholder resolutions and make recommendations to institutional shareholders on how to vote. Their recommendations have been influential with institutional investors, and both have been paying more attention to issues relating to corporate social responsibility in recent years.

Ethical investors can and do use this same route. According to a report by the Interfaith Center on Corporate Responsibility, in 1999 SRI managers filed about 220 shareholder resolutions with more than 150 U.S. companies. The largest number covered environmental issues, with equity and corporate responsibility taking the next two places. Most of these resolutions are not passed by the shareholders—and even if they were, they would not be binding on the corporation. But the aim is not to pass resolutions; it is to get an issue on the agenda of the board of directors and to start the company thinking about it. The proponents of the resolution see this as the start of a dialogue that may last years before it is productive, although there have been occasions on which shareholder activists find themselves knocking on an open door. A notable case of this type was the decision by Home Depot, a major U.S. Do-It-Yourself outlet, to stop buying mature wood from endangered forests. In this case, shareholder activism was accompanied by a consumer boycott organized by rainforest-related NGOs. Baxter International, the manufacturer of health-care products, also agreed to stop using polyvinyl chloride (PVC) in some of its products. PVC releases carcinogens when it is burnt. Chevron and Exxon are facing similar actions by environmental NGOs intended to force them to abandon plans to drill in the Alaskan Arctic wildlife refuge. Another interesting achievement of shareholder activism can be seen in a project run jointly by two major brand names, Disney and McDonald's. McDonald's has exclusive restaurant industry marketing rights to Disney properties, including film, home video, theme parks, and television, so that the two are in effect running a joint venture in the manufacture of Disney items for sale in McDonalds' branches. At the instigation of several faith-based investment funds that are shareholders in both groups, and in collaboration with these groups, the two companies are investing considerable effort and resources in monitoring the labor conditions under which these products are made. This is not an easy undertaking: many companies have gone public with the problems they have encountered with ensuring compliance with labor standards in China. In this process they have enlisted the help of Chinese groups that are also concerned about labor standards.

Another good illustration of the role of active SRI funds comes from a review of the Domini fund's activities (available at http://www.domini. com/shareholder-advocacy/Current-Wo/index.htm). Domini was one of the first SRI funds and is still one of the largest and has been a trendsetter in this business. Currently, they are engaging companies in their portfolios on the following issues: global warming, global labor standards, global poverty and trade, diversity, corporate political contributions, fair trade coffee, recycling, proxy voting, transparency, and human rights. In most of these campaigns, they are allied with other groups, often the Interfaith Center on Corporate Responsibility, another of the heavy hitters in the area of shareholder activism. Among their recent successes were agreements by two oil companies, Apache and Anadarko, to report their responses to climate change, an agreement by Wendy's International to produce a report on its social and environmental performance, the production by Target of its first sustainability report, and an agreement by BellSouth to post its public policy positions and its political contributions policy on its Web site. Although none of these is individually a major achievement, all of the impacts just listed were obtained in one quarter, and a continuous stream of similar achievements, taken together with similar attainments by other SRI groups, can amount to a significant change in the corporate responsibility landscape.

A more striking example is provided by the fate of a Canadian oil company, Talisman. Until 2002, Talisman owned a stake in the Greater Nile Oil Project, an oil company operating in Sudan. This company was supplying 10,000 barrels of oil per day (420,000 gallons) to the Sudanese government, and it was widely believed that this oil was used by the Sudanese air force to fuel aircraft that attacked civilians and aid agencies during the bloody and vicious civil war in Sudan. Human rights groups in Canada pressured Talisman to sell its stake, placing resolutions on the agenda at annual meetings and claiming that Talisman's involvement violated Canada's International Code of Ethics for Canadian Business. During this period, Talisman's share price was depressed by the controversy centered on the company: the *Globe and Mail* reported from Toronto on June 26, 2000, that oil analysts as a group felt that the Sudan discount in Talisman's share price was in the range of Canadian $15 to $25,[10] an effect serious enough to make the company a candidate for a hostile takeover. Ultimately, Talisman conceded defeat and sold its stake in the Greater Nile Oil Project in October 2002 to ONGC Videsh Limited, a subsidiary of Oil and Natural Gas Corporation Limited, India's national oil company.[11] But this was not the end of the matter for Talisman. The U.S. Alien Tort Claims Act permits victims of international human rights abuses to sue both U.S. and non-U.S. companies in U.S. courts.[12] In *The Presbyterian Church of Sudan v. Talisman Energy,* villagers and the Church are suing Talisman for its participation in the Sudanese government's ethnic cleansing of Christian and other non-Muslim minorities in southern Sudan.[13] The lawsuit is seeking class action status and alleges that the company conspired with, or aided and abetted, the government of Sudan in committing violations of international law in connection with the company's now-disposed-of interest in oil operations in Sudan.[14]

The bottom line is that SRI funds appear to be influencing corporate policies through shareholder advocacy, although the effect of shareholder advocacy appears to be most effective when accompanied by a credible threat of consumer responses. The responsible consumer and the responsible investor form a team that is more than the sum of its parts.

Conclusions

Socially responsible investors are a significant presence in capital markets. The amounts in SRI funds are large and growing. What are SRI funds seeking, over and above a competitive return? What returns are they actually achieving? What impact have they had to date, and how might this change if the practice spreads? The aims of SRI funds are as diverse as the aims of political pressure groups and nongovernmental organizations. There are funds for all persuasions. A company might appeal to some but be anathema to others. There does seem to be general agreement among funds on a set of criteria that are used to define social responsibility. Weapons, pollution, and abuse of human rights are all seen as unethical as is gambling. Executives who want to court socially responsible investors should place their corporations strategically on these issues.

On average, socially responsible funds have performed well. There are several possible explanations for this and whether this is likely to continue depends on which are valid. An interesting possibility is that socially responsible behavior proxies for general managerial competence, and several studies seem to confirm this. There is also the fact that socially responsible investing interacts with similar behavior by consumers, each reinforcing the former. This is part of the process of consumers thinking about all dimensions of their choices. It is not clear yet what effect SRI has. Certainly, shareholder activism by socially responsible investors, along with consumer activism, has affected the choices of influential corporations. Socially responsible funds adopting a passive role toward their shareholdings are imposing some costs on the companies that they boycott—the "sin stocks"—but it is not clear whether they are helping the companies that they aim to support.

4

Financial Institutions and Social and Environmental Performance

For financial institutions, external costs are typically not important and not a source of conflict with society. But for the clients of these institutions, this is not the case. Banks may finance companies involved in deforestation or polluting energy production and thus indirectly cause external costs. If aggrieved groups "follow the money," they find a trail leading to banks and often point a finger at them, a process that has lead to the development of the Equator Principles (EP), one of the most interesting developments in the area of managing environmental impacts. Much of this chapter is about the Equator Principles.

Although there are few direct external costs associated with the financial sector, there are, nevertheless, many cases in which it does generate distributional conflicts. To deal with the simplest first: currently, several large U.K. and U.S. investment banks are the targets of lawsuits alleging gender discrimination and sexual harassment, and the abundance of such suits in the investment-banking industry for a decade or more suggests that they could clearly benefit from applying some of the most elementary ideas of social responsibility to their own human resources policies.

Investment banks and insurance companies have also been accused and indeed found guilty, of other forms of inequity, most of which arise from unfair treatment of some of their clients. Insider trading, common in many financial markets, is an example. People with privileged access to financial information (not always but often in financial institutions) may exploit this at the expense of their clients and the trading public. At the heart of arguments about insider trading is a conflict about the fair or proper distribution of the gains from participation in financial markets. Recent U.S. cases concerning the allocation of shares in initial public offerings (IPOs) are of the same type: the allegations here were that brokers issued undervalued shares preferentially to people who would bring them additional business, although purporting to issue them in a manner giving equal access to all. Again, the issue is the distribution of the benefits from market participation. Fake bids, rigged auctions, and volume-contingent commissions in the insurance industry are also of this genre—moves by brokers to appropriate to themselves rewards that are commonly considered due to others. So although financial institutions are not normally sources of private–social cost conflicts by their own actions, they clearly can be and often are sources of acute distributional conflicts by their control over access to the gains from trading in financial markets.

A different set of issues arises when we look at the operations of banks' clients, operations that are often financed by the banks. Did Nike's banks finance sweatshops? Do Exxon's banks finance environmental degradation? Banks are vulnerable to charges of socially inappropriate behavior by the actions of their clients, for which the banks are sometimes held responsible on the grounds that without their knowledge and financial support these actions would not occur. This explains the Equator Principles, which were agreed to by ten major banks in June 2003 and are now agreed to by a total of fifty-three.[1]

Background to the Equator Principles

The story of the Equator Principles at Citigroup illustrates how one industry, commercial banking, and one firm within that industry, has managed criticism of the social and environmental impact of its operations and how this has led to collective action within the industry and the emergence of a new framework for managing environmental and social impacts.

Over the last fifty years many infrastructure investments in developing countries have been controversial because of their environmental and social impacts. Typically, these have involved the construction of new roads, dams, power plants, or pipelines, and controversy has arisen from their disruptive effects on local communities and ecosystems. Many such investments are funded by project finance techniques, which involve establishing the project as a corporate entity financed by both equity and debt. Usually supplied by syndicates of international banks, debt typically provides the majority of financing. Nongovernmental organizations and other groups concerned with the environmental and social effects of these projects concluded that the best way of exerting pressure for higher social and environmental standards was to follow the money and put pressure on the banks supplying finance, rather than on the project sponsors, the companies behind the projects. Many major international banks were heavily invested in project finance and so were in this business repeatedly, whereas most sponsors were involved with only a few projects. As a consequence, from early in the new century Citigroup and other major players in project finance faced increasing pressure from socially and environmentally oriented nongovernmental organizations, and from socially responsible investment funds, because of their roles in facilitating environmental damage through project finance. SRI funds moved motions on the environment at several Citigroup annual general meetings, and then the NGO Rainforest Action Network (RAN) launched a campaign against Citigroup, protesting about the bank's alleged involvement in the destruction of tropical rainforests. Part of this campaign was an advert broadcast on cable television in New York, Citigroup's home base, in which celebrities Susan Sarandon and Daryl Hannah urged Citigroup credit card holders to destroy their cards. Simultaneously, RAN publicized photos (believed to be stock photos) of clear-cut forests, implying that the cutting was financed by Citigroup.

Around this time, the drumbeat of critical comments about the environmental and social impacts of bank-financed projects was getting louder. The cumulative effect of demonstrations, petitions and negative advertising by RAN played a role in persuading Citigroup executives to begin discussions of this issue. Chris Beale, who was then the global head of project finance, and also the son of a former Australian environment minister, felt the need to take defensive action before the situation reached a crisis level and attracted more attention. At that point, there was no frame of reference or internal process at Citigroup to address this kind of criticism from external groups. So in response, Citigroup established an internal Environmental and Social Policy Review Committee, consisting of representatives from Community Relations, the Corporate and Investment Banks, the Legal, Risk Management, Asset Management and other departments to address these issues. Citigroup also initiated a dialogue with a group of SRI funds and one nongovernmental organization, Friends of the Earth (FoE), which was called the "Shareholder Dialogue Group." Once this committee was in place, Citigroup initiated a "Shareholder Dialogue" with SRI funds and Friends of the Earth (FoE) to explain its existing procedures for evaluating candidates for project finance deals.

The existing methods were illustrated by the example of a Latin American native claim on land used in a candidate project and a discussion of how Citigroup had required that this be resolved before they would fund the project. In this case, the funding of the project was via a debt private placement and a bank syndication, rather than project finance. Citigroup felt that the external groups were positively impressed by the way it had resolved the complex issues posed by this case and thought of this as a possible precedent. Further discussions with external groups led to a commitment by Citigroup to enhance due diligence for projects in "high-caution zones," zones particularly sensitive to environmental or social damage; to implement new lending practices for areas occupied by indigenous peoples; and to reporting greenhouse gas emissions from all power-sector projects it finances.[2] An important message from this was that no commercial institution, not even a global bank of the size and influence of Citigroup, is immune from pressures arising from adverse public opinion. This message is even today proving to be an important catalyst for a more proactive approach on the part of banks toward sustainability, human rights, and social impacts.

Development of the Equator Principles

Many international banks went through experiences similar to Citigroup's at about the same time. As a result, Herman Mulder, senior executive vice president of the Dutch bank ABN AMRO in the bank's risk organization, urged Peter Woicke, head of the International Finance Corporation (IFC), to invite a small group of leading project finance banks to come to London on October 21, 2002, to discuss for a day environmental and social issues related to project finance in emerging markets. Representatives of nine banks from six countries attended this meeting—ABN AMRO, Barclays, BNP Paribas, Citigroup, Deutsche Bank, Rabobank, Societe General, Sumitomo Mitsui Banking Corporation, and WestLB. The bankers present included four global heads of project finance or structured finance, one head of export finance, a financial markets head, and three senior risk managers. IFC was represented by Woicke Bernard Sheehan (director of Operational Strategy), Suellen Lazarus (director of Syndications), Rachel Kyte from IFC's ombudsman's office, and Glen Armstrong, a former IFC environmental specialist serving as a consultant to IFC on sustainable development. Herman Mulder chaired the meeting, which was held at ABN AMRO's offices at Bishopsgate in London.

Several banks and the IFC presented case studies of projects where environmental or social issues had arisen, and spoke about how the project sponsors and banks had dealt with the issues and the controversies that surrounded the projects. ABN AMRO discussed the Chad Cameroon oil pipeline (a $3.7 billion project in West Africa involving oil extraction and a 670-mile pipeline), WestLB talked about Oleoducto de Crudos Pesados (OCP) oil pipeline in Ecuador, and IFC talked about the Yanacocha gold mine in Peru, where mercury spillage from a truck had posed a health threat and led to the mine being closed for five days. Delays such as these are costly from a financial and reputational standpoint. Several bankers spoke of stakeholder pressures their banks faced on environmental issues. The pressures included shareholder resolutions at annual meetings, questions from political parties, articles in the mainstream press or on Web sites, and campaigns by nongovernmental organizations. One bank spoke of inconsistent standards applied by competing banks in assessing environmental and social risks, and of the need to have a level playing field on these issues.

When it came to Citigroup's turn to present a case study, rather than talking about Citigroup's experience Chris Beale used his time to propose that they work on a framework to guide project finance banks in dealing with these issues on a consistent basis. Woicke said later that he knew at that point there was going to be some accord reached by the banks. "When I heard Citigroup propose this, I knew we had made a breakthrough. A big bank—the biggest, and an American bank—was on board. Others would follow." After discussion, Mulder proposed that a committee of four banks—ABN AMRO, Barclays, Citigroup and WestLB, known as the "Gang of Four"—try to develop a framework focusing on the oil industry, where many of the issues had arisen recently. ABN suggested a topic-by-topic approach—rules for forestry, rules for oil for pipelines, and so on.

Chris Beale suggested instead an approach that tackled all industries at once and on a global basis. The original focus was on emerging markets, but it quickly became clear that consistent worldwide standards were needed.

Drafting the Equator Principles

The four banks, the "Gang of Four," met several times in November and December 2002 and January 2003 by conference call. Chris Beale led the calls, which included Richard Burrett, global head of project finance at ABN AMRO, Chris Bray, head of environmental risk management at Barclays, and Hans Höveler, global head of specialized finance at WestLB. The Gang of Four quickly decided two things:

- To draft a framework for all industry sectors, not just oil and gas. The group wanted to do something comprehensive and not to have to do this all over again for every sector involved in project finance.
- That it made no sense for banks to invent new environmental standards; it was better to adopt an existing set of standards.

After surveying the policies of various multilateral agencies and supranational bodies, they decided to focus on the World Bank group's policies, specifically the Pollution Prevention and Abatement Handbook of the World Bank, and the Safeguard Policies of the IFC (the World Bank Group investment arm that focused on the private sector) and the Sector Guidelines of the World Bank and IFC. The World Bank Group had been developing environmental policies for more than thirty years and IFC had been developing social policies for thirteen years, and they had a body of standards that was comprehensive and applied to all sectors. These were not the only international environmental standards, but they were widely referenced. There were other multilateral agencies (MLAs) with excellent policies, but most MLAs focused on a region, such as Europe only or Latin America only, whereas IFC's policies applied throughout the emerging markets (technically to low- and middle-income countries, as defined by the World Bank). Only the IFC had comprehensive social policies dealing with matters such as resettlement of people. Most MLAs did not have explicit social policies but often applied IFC policies when social issues arose in their lending activity.

The group also looked at various environmental declarations (for example, the United Nations' UNEP-FI) but found they were essentially aspirational statements with no substantive implementation steps because they were not written with project financing in mind. They wanted something that involved a process or a methodology that project finance bankers could follow. The Collevecchio declaration by a group of NGOs did not exist at the time—it was announced on January 27, 2003—but when the banks reviewed it, they found that it had the same limits as the other declarations, being aspirational with no implementation steps and no process. The six principles of the Collevecchio Declaration were: sustainability; do no harm; responsibility; accountability; transparency; and sustainable markets and governance.

The banks had a difficult time finding common ground with the IFC over the language and mechanics of the draft document. The banks were focused on establishing a set of principles that included specific procedures, performance standards, and metrics that were straightforward to measure and adopt. By November 2003, however, the gang of four had drafted the "London Principles," found the name already taken, and renamed it the "Greenwich Principles." Simon Elliston, a managing director in Project Finance at Citigroup in London, was the initial draftsman, but many others contributed to the drafting over the following months, including Sanjay Khettry, a managing director in Project Finance at Citigroup in New York. Barclay's Chris Bray suggested changing the name from "Greenwich" because it was too close to the word *greenwash*. "We are doing something substantive here," he said, "but critics could be mischievous with the name." Simon Elliston invented a new name for the principles: the Equator Principles. The Gang of Four liked it.

A draft based on these was prepared and shown to some NGOs, the Worldwide Fund for Nature among them, and to the Shareholder Dialogue group. There was a positive reaction at first, recognizing that this proposal went beyond anything that had been suggested before. It, however, did not take long for critics to emerge and try to up the ante.

Second Meeting of the Banks—February 12, 2003, at Citigroup's office in Canary Wharf, London

Representatives of eight banks attended a meeting in London on February 12, 2003.[3] The IFC was again represented by Woicke, accompanied by Gavin Murray (head of IFC's Environmental & Social Development department), Sheehan, Lazarus, and Armstrong. Beale chaired the meeting, which was held at Citigroup's office in Canary Wharf, London.

The Gang of Four presented the draft principles to the group. IFC's advisor, Glen Armstrong, critiqued the draft. The banks discussed the feedback received from clients and from NGOs and discussed the revisions that the draft needed. Woicke committed that the IFC would provide training in environmental and social risk assessment and project categorization to banks that adopted the principles. The meeting talked about a target date for the adoption of the principles, and IFC proposed June 4, 2003, the date for IFC's annual bankers' meeting, when IFC hosts the banks with which it has done business during the year. "It was an ambitious target, but we didn't want this drafting process to drag on for years," said Beale. "We treated it like a financing deal. Let's get it structured, get it closed, and get it syndicated."

Financial Times Articles

On April 7, 2003, the *Financial Times* ran a story saying it had obtained a copy of a draft of the EP, and that four banks, ABN AMRO, Barclays, Citigroup, and WestLB planned to

> "sign an agreement" called the EP which would adopt IFC's social and environmental rules for sustainable development, which include guidelines on issues ranging from environmental assessment and natural habitats to indigenous peoples and child and forced labour.

The article quoted Fred Krupp, head of Environmental Defense, as saying, "This is a major step forward in trying to achieve environmental standards for the global economy."

On April 9, 2003, the *Financial Times* ran a second story on the EP, saying,

> ABN AMRO, Barclays, Citigroup and WestLB are trying to build support across the financial community to ensure that they are not at a competitive disadvantage. Credit Suisse First Boston said yesterday that it was looking at the agreement. "We have a record of supporting socially and environmentally responsible business practices," said a spokesman.

Third Meeting of the Banks—April 29, 2003, at WestLB's Offices in Düsseldorf

Representatives of sixteen banks attended the third meeting of the banks, which was hosted by WestLB at its headquarters in Düsseldorf on April 29, 2003. The publicity from the two *Financial Times* articles had created a lot of interest among bankers.[4] IFC was represented by Suellen Lazarus and Glen Armstrong. Hans Höveler chaired the meeting.

The meeting discussed the provisions of the draft Equator Principles and the feedback from sponsors and NGOs. Glen Armstrong gave a presentation on IFC's Safeguard Policies and its categorization process. The meeting debated whether the EP should apply globally or just to emerging markets. Although most of the problems that had arisen on environmental and social issues had arisen in emerging market projects, the meeting decided that the Equator Principles should apply globally. The meeting also debated whether using a $50-million-project cost as the cutoff point for application of the Equator Principles was too high or too low and decided to leave it at $50 million. According to Dealogic's league table data, 97 percent of projects financed in 2002 and reported to it cost $50 million or more. Most bankers felt transactions below that size were unlikely to have major developmental, environmental, or social impact, and anyway they could always apply aspects of the Equator Principles to them if it seemed warranted. The meeting also endorsed June 4, 2003, as the launch date. It was agreed that the bankers should direct questions to the Gang of Four or the IFC until May 22, a final draft of the Equator Principles would be circulated on May 9, and banks wanting to be in the initial group—the "lead banks"—would confirm by May 23 their preparedness to adopt the Equator Principles.

In adopting the Equator Principles, the banks would not sign an agreement, as the *Financial Times* had suggested. Rather, they would individually declare that they had or would put in place policies consistent with the principles. For antitrust reasons, each bank would adopt the Equator Principles as its own set of "voluntary" policies rather than all banks agreeing on standards. The standards indicated in the principles were in many countries above the legally required minimum, and even above legal requirements in some cases in the United States.

Elements of the Equator Principles

The preamble to the Equator Principles acknowledges that financial institutions play an important role in financing development and that, particularly in the emerging markets, project financiers often encounter environmental or social policy issues. The preamble states that the institutions "recognize that our role as financiers affords us significant opportunities to promote responsible environmental stewardship and socially responsible development." This was a significant statement by project finance banks, going beyond UNEP-FI and any previous statement by banks on these issues. An important element of the EP is that they require a covenant in the project loan agreement that the project borrower will comply with its environmental and social risk management plan. A violation of this plan is therefore a violation of the terms of the loan and can be a cause of default and justify a foreclosure on the loan by the lending banks. This feature of project finance loans, which is not replicated in other types of financing, gives the lending banks unusual leverage to enforce their standards.

The Equator Principles require banks to categorize the risk of a project in accordance with guidelines based on the IFC process, which uses a threefold division into Category A (high risk), Category B (medium risk) and Category C (low risk). A project is Category A if it is likely to have significant adverse environmental impacts that are sensitive, diverse, or unprecedented. The impacts are typically irreversible, such as the loss of a major natural habitat, affecting vulnerable groups or ethnic minorities, involving involuntary displacement or resettlement, or affecting significant cultural heritage sites. A project is Category B if its potential adverse environmental impacts are less adverse than those of Category A projects. Category B impacts are site-specific, few if any of them are irreversible, and in most cases mitigatory measures can be implemented. A project is Category C if it is likely to have minimal or no adverse environmental impacts.

The principles require that for all Category A and B projects the borrower undertakes an environmental assessment (EA), which addresses the issues raised in the categorization process to the financial institutions' satisfaction. The EA must have made reference to the World Bank Pollution Prevention and Abatement Handbook (an empirical set of emission and effluent standards), the IFC Safeguard Policies (processes for addressing social issues), and World Bank and IFC Sector Guidelines (environmental standards for certain industry sectors).

All Category A projects and certain Category B projects must develop an environmental management plan (EMP) that draws on the conclusions of the EA and addresses mitigation and action plans. This mirrors the IFC process. Going one step beyond that process, the financial institutions require that the borrower covenant in the project loan agreement to comply with the EMP and to report regularly on its compliance. "This is where the Principles differ the most from all the other accords and declarations—this is where they have teeth," said Beale. "Failure to comply with the EMP could lead to an event of default." When a borrower is not in compliance with the EMP, the Equator Principles require banks to engage with the borrower in its efforts to seek solutions to bring it back into compliance. The Principles also say that the financial institutions will not provide loans to projects where the borrower will not or is unable to comply with the institutions' environmental and social policies. This addressed the issue of sponsor capacity and was the area where the Equator Principles went beyond the written IFC policy but reflected current IFC practice. The Equator Principles require that:

In adopting the Equator Principles, a bank undertakes to provide loans only to those projects whose sponsors can demonstrate to the satisfaction of the bank their ability and willingness to comply with comprehensive processes aimed at ensuring that projects are developed in a socially responsible manner and according to sound environmental management practices.

The Equator Principles will use a screening process for projects which is based on IFC's environmental and social screening process. Projects will be categorized as A, B or C (high, medium or low environmental or social risk) by the banks, using common terminology. For A and B projects (high and medium risk), the borrower will complete an Environmental Assessment addressing the environmental and social issues identified in the categorization process. After appropriate consultation with affected local stakeholders, category A projects, and category B projects where appropriate, will prepare Environmental Management Plans which address mitigation and monitoring of environmental and social risks.

The Environmental Assessment will address such issues as:

- Sustainable development and use of renewable natural resources.
- Protection of human health, cultural properties, and biodiversity, including endangered species and sensitive ecosystems.
- Use of dangerous substances.
- Major hazards.
- Occupational health and safety.
- Fire prevention and life safety.
- Socioeconomic impacts.
- Land acquisition and land use.
- Involuntary resettlement.
- Impacts on indigenous peoples and communities.
- Cumulative impacts of existing projects, the proposed project, and anticipated future projects.
- Participation of affected parties in the design, review, and implementation of the project.
- Consideration of environmentally and socially preferable alternatives.
- Efficient production, delivery, and use of energy.
- Pollution prevention and waste minimization, pollution controls (liquid effluents and air emissions), and solid and chemical waste management.

The borrower will be required to demonstrate to the bank that the project complies with host country laws and the World Bank and IFC Pollution Prevention and Abatement Guidelines for the relevant industry sector. For projects in the emerging markets, the borrower would also have to demonstrate that the Environmental Assessment has taken into account the IFC Safeguard Polices, which provide guidance on issues such as natural habitats, indigenous peoples, involuntary resettlement, safety of dams, forestry, and cultural property.

Test-Marketing the Principles with Project Sponsors and NGOs

In January and February 2003, the G4 began to test-market the principles with selected clients who were sponsors of major projects in the energy and mining sectors. "Before presenting the principles to the next bank meeting, we wanted feedback from industry people who had firsthand experience of implementing IFC policies in sensitive projects," said Beale. "We wanted to know what worked and what didn't, and whether the principles we were drafting could be implemented by sponsors. We received good feedback and adjusted our draft."

On February 5, 2003, bankers from ABN AMRO and Citigroup approached several NGOs in Washington, DC to get their feedback on the principles.[5] "The initial reaction of NGOs was one of surprise," said Beale

They said, 'We didn't expect this,' and 'We didn't ask you to do this.' They were amazed at the scope of what we were attempting. They were impressed that private sector banks were aiming to go beyond the policies of the government-owned export credit agencies.

The government-owned export credit agencies (ECAs) in the OECD had been negotiating a common approach to the environment for several years without being able to reach an agreement. The banks received comments from several of the NGOs over the next week. Among the comments were that the EP should (i) address more human rights issues, such as conflict zones, security needs of projects, and land issues in nondemocratic states; (ii) consider addressing the corruption issue in monies received by governments from projects; (iii) apply globally, not just to emerging markets; (iv) adopt "no go" zones, that is areas where project development would be excluded; (v) require banks to publicly disclose sponsors' environmental impact assessments and sponsors' environmental management plans; and

(vi) create a permanent NGO advisory group to independently monitor and audit banks' implementation of the Equator Principles. Later, the gang of four also contacted several consulting firms that provided independent engineering services to bank syndicates in project finance.

Marketing the Principles to Other Banks

The Gang of Four commenced marketing the EP to other banks, led by Beale and Burrett. "I found the best way to market the Principles was to fly in to a bank's head office and meet with the project finance head and the risk head," said Beale. "There had to be both a risk case and a business case for the Principles." The risk case was a reduction in credit risk by ensuring that sponsors constructed and operated projects to a high standard.

> The Principles should lead to safer loans, because if banks finance projects which don't meet high environmental standards or which harm people, there's a likelihood that a host government or local people will interfere with the project or even shut it down.

The business case was that environmental and social difficulties emerging during a project could cause lengthy delays, six to eighteen months in some cases. Beale argued that by "getting it right the first time" there could be large financial benefit to sponsors in receiving project cash flow earlier. IFC's Suellen Lazarus also contacted banks to urge them to consider adopting the EP.[6]

The Management Decision—Go It Alone or Not?

The final draft of the EP was circulated to banks on May 9, 2003. An "adoption form" allowed banks to declare their intention to adopt the EP on June 4, 2003. A draft Web site for the EP was created, to become active on the launch date. All told, over thirty banks had been contacted by the Gang of Four or by IFC. On May 25, 2003, ten days before the scheduled launch of the Equator Principles, only three of the banks canvassed had committed to adopt the Equator Principles. Several others were expected to do so, but would they be ready by the intended launch date, June 4, 2003? Citigroup and the other banks leading the EP effort wanted a critical mass of banks, of ten to twelve banks, to launch the EP. IFC, which had been working closely with the banks on the EP and on whose policies the EP were based, was keen to have the EP launched at its annual bankers' meeting on June 4 and was pressing for a launch if there were five to six banks on board. Should the three banks (which included Citigroup) go it alone, or should they wait for more banks to come in? The tension was resolved when in the last few days before the launch date another seven banks had signed up, for a total of ten. At the launch, the signatories had about 30 percent by value market share in the project finance field.

Reaction to the Equator Principles

Ironically, in the first year after the release of the Equator Principles the member banks encountered more NGO criticism than ever before. This was worrying to some of the banks new to this process and to some of the smaller banks who were not used to this kind of public scrutiny. It did indeed seem that "No good deed goes unpunished." Following their decision to adopt the Equator Principles, and having stuck their heads above the parapet while other banks had been content to remain below the NGO radar screen, the Equator Principles banks were not portrayed by NGOs as a force for good or as demonstrating good environmental stewardship. Quite to the contrary, they were portrayed as opponents of social and environmental progress and as a pressure group of powerful financial institutions that lobbied the IFC and World Bank in order to limit or prevent positive social and environmental change, which, if adopted, would be disadvantageous to banks and sponsors.[7] NGOs were more supportive privately than publicly. They, however, wanted to see more disclosure about those deals/clients that were turned down as a result of the principles, a request that according to the banks goes against any commercial bank's commitment to confidentiality in its dealings with its clients. Disclosure, the banks argue, would jeopardize client relationships and compromise other business units' ability to win business from clients rejected for project finance deals.

Client reaction was mixed, especially among those such as state-run oil companies, which do not feel NGO pressure, and therefore, consider the Equator Principles an unnecessary hurdle. Many clients, however, have been supportive of Citigroup for being involved and acting as an advocate to keep policies from becoming too extreme. Most, including the more sophisticated clients, welcomed the principles after a time as a valuable clarification and something that could expedite necessary clearances.

Equator Principles at Citigroup

The implementation of the Equator Principles in Citigroup is now overseen by the project finance and risk management divisions. As Citigroup sees it, what is at stake in implementing these principles is "franchise risk" or "reputation risk," a form of risk that is very significant to a large financial institution. In addition to managing franchise or reputation risk, Chris Beale felt a need to supplement Citigroup's charter, which aims to make a profit while "doing no harm," with the additional aim of being a good influence in society whenever possible. Though the CEO Chuck Prince had been committed to the idea of the Equator Principles from the beginning, adopting them was a risk for Citigroup—and also a real risk for Chris Beale, whose division would have to meet the costs of implementation. Though the principles would benefit Citigroup's business in the long term, there were implementation risks to consider in the short term, including potential backlash from clients. The business case for adopting the EP, however, was strong: dealing with environmental and social issues upfront could avoid costs associated with project delays (and lawsuits) and generate more revenue through efficiencies.

Since the adoption of Equator Principles, Citigroup has used them to guide overall corporate policy where applicable. Within Citigroup, the reach of the principles has extended and a version known as "EP Lite" is now used in the corporate lending area. But there is a limit to how far the principles can be extended away from project finance: in project finance, loans are project-specific and there are covenants that regulate how the loan is used. In corporate lending to investment-grade companies, however, the lender may not know how loans are to be used. "EP Lite" is used when the use of the loan proceeds is known, in which case the rating A/B/C is used. The adjective "lite" in this context means that there is no covenant imposing the EP and that violation of the EP is therefore not automatically an event of default. In only 2 percent of corporate—as opposed to project finance—deals is the use of proceeds identified, so "EP Lite" is in fact rarely applied to corporate business. The private equity group at Citigroup has also used ideas from the Equator Principles as a franchise risk control. There is also some use in the bond area, on occasions, for project-specific bonds rather than for general corporate bonds. Strategically, it was important to apply the Equator Principles to bonds in order to bring Credit Swiss First Boston, a big bond house, on board.

After the adoption of the Equator Principles, Citigroup ran extensive training sessions for staff who worked in project finance, trade functions, oil and gas, and corporate lending. They used an IFC staffer to teach a set of cases, taking advantage of a commitment made by Woicke of the IFC at the second meeting of the banks in February 2003. Cases were analyzed by splitting the audience into two groups, a deal team and a risk management team, and with the members of each team initially developing the perspective appropriate to their section of the company, and then working to understand that of the other group.

In the summer of 2005, Citigroup has probably walked away from two deals because of the Equator Principles. The first of these was downstream from a project with dubious environmental and social impacts but may not of itself have been bad.[8] The implementation of the principles has probably cost Citigroup about $5 million. It is symbolic of the way the market has evolved that two large clients were originally hostile but are now supportive and see principles as a guard against interference in projects by NGOs.

Consequences and Implications of Equator Principles

Credit risk management is undergoing an important transition. Banks are no longer treating environmental and other social issues as peripheral to their business concerns; they no longer focus simply on recycling paper or using energy-efficient light bulbs... the majority of the world's large banks agree that integrating environmental and broader social issues into their core credit risk management is essential to managing credit risk in the 21st century.

Reed Huppman, Partner, ERM[9]

ERM sees the beginning of a paradigm shift among lending institutions and in credit risk assessment, triggered by the adoption of the Equator Principles by leading international commercial banks. The Equator Principles are likely to act as a stepping-stone for inserting environmental and social considerations into other aspects of bank's policies, as is already happening at Citigroup. For example, according to the Freshfields Bruckhaus Deringer report on the Equator Principles:

> at its Annual General Meeting held on 28 May 2004, HSBC launched a new international guideline for the forest land and forest products sector, with a view to ensuring that HSBC's involvement in this potentially sensitive sector is consistent with sustainability principles. The guideline, briefly, states that HSBC's preference is to deal with forest-owner customers who are either operating managed forests certified by the Forest Stewardship Council (FSC), or who meet equivalent FSC recognised standard, or who trade in products that are FSC certified or equivalent.[10]

In addition to Citigroup, Barclays and Bank of America are making similar moves. Both HSBC (in April 2004) and Bank of America (in May 2004) adopted targets and deadlines for the reduction of greenhouse gas emissions. ABN AMRO claims to have extended the application of the Equator Principles by bringing within their jurisdiction all corporate lending in the oil, gas, and mining sectors. And again according to the Freshfields Bruckhaus Deringer report:

> In areas such as upstream oil and gas projects (historically carried out largely through balance sheet financing), there is also an observable trend towards a similar approach to that required by the Equator Principles ('Equator-Lite') being taken.... WestLB thought it likely that the Equator Principles would be applied to more of the bank's products in the future, including commodity trade financing and export financing.[11]

Concern for environmental and social issues on the part of banks has led to increased awareness of these issues on the part of project sponsors. One of the sponsors historically most concerned with environmental and social issues is BP: in response to the Equator Principles, BP developed a new Human Rights Impact Assessment procedure for the Tangguh Indonesian LNG plant project.[12] They were advised on this by an independent legal counsel. An independent panel, the Tangguh Independent Advisory Panel, reviewed the impact on human rights and other aspects of the project.[13] BP is also a major player in the very controversial Baku-Tbilisi-Ceyhan (BTC) pipeline, which takes crude oil from the central Asian oilfields to the Mediterranean. In this context, BP established the independent Caspian Development Advisory Panel (CDAP) to monitor BTC and other related BP activities in Azerbaijan, Georgia, and Turkey. Although the CDAP has no executive authority, it reports directly to the BP group chief executive. According to the Freshfields analysis:

> The CDAP has made more than 100 different recommendations in order to help ensure that BTC and related projects serve as a template in the future for major investments in developing and transition countries by multinational companies in extractive industries. These recommendations have included that BP and BTC establish an ombudsman in each host country and a special human rights coordinator to implement, co-ordinate and monitor human rights commitments related to the projects and to interact with all key stakeholders, including host governments and non-governmental organisations.[14]

The report concludes that

> BP has also entered into voluntary principles on security and human rights which they have applied in both the BTC pipeline project and the Tangguh gas project in Indonesia. These important innovations and developments by BP should be recognised fully, as BP and the other sponsors of the BTC pipeline and the lenders to the BTC pipeline projects have been subjected to widespread and often unfair criticism in respect of the assessment and management of the BTC pipeline project.

Another interesting consequence of the Equator Principles is that they have affected the behavior of banks that have not subscribed to them. Several of these banks often justify their decision to lend along Equator Principles lines, even though they have not formally adopted the principles. The

BTC pipeline project illustrates this well. Given intense criticism of the project by NGOs and other stakeholders,[15] several banks, both Equator and non-Equator, disclosed[16] for the first time why they decided to support the project. ABN AMRO, one of the original equator banks, issued a press release explaining why it decided to participate in the BTC pipeline funding. Surprisingly, a number of nonequator banks then followed suit. Société Générale, a lead bank on the BTC pipeline project and a nonequator bank, explained in its Sustainable Development Report that it decided to participate because the project had been assessed by independent consultants and the IFC and European Bank for Reconstruction and Development. It also took comfort from the fact that public bodies with extensive experience in the field and extremely high environmental, social, and human rights standards were involved in funding the project.[17] Institutional investors also entered the debate about the BTC pipeline: Insight Investment, Bank of Scotland's fund management arm with an active presence in SRI investing, organized meetings between sponsors, lenders, institutional investors and NGOs to discuss human rights, environmental impacts, and legal issues relating to the BTC pipeline.

Evolution of the Equator Principles

In late 2004 the IFC started to revise their social and environmental standards, a natural evolution in their business practices, but nevertheless an event that posed unanticipated problems for the Equator banks, which having only recently adopted the current standards were not anticipating changes so soon. Yet the Equator banks wanted to be able to say that they were working to IFC standards because of the broader community's respect for those standards, and to do this they would clearly have to move to the new IFC standards. The IFC also gained kudos and influence from having the Equator Principles based on its standards, and so wanted the banks to accept its proposed revisions. It could not live with major commercial banks rejecting the new standards. The principles had made commercial banks and the IFC strongly interdependent, a result that neither had anticipated when they were adopted. In the proposed revisions, the IFC wanted to incorporate labor standards from ILO (International Labour Organization), standards that were aimed at the garment industry, sweatshops, and a range of problems associated with manufacturing plants in low-wage countries. The Equator banks had a problem with this, as their projects rarely involved the issues at which these standards are aimed. After much discussion, the IFC finally dropped the ILO provision.

This incident shows that the Equator Principles need an organization and a structure, a formal process for updating, all of which are currently lacking. At present, the responsibility for chairing the group and for maintaining Web site rotates among member banks. The organization really needs a secretariat to maintain the Web site, act as a custodian of precedents and processes, prepare position papers, and liaise with the IFC, NGOs, and other relevant groups. Functioning as a stand-alone NGO would enable the Equator banks to foster the best practices and to establish a consistent format for sustainability reports. As part of this, Equator Principles would set out a process for revision of standards, with an agreement that, for example, if more than X percent of member banks agree to new standards, then these are the new Equator Principles and any bank not agreeing to these will no longer be an Equator bank.

The Business Case for the Equator Principles

Why did thirty large commercial banks put the time and effort required into designing and implementing the Equator Principles? They were clearly under no legal obligation to do so and there was no sign that this was about to change: it is most unlikely that their home governments would have passed legislation requiring anything close to what was involved in the equator principles. Governments do pass legislation requiring the internalization of external costs, which as we have seen is what is involved in most environmental conflicts, but usually only when the external costs fall on the citizens of the home country. An interesting exception is the U.S. Foreign Corrupt Practices Act, which penalizes the payment of bribes in foreign countries. There are few other examples of an industrial country passing legislation that penalizes its companies for misbehaving in foreign countries. There was undoubtedly an element of idealism on the part of the EP founders: each of the companies in the gang of four was led in its efforts to design and implement the EP by someone whose personal values were sympathetic to this goal. Chris Beale of Citigroup, as mentioned, is the son of an Australian environment minister and describes himself as "not a tree hugger, but someone with a green streak, concerned about environmental issues, and who wants my kids to enjoy healthy air and clean environment." While working for his MBA at Harvard, Beale wrote two term papers on pollution control methods.

At Citigroup, which was perhaps most important of the initial gang of four, Chris Beale was backed 100 percent by the new chief executive officer, Charles Prince, who had pledged to make honesty and integrity core values at Citigroup. Prince was in the process of trying to change Citigroup's image in this respect: just a few years before he took over as CEO, Citigroup was mired in an embarrassing number of scandals, namely:

- In 2002, the Federal Trade Commission charges in connection with sub-prime lending led to a settlement of $215 million.
- In 2003, the Securities and Exchange Commission charges in connection with biased securities research led to a settlement of $400 million, charges in connection with Citibank's action in the Enron case led to a settlement of $145 million, and charges of biased research led to a settlement of $325 million.
- In 2004, Federal Reserve charges in connection with sub-prime lending led to a settlement of $70 million, and a settlement in the WorldCom scandal led to a settlement of $42.58 billion.

As if these were not enough, in August 2004 Citibank bond traders in London, according to *Business Week,*

dumped at least $13.3 billion worth of European government bonds onto the market, then bought a third of them back at lower prices within about a half-hour—scooping profits that rivals say could be up to $24 million. As Citi traders high-fived each other in triumph, pandemonium broke out in the market. Citi's actions weren't illegal, but broke an unwritten understanding not to whipsaw markets or take advantage of the thin summer trading. When a rival trader called to ask what was up, the Citi crew laughed and hung up.

And only next month, in September 2004, Japanese regulators shut down Citigroup's private banking operation in Japan, citing extensive legal violations over seven years, including lax governance and money laundering controls and "numerous instances of unfair transactions... in which large profits were obtained through unsound means."[18] It is clear from this background that Citigroup was in serious danger of developing a reputation for unethical behavior and of running foul of regulators and quite possibly ultimately of legislators in several countries, including such key markets as the United States, the United Kingdom, and Japan. For Citigroup, there was therefore a real payoff to changing the group's image and making clear that there was a behavior change under way. Pushing for the Equator Principles was a high profile, cost-effective way of signaling this. CEO Prince's enthusiastic endorsement is therefore not surprising:

> This is about good business practice, it is about leadership and it is about doing the right thing. We are extremely proud to be part of this voluntary, private-sector initiative and we are confident that we will see more and more banks active in project finance adopt these principles in the coming months.[19]

More generally, there are a number of elements that together constitute a powerful business case for the Equator Principles. These include the impact on the bank's reputation, maintaining good relations with stakeholders and NGOs and avoiding activism that targets the bank, a belief that once the principles were in place project sponsors would learn to prepare projects that conformed to environmental and social standards so that the EP would almost become redundant and a desire to establish an industry standard and a level playing field with respect to the treatment of social and environmental issues. There was also a perception that the Equator Principles would reduce the political risks associated with project finance and could in the long run reduce the cost of capital.

In their survey of the Equator Principles, Freshfields Bruckhaus Deringer[20] report that

> banks and project sponsors returned repeatedly to the value and importance of reputation, the need to protect a good reputation and the difficulty in regaining

a good reputation if tarnished. In this context, banks used "reputation" in two different senses: first, the need to protect the public image of the institution by what the banks do; and, second, the vulnerability of the reputation of the bank to what the bank's clients do. The capacity of sponsors to adopt and implement high environmental, social and human rights standards was seen as critical to the reputation of the banks.

Conversely, it was recognized that stains on reputation are particularly stubborn and difficult to remove. For example, discussing the long-term effect of the student boycott of Barclays in the 1970s and 1980s over apartheid in South Africa, Chris Lendrum, group vice-chairman, remarked in February 2004 that "even today we are dogged by the perceptions about South Africa."[21] In addition, the seizure of Nazi gold held by certain Swiss banks still haunts the imaginations of many bankers.

Another interesting result to emerge from this survey is that financial institutions and sponsors viewed the approval of ethical funds, such as F&C and Insight Investment, as being important and also view inclusion in FTSE 4 Good and the Dow Jones Sustainability Index to be beneficial to their reputation (an issue mentioned in the previous chapter). For the Equator banks, adoption of the Equator Principles facilitates this inclusion.[22]

A connection between the EP and the reduced cost of finance could emerge from the international banking regulatory framework and was referred to by some banks in the Freshfields Bruckhaus Deringer survey. An important element in this is the Basel II Framework Agreement, incorporated into European Union law under the EU Capital Requirements Directive. This agreement requires that internationally active banks satisfy minimum capital requirements against credit risks and operational risks. What this means is that the amount of credit and operational risk that a bank is permitted to take depends upon the amount of capital it has available. The amount of capital reserved for credit risk can be reduced if a bank can show that it has acceptable internal risk assessment and management procedures that have been in operation for a minimum period of at least three years. In this case it qualifies for the Internal Ratings Based (IRB) approach. Equator banks may regard compliance with the Equator Principles as a discipline that will improve their internal risk assessment and management procedures and thus contribute to their qualifying for the IRB approach. Certainly, if a bank has historical experience that projects which satisfy the Equator Principles have lower default rates and loss estimates than similar projects which are not compliant, it may need to hold less capital against the risks of these projects, which could mean that it could offer more competitive pricing for Equator-compliant projects.

At Citigroup, Chris Beale sees the EP as a way of managing business risks but believes that to date there is no quantitative data that can confirm this.

> Well defined environmental and social policies, such as Equator Principles, clearly make it less likely that we will find ourselves in trouble in the future, but there is no historical cost that we can quantify. We could take a view on default risk in the future but this too is difficult to measure. However, Equator Principles presents a framework for business risk reduction, primarily more quantifiable as reputational risk... Banks face both credit and reputation risk when they finance development around the world. If sponsors adopt and follow Equator Principles for sensitive projects, they might well enjoy a faster implementation period, with the end result being that the project starts generating revenue streams earlier, avoiding the specter of costly interruptions, delays and retrenchments.

The belief is that "EP will lead to more secure investments on the part of customers and safer loans on the part of banks." Mr. Beale implies that the downside to not paying heed to EP concerns could be disastrous: "If banks finance something dirty or that harms people, it's possible the host government or local people will interfere with or even confiscate the private development project."[23]

Evaluation of the Equator Principles

The business case for the Equator Principles, from the perspectives of the participating banks, seems clear, and although it is still too early to pass a definitive judgment, it is likely that the banks will gain from developing and implementing these principles. The costs of implementation are low, little business has been lost, and the gains to reputation have been significant. And no doubt some significant pitfalls will be avoided. Looking from another perspective, how well have the Equator Principles served the environmental and social concerns that motivated the NGOs to press for action on project finance in the first place? Could the principles be improved in this respect? And what do they tell us about the possibilities for similar developments in other industries?

Again, it is too soon to reach any definitive conclusions here. By focusing so much attention on social and environmental issues, the Equator Principles must have done some good: all of the major international banks based in Europe, Japan, or the United States are now well aware of the sensitivity of these issues and their potential for complicating a project. So at very least we can be sure that environmental and social issues are receiving more and more careful attention than before. Some NGOs claim that in spite of this the Equator banks are violating the principles to which they have committed themselves: perhaps the biggest claim of this type being in connection with the Baku-Tbilisi-Ceyhan pipeline, which runs 1,100 miles from the Sangachal terminal near Baku, the capital of Azerbaijan, through Georgia, and to the Turkish Mediterranean port of Ceyhan. Costing $3.2 billion, the pipeline, which was formally opened in May 2005, carries 1 million barrels a day from the Caspian Sea, which contains the world's third largest oil and gas reserves. NGOs claim that there are unacceptable environmental risks, mainly associated with possible leaks, and that within Turkey in particular the pipeline opened up possibilities of human rights abuses because of the need to displace local populations while the pipeline was built. To date, there is no evidence that any of these dangers have been realized, and of course they must be offset against the very considerable economic gains to the countries crossed by the pipeline and to Azerbaijan from better access to international oil markets. All countries affected by the pipeline are poor and in need of extra income.

While recognizing that it is too early to call the score on the impact of the Equator Principles, there are some limitations that have been highlighted by NGOs. The scope of the principles is limited: they apply only to investments funded by the project finance mechanism. As we noted above, some banks are extending the coverage in limited ways, but project finance probably covers only 10–20 percent of all capital expenditures.

The principles are voluntary rather than mandatory, so there is no redress against a bank that violates them and no enforcement mechanism. Nor is there any appeal mechanism if NGOs believe that an environmental assessment carried out under the principles is inadequate or inaccurate. Finally, NGOs have argued that they need to see the environmental impact assessments carried out for project sponsors and be able to critique these and have, in addition, argued for access to data on projects not accepted by the Equator banks.

Another limitation is that the Equator Principles are probably most needed among second-tier banks, for whom an analysis of environmental and social impacts of projects is often not a major priority. But they are still underrepresented. So far, there is only one Middle Eastern bank on board—largely because of an unwillingness to criticize governments in that area. Nevertheless, in one large Middle Eastern project the Equator Principles were successfully imposed on the client. Banks in the Middle East are big enough to do deals outside the Equator Principles group of up to about $500 million. Currently, there are no Chinese banks in the Equator Principles group, and Chinese banks acting alone could finance deals up to $1 billion. This is a potential weakness in the structure of the Equator Principles.

Many of these criticisms have some substance to them. Yet it is difficult to see scope for great improvement without radical changes in the banking industry. The scope of the Equator Principles is indeed limited, but extending this mechanism beyond project finance is hard: in project finance the lending banks, which usually operate in groups, have a very specific contractual relationship with the project that gives them great power to enforce standards as part of the loan conditions. This is not true for more widely practiced corporate lending: if a bank believes that a client is using its loan proceeds in inappropriate ways, then its only real sanction is to stop doing business with the client, very much a "nuclear alternative" for banks dealing with major clients. There would always be a fear that other banks would welcome a profitable client. There have been some cases of banks cutting off a client because of what is perceived as environmental misconduct, but this will always be a last resort, adopted when the embarrassment of being associated with the client outweighs the profits from the relationship. The lack of enforceability of the principles is also an almost unavoidable feature of a voluntary scheme. Why would banks voluntarily give NGOs the right to sue them?

My sense is that the Equator Principles are a very positive first step toward bringing social and environmental factors into banks' decisions, and they have taken this step partly out of altruism but also substantially because there is a strong business case and because in the area of project finance it is practical to make real progress. If the business case for additional steps becomes strong enough, we may see them. Otherwise, we will probably not see much extra progress until there is an international treaty on these issues.

On the question of whether the Equator Principles can serve as a model or at least guide as to what might work in other industries, there are certainly some lessons that stand out. One is that the business case for environmentally responsible behavior is powerful, powerful enough to convince a group of important international banks to take it very seriously. Another lesson is the need for collective action: the development of the principles was driven by a group of banks that were major players in project finance. No one bank would have implemented such a system on its own: it would have feared losing clients and being undercut by competitors. But when several major players moved together, these fears were allayed. Collective action by a leading group is therefore imperative in cases like this: ironically, the same applies to such antisocial practices as price setting. If one company in a competitive business tries to raise prices, it will fear losing customers and being undercut, just as a single Equator bank would. But if several big players move together, there is a real chance that they can make a price rise stick. This is why antitrust laws are so strict about conspiracies! But conspiracies are needed for initiatives such as Equator. Currently, there is another such initiative being developed in the toy industry, trying to address problems associated with monitoring working conditions and ensuring compliance with labor agreements in factories in China. And, interestingly, progress on improving working conditions in the garment industry worldwide has needed coordinated actions by most major purchasers through groups such as the Fair Labor Association (see Chapter 9): again, as in project finance, no one on its own has the power to insist on changes along its supply chain. Another lesson is that the whole process was started by NGOs, who managed to attract the public's attention and use this to force banks to pay attention. Clearly, there were people in the banks who were already concerned about environmental and social issues, but without the outside leverage, progress would have been far slower. The threat of consumer boycotts created a clear and visible cost to continuing business as usual, clear enough to start a process of change, even if there was anyway a distinct but less dramatic business case for change.

5

Pharmaceuticals and Corporate Responsibility

Doing Well and Doing Good

"We try never to forget that medicine is for the people. It is not for profits. The profits follow, and if we have remembered that they never fail to appear. The better we have remembered, the larger they have been." These are the heartwarming words of George W. Merck, founder and past president of the eponymous pharmaceutical company. Heartwarming—but are they true? They imply that pharmaceutical companies do well (financially) by doing good (medically). There does seem to be truth in this.

Certainly, they have done well: pharmaceutical companies are always among the most profitable, with rates of return on equity and on investments that are among the highest of all industries. And they have also done good: they have contributed to the quality of life and to the increasing of life expectancy over the last half-century.

The pharmaceutical industry has been one of the most profitable in the world for most of the last quarter of a century. Table 5.1 shows three measures of return for the pharmaceutical industry and for five other industries, money center banks, personal computer makers, aerospace and defense, automakers, and semiconductor makers. The measures of return are returns on sales, equity, and assets. The first of these is profit as a percentage of sales, and the second and third are respectively profits as a percent of shareholders' equity, and total corporate assets. Return on assets is usually less than return on equity, as the value of assets usually exceeds the value of equity.[1]

From Table 5.1, we see that the pharmaceutical industry has the highest return on sales, and the second highest returns on equity and assets. Makers of personal computers have a much higher return on equity and a slightly higher return on assets: all other industries shown score lower on all

TABLE 5.1 The Three Measures of Return for the Pharmaceutical Industry and for Five Other Industries

	Drugmakers (Major)	Money Center Banks	Personal Computers	Aerospace Defense	Automakers	Semi-conductor Makers
Return on sales	16.83%	16.48%	6.41%	4.13%	2.39%	13.45%
Return on equity	22.43%	13.81%	35.18%	12.39%	9.73%	13.99%
Return on assets	11.07%	1.09%	12.69%	4.16%	1.49%	9.84%

measures. Pharmaceuticals, then, are certainly profitable and have been for at least two decades. Pharmaceuticals have also been a central contributor to the improvement in health and life expectancy over the last half-century. As we tend to take for granted much of what they have brought us, it is worth recalling their contributions.

Many diseases that were common fifty or more years ago are now rare because of vaccines. Smallpox, once a worldwide killer, has been eradicated. Common childhood diseases such as mumps and measles have been all but eliminated. Tuberculosis is under control in the developed world. There are vaccines for most dangerous diseases.

Many conditions that were dangerous and untreatable thirty years ago are now routinely treated by drugs. Acid suppressants treat a range of gastric problems that were once serious and possibly deadly, but are now harmless. A wide range of cardiovascular problems can be remedied with drugs to reduce cholesterol, thin the blood, or reduce blood pressure. Drugs can cure most cases of depression. AIDS, a death sentence when it appeared and also a complex and novel disease, can now be contained and need no longer be a death sentence. Even cancer, one of the most frightening of all diseases, is beginning to yield to pharmaceutical attacks. We have progressed to the point where most people today expect that if they are sick, there is a pill that will make them better and are surprised and disappointed to hear otherwise. This radical change from fifty or fewer years ago is a measure of what the pharmaceutical industry has wrought for society.

My colleague Frank Lichtenberg has studied the effect of new drugs on longevity in the United States[2] and concluded that they have made a major contribution to increased life expectancy. Between 1960 and 1997, life expectancy in the United States increased from 69.7 to 76.5 years, an increase of 9.7 percent over about forty years. The other major contributor to longer lives, according to Frank's study, was increased expenditure on health care. But of the two, expenditure on the development of new drugs was by far the more cost-effective. To gain one life-year[3] by increasing health care expenditure cost $11,053, whereas to do the same by developing new drugs cost $1,345.

The Fall from Grace

There is no question then that the pharmaceutical industry has done well financially and has done good—eliminating common diseases through vaccines, curing life-threatening diseases, improving the quality of life, and also increasing the length of the average person's life. It seems then that the pharmaceutical industry ought to be the poster child for capitalism—making money while improving the human condition, in the best traditions of Adam Smith. Yet ironically it is not, and indeed is far from that position. It is under attack from many angles, and a recent Harris Interactive poll[4] showed that the U.S. public's perception of the pharmaceutical industry is low and has declined dramatically. In 2005, less than 15 percent of the population agreed that the pharmaceutical industry does a good job of serving its customers, whereas in 1998 that percentage had been about 50. By comparison, about 70 percent feel that the computer industry does a good job of serving its customers. Remarkably, slightly over 60 percent even agreed that the airline industry does a good job. Of the companies mentioned in the survey, only health insurance, tobacco, and oil were rated lower by the respondents. A recent survey of the industry by *The Economist* stated that pharmaceutical firms

stand accused of focusing on "me-too" drugs which confer little clinical benefit over existing medicines; rushing these to market through cunning clinical trials designed to make them look better than they are; and suppressing data to the contrary. The industry is also lambasted for expensive, aggressive and mis-leading direct-to-consumer advertising, which sometimes creates conditions to fit the drugs rather than the other way around. Hobnobbing with doctors means giving them "food, flattery and friendship" at best, and outright bribery at worst.

This litany of charges was reinforced by New York Attorney General Elliot Spitzer's suit against GlaxoSmithKline for allegedly suppressing data link-ing the use of antidepressants to increased incidence of suicide among teen-agers and by the withdrawal of Merck's Cox-2 inhibitor Vioxx because of the risk of heart problems. Merck—whose founder's sentiments on doing good and doing well opened this chapter—now faces that peculiarly American death, annihilation through lawsuits.

There is a real irony in the position of Merck. Not only did its founder express very clearly estimable sentiments that have to some degree guided the company since then, but also Merck played a leading role in the development and introduction of one of the most valuable categories of new drugs of the last few decades, the cholesterol-lowering drugs. In addi-tion, in the 1980s Merck went out of its way to eliminate, at a cost of over $200 million, a disfiguring, disabling, and painful disease common in many tropical regions, river blindness. Caused by a parasitic worm that can enter the body when a fly bites, river blindness is the result of these worms growing and breeding within the body. They can grow to over two feet in length, and when they reproduce they release millions of offspring called microfilariae that swarm through the body, causing itching so bad that vic-tims have been known to commit suicide. Eventually, these microfilariae reach the eye and can cause blindness. In parts of West Africa, the majority of those over forty-five were blind from river blindness.

Merck's research scientists realized in the late 1970s that a drug they had developed to kill parasitic worms in animals might kill the worms that cause river blindness. The company's top management decided to carry out clinical trials in Africa, which meant establishing the local infrastruc-ture required for these tests, and discovered that a derivative of their drug, which they called Mectizan, was indeed completely effective in curing this painful and damaging illness. They realized early on that there would be no market for the drug, as the affected population had no money to pay, and sought to give the drug away free to local governments or the World Health Organization, so that they could distribute it to people who needed it. For reasons too complex to summarize here (but that are not to their credit) neither organization rose to the occasion. Rather than leave the disease untreated, Merck not only gave the drug away but also put in place a distribution system, no small task in tropical regions with no health system and no vehicular access.[5] Of the rationale for this donation, the then chief executive officer Roy Vagelos said:

> Some argue that corporations should not be in the business of making donations, contending that their first obligation is to reward stockholders with higher dividends and not squander company resources on gifts. I disagree. Our policy on Mectizan and other gifts made Merck a place where people were proud and excited to work because they wanted to make lives better around the world. It helped us recruit the best people and build company morale. It was consistent with Merck's fundamental corporate philosophy of doing well by doing good. It served the global society Merck serves. It also served Merck's stockholders because corporate social generosity is often followed by higher profits as the corporation becomes a better, more attractive workplace for the best talent.[6]

An interesting statement, touching on many themes we have already addressed, and, as I said before, a painfully ironic story given Merck's present predicament.

   Why is the pharmaceutical industry held in such low esteem, with prominent firms in danger of legal annihilation, when in fact it has contributed so much and will probably do so again in the future?

Access to Medicines

The pharmaceutical industry has made a number of serious mistakes, all readily identifiable from the perspective we have developed on corporate responsibility. One that is easy to identify is its position on the pricing of AIDS drugs in South Africa. It is difficult to imagine a more morally indefensible position than suing the government of the charismatic and widely loved Nelson Mandela, shortly after his masterminding the transition of South Africa from racial segregation to a multiracial democracy, for seeking to prevent the poorest members of its society from dying. Yet that is the position assumed by the pharmaceutical industry. Tone-deaf is an understatement: such a move was always bound to come back and haunt them.

The background is that in the late 1980s and early 1990s anti-AIDS drugs became available, not cures but drugs that, nevertheless, reduced the presence of AIDS viruses in the body and turned AIDS from a death sentence to a controllable chronic illness. They were sold at a very high price in the United States—in the region of $10,000 for a year's treatment. The incidence of AIDS in South Africa was high—far higher than in the United States. Yet clearly the vast majority of AIDS sufferers there could not afford even a small fraction of this price. Drug companies initially refused South African government requests to reduce prices. Rather than leave its citizens to die of AIDS, in 1997—four years after the failure of negotiations on price—the South African government granted its Ministry of Health the right to allow the import of AIDS drugs made under license in other countries. This meant, for example, that an Indian company, Cipla, was able to supply AIDS drugs at a small fraction of the U.S. list price. (U.S. patents were not valid in India.) Shortly after the government gave the Health Ministry this power (in February 1998 to be precise), thirty-nine major drug companies filed a lawsuit against the government of South Africa, claiming that this new law violated international trade agreements, such as the Trade Related Intellectual Property (TRIPs) provisions of the World Trade Organization.

The lawsuit was a serious mistake by the drug companies. Médecins sans Frontières, an international NGO dedicated to providing medical treatment to those in need, presented the companies in the trial with a petition of 250,000 signatures asking that they drop the case. Oxfam, a British charity and NGO dedicated to the relief of poverty, pressured GlaxoSmithKline into changing its hitherto strict policy on patent enforcement in poor countries. ACT UP!, an AIDS activist group, stormed the office of the chief executive of Pfizer, one of the more recalcitrant drug companies, and demanded that the company drop the price of an AIDS-related drug in South Africa. Media treatment of the lawsuit in the West was almost universally negative. The influential and conservative magazine *The Economist* commented bitingly that

Powerful medicines can have powerful side-effects, sometime clouding the judgment or blunting reactions. As the public debate over how to get expensive rich-world medicines to poor countries shows, this is as true for those who make the drugs as for those who take them.[7]

The trial started in March 2001, and after six weeks the drug companies realized that they had a public relations disaster on their hands and withdrew their suit, paying the legal costs of the South African government. Nothing was gained, and a great deal lost in terms of public esteem and trust, by this episode. It should have been obvious to the drug companies from the start that the world would not tolerate millions of poor people dying from AIDS just because they could not afford the prices charged for medicines by Western companies and that they would have to find a way of accommodating to this reality.

Although the pricing of AIDS drugs in South Africa was perhaps the most egregious of their misjudgments, the drug companies made many others. Year in and year out they raised the prices of existing medicines faster than the rate of inflation—not the prices of new drugs, but of old medicines that had been on the market for years and which were in no way changed from year to year. The American Association of Retired People claims that from 2001 to 2004 the prices for the most commonly used brand name drugs increased 28 percent, and again none of these were new drugs: this was just the result of companies increasing profit margins where they thought the market would bear it.

Roy Vagelos, who was the CEO of Merck when it developed and marketed the first cholesterol-lowering drug, comments in his book *Medicine Science and Merck* on the pressures he experienced to raise prices for no reason other than that it was possible and on the struggle he had to resist these pressures. His successor, and his fellow CEOs at Merck's competitors, clearly did not struggle or at least gave up more easily. Financially desperate U.S. senior citizens started to buy medicines from Canada, where the prices were often less than half those in the United States, and in response drug companies sought and obtained a law blocking the import of medicines from Canada. And when Medicare was extended to cover some of the costs of prescription drugs, they lobbied to insert in the legislation a provision that the government not use its bargaining power to negotiate prices lower than the list prices—something done by every other government in the world and by most hospitals and health plans. When Maine passed a law allowing the state to negotiate the prices of prescription drugs with manufacturers on behalf of its citizens, the pharmaceutical companies filed a lawsuit to prevent this, won at the first round, but lost at the Court of Appeals.

Behind the public fury that built up over drug pricing is the issue of access to medicines: high prices limit access, particularly for those in the United States without health insurance, a large and growing number, and for those in poor countries without universal health services provided by the government.

Transparency

This is not the end of the charges. There is ample evidence that the drug firms almost bribed doctors in attempts to persuade them to use their drugs, offering thinly veiled free vacations and remunerative consultancies to those who would play along. Perhaps worse was evidence that some companies had suppressed evidence about dangerous side effects of their drugs, putting their customers' lives at risk in the search for profits. In response, major scientific journals tried to force drug companies to allow researchers to disclose unfavorable as well as favorable results—not an easy task as the companies paid for clinical trials and owned the data.

Merck again acts as a case that illustrates well what is at issue here with its painkiller Vioxx, which was withdrawn voluntarily in September 2004. Vioxx was developed as an alternative to conventional painkillers such as Aspirin and Advil, which had been available without prescription for many years. Both Aspirin and Advil, and other members of the NSAID[8] family, had the unfortunate side effect of irritating the lining of the stomach and causing bleeding in some patients when taken for long periods. This limited their use as treatments for chronic pains, such as those associated with arthritis. Merck and several other companies therefore developed a new family of painkillers called Cox-2 inhibitors, of which Vioxx was one, that were as effective as the traditional painkillers, but did not irritate the stomach lining. The U.S. Food and Drug Administration (FDA) approved of Vioxx in

1999. Merck then had the option of promoting it as an alternative to Aspirin and Advil just for those with reactions to these drugs, or promoting it as a replacement for them even for those for whom the traditional medicines worked fine. As the latter strategy lead to a larger market, it was Merck's chosen route. Vioxx was therefore promoted by heavy direct-to-consumer (DTC) advertising and became one of Merck's most profitable products, yielding a surplus over manufacturing costs of about $2 billion annually.

In 1999, Merck started a clinical trial called VIGOR, checking the effectiveness of Vioxx in patients with gastrointestinal problems, and in this trial they noted for the first time that patients taking Vioxx suffered roughly twice as many heart attacks and strokes as those taking the control, Naproxen, one of the traditional painkillers. Merck argued that this was due not to the tendency of Vioxx to cause cardiovascular problems but to the heart-protecting effects of Naproxen, although there was no evidence of such effects from Naproxen. They even went as far as issuing a press release titled "Merck confirms favorable cardiovascular profile for Vioxx," leading to strong criticism from the FDA, who described the press release as "simply incomprehensible" and part of "a promotional campaign for Vioxx that minimizes the potentially serious cardiovascular findings that were observed." They also remarked that "patients on Vioxx were observed to have a four- to five-fold increase" in heart attacks.[9]

Early in 2000, Merck began another clinical trial intended to test for the effectiveness of Vioxx as a possible cure for colon cancer. By 2003, the panel monitoring this trial noted that the incidence of heart attacks and strokes was 20 percent higher among patients on Vioxx than on the placebo and by 2004 this difference was 80 percent; in September of that year Merck withdrew Vioxx from the market.

By the time Merck withdrew Vioxx, they had known of evidence that it lead to increased cardiovascular risks for at least three years and possibly more and had publicly denied that there was any risk associated with Vioxx. The responsible move would have been to disclose these risks to the medical profession and to the FDA as soon as they were known, so that doctors and patients could have made their own informed decisions whether to take the risks or not. Some with severe pain and sensitivity to NSAIDs would have continued and others would have stopped. Merck's profits would have dropped, but patients would have lived and Merck's legal liabilities would have been far less: it and its shareholders would have been better off in the end.

In August 2005, a Texas jury awarded damages of $253 million against Merck in a case that many legal experts thought unwinnable because of a lack of evidence that Merck's product Vioxx was directly responsible for the heart arrhythmia that killed the plaintiff's husband. Merck's withdrawal of Vioxx led to a drop in its stock-market value of almost $30 billion. This was in response to the loss of profits from the withdrawal of this erstwhile very profitable drug and to the threat of thousands of lawsuits arising from the admission that Merck understated the risk of cardiovascular complications arising from its use. The loss in stock-market value, incidentally, was greatly in excess of the present value of the profits that would have come from the sale of Vioxx had this been continued, so that Merck would have been better off never to have put the drug on the market. Better still would have been to put the drug on the market with a clear assessment of the risks associated with it.

The Way Ahead

All the moves I have described—raising prices in the United States, charging high prices in poor countries, and holding back evidence of dangerous side effects—portray the industry as grasping, seeking to squeeze the last cent out of its sick customers, who not surprisingly resented this deeply and developed a strong antipathy that is the basis of the Harris Interactive poll results cited earlier.

Everything we have seen so far is consistent with the way we have thought about corporate responsibilities in earlier chapters. Central to the tensions between drug companies and society is a distributional conflict arising from the inability of the poor to pay the prices charged by profit-oriented pharmaceutical companies. This conflict is at its sharpest in developing countries, where people are living on a few dollars a day and clearly cannot pay prices that make drug distribution commercially viable. It also arises in the United States, as the number of people without health insurance rises: this figure is currently in the region of fifty million. The uninsured, usually also poor, again cannot pay the prices demanded by drug companies.

Drug companies are in a unique situation here: it is true of most industries that many people cannot afford their products, and neither they nor the rest of society are concerned about this. Most people cannot afford expensive cars or houses, a fact of little consequence. We don't worry that most people can't afford Ferraris or Aston Martins or Manhattan penthouses. But drug companies are different because drugs are different; they are not just ordinary commodities: they can make the difference between life and death, or between being sick and being well, and most of us do not accept that these differences should be determined by income. This puts drug companies in a unique and difficult position: we expect that everyone will have access to their products, even people who cannot afford them. As long as this expectation is unfulfilled, drug companies will be censured and the conflict will remain unresolved.

In many countries this conflict is resolved by governmental action: the government undertakes to buy medicines from drug companies and to distribute them to consumers through a national health service. Drug companies negotiate a profitable price with the government purchasing agency and do not have to worry that anyone will be unable to pay this price—distribution to consumers is the government's responsibility, not the companies'. If the government wants to subsidize the purchases of some groups, it can do so. Systems like this operate in most industrial countries other than the United States. There are obvious advantages, but there are disadvantages too: such systems in effect regulate the pharmaceutical industry, determining both what it can sell and the price at which it is sold. Whether a fully regulated industry would be as innovative as the current pharmaceutical industry is an open question. There is now active debate about whether such a system should be implemented in the United States.

Governmental action can resolve the dilemma faced by drug companies in industrial countries, and has done so in many countries even if not in the United States, but has not so far addressed the conflict between access and profits in the developing countries. Most poor countries do not have effective national health services and probably do not have the experience and bargaining power to make attractive deals with big drug companies. So the conflict between access and profits remains unresolved in both the United States and developing countries, a thought-provoking conjunction.

TABLE 5.2 2005 Poverty Guidelines for Forty-Eight Contiguous States and the District of Columbia

Persons in Family Unit	Poverty Guideline
1	$9,570
2	$12,830
3	$16,090
4	$19,350
5	$22,610
6	$25,870
7	$29,130
8	$32,390

For family units with more than eight persons, add $3,260 for each additional person.

In the United States the drug companies are making some moves to resolve the problem, through programs in which they make medicines available free or at reduced costs to uninsured families with low incomes. Most major drug companies now run such programs. The details vary, but typically to be eligible a family needs to show that it has no health insurance and an income that, in the case of the program run by Pfizer, is no more than twice the federal poverty guideline. Here are the federal guidelines, taken from http://aspe.hhs.gov/poverty/05fedreg.htm (Table 5.2).

So a family of four would be eligible for free medicines from Pfizer provided that it is uninsured and earns less than $38,700, and a couple with no children would have to earn less than $25,660. GlaxoSmithKline (GSK) has similar programs: as they say on their Web site

Access to medicines is not just an issue for the developing world. Even in developed countries some patients cannot afford the medicines they need. This is particularly a problem in the U.S. where many people do not have health insurance. GSK has developed Patient Assistance Programs and discount cards in the U.S. to help patients without insurance.

GSK's Patient Assistance program makes medicines available free or nearly free to the eligible uninsured: its discount cards give a 40 percent discount. This sounds generous, but in evaluating this we must remember that expensive drugs can cost $10,000 per year and more, so a 40 percent discount, while significant, would probably leave many families unable to pay.

Both GSK and Pfizer are part of a system called Together Rx, through which a group of twelve pharmaceutical companies[10] provide certain medicines at reduced cost to eligible families. Eligibility criteria are as follows (for more details see http://togetherrxaccess.com/en/eligibility.html):

- Not eligible for Medicare
- No prescription drug coverage (public or private)
- Household income equal to or less than
  - $30,000 for a single person
  - $40,000 for a family of two
  - $50,000 for a family of three
  - $60,000 for a family of four
  - $70,000 for a family of five
- Legal U.S. resident

I have not been able to find data on the size of the discounts to which eligible families are entitled, nor on how many people use this and other systems designed to help the poor and uninsured. GSK's Web site suggests that about seven hundred thousand people benefit from its Patient Assistance program and discount cards. As about fifty million are uninsured, this is less than two percent of those who need help—nice as far as it goes, but hardly a resolution of the problem.

Although these medicine access programs in the United States are limited, they are clearly a move to reduce the distributional conflicts inherent in the sale of medicines. They are moves in exactly the direction a corporate responsibility strategy would recommend. But in fact a key point is that it is not really clear if it is the responsibility of corporations to reduce these conflicts. As I noted earlier, in many countries the government takes care of this. America has drawn the line between public and private responsibilities differently from other industrial countries, and with the number of uninsured at fifty million and growing, one has to wonder if it has drawn it well.

This issue will clearly remain on the political agenda for some time, and if the line is eventually redrawn, it could change corporate responsibilities in this area. The assumption of greater responsibilities by the public sector could remove the conflict that drug companies now face in the United States. Drug companies should be supporting further intervention in the provision of medicines by the federal government in the United States rather than opposing, as has generally been the case.

This would not, however, reduce the conflicts that they face in the international arena, where it would still be the case that most people in poor countries cannot afford modern medicines and yet need them desperately. Indeed, it is not just a case of providing medicines to poor countries but also of developing medicines for these countries: as we saw in the case of Merck and river blindness, there are diseases that are crippling to inhabitants of tropical countries and which do not occur in advanced countries. Big drug companies have no incentive to develop medicines for these diseases, even if this is possible. The most dramatic case is certainly malaria. Afflicting tens of millions people in forty-four countries, my colleague Jeffrey Sachs has estimated that malaria costs the countries in which it is endemic a 1.3 percent reduction in the growth of their gross domestic product each year and plays a major role in holding back their economic development.[11] Yet, until recently, drug companies made no serious effort to develop vaccines or a cure, simply because there was no prospect of ever earning enough from sales to recoup their investments and earn a good return.

Again, it is not evident that it is the responsibility of drug companies to develop drugs for which there is, in the financial sense, no market—just as it was not clear that it is up to them to solve the problem of the uninsured in the United States. Drug companies are market-based entities. I noted in Chapter 1 that, while the invisible hand is effective in many ways, it can meet needs only if they can be expressed in money terms. In a market economy, others supply us with what we want because we can pay them to do so and this payment gives them an incentive. But if we are too poor to pay, this logic fails. Our needs cannot be expressed in the market and so the market cannot meet them. Paul Samuelson, a famous economist, once said that in a market economy we vote with our dollars. Those with no dollars are then disenfranchised.

If we hold corporations responsible for solving the problems of developing and providing medicines for poor countries, we expect their shareholders to pay for the solution. They certainly have no legal obligation to do this, nor do they seem to have a moral obligation, and least no more than any rich person, shareholder or nonshareholder, has a moral obligation to help here. Nevertheless, as we saw in the case of Merck and river blindness, some corporations do anyway go ahead and develop products for which they will not be remunerated. Merck's CEO, Roy Vagelos, argued that producing and distributing the river blindness drug was good for Merck's shareholders, as it enabled the company to recruit and retain superior scientists, and boosted morale in the company. While I have am sure he was correct in that one case, it seems unlikely that there would be no cost to shareholders if a drug company continually adopted major research and development projects that lead to no revenues, and then paid for the distribution of the resulting drug. So ultimately there would be a cost to shareholders.

Foundations and international organizations have recently assumed financial responsibility for the development and distribution of medicines to combat HIV–AIDS and malaria, two of the most damaging and deadly diseases of the third world. The Bill and Melinda Gates Foundation has made large sums available for research into malaria vaccines and treatments, substantially through grants to the Malaria Vaccines Initiative, and others have also funded this initiative. So research into malaria vaccines now has momentum, with some already in field trials. *Business Week* put it this way:

> Enter the Gates foundation, which has brokered a truce between industry and the public sector. Since its creation four years ago, it has invested more than $1.6 billion to speed the development of vaccines and procure existing ones for the world's poor. One of many Gates-backed initiatives is the Global Alliance for Vaccine & Immunization (GAVI), a partnership between industry and the private sector that says it has provided more than 8 million children with access to basic vaccines. A study by the Center for International Development at Harvard University notes that the Gates foundation is outspending the seven most powerful economies in the world combined—helping create a market where none existed.[12]

The last sentence of this comment is the key to what is happening here— creating a market where none existed, by providing a demand with a dollar value where there was previously none, in Samuelson's terms giving votes to the poor. The Gates foundation plays a pivotal role here. Other foundations have also contributed to medicine in the third world, notably the Clinton Foundation run by ex-president Bill Clinton. This has played a central role in the treatment of AIDS in Africa: the foundation has purchased AIDS drugs cheaply from generic manufactures, bargaining to bring the cost of some common treatments below $0.5 daily. Suppliers such as Aspen Pharmacare Holdings, Cipla, Hetero Drugs, Ranbaxy Laboratories, and Matrix Laboratories have agreed to accept reduced margins and even to reduce prices further as volumes rise. The foundation has also worked to organize the logistics of diagnosis and treatment, with Western companies providing diagnostic drugs and equipment at a reduced profit margin.[13]

Governments are also beginning to play this role. The Global Fund for AIDS, Tuberculosis, and Malaria is funded primarily by government grants, some in the billions, and uses these to purchase and fund the distribution of medicines. The United Nations' arm UNAIDS acts likewise. Through both of these groups, rich-country governments are providing money to transform the latent demand of poor people for medicines into manifest demand of the type that moves the corporate world. The most recent development is the formation of the International Finance Facility for Immunization, established by the Group of Eight leading industrial countries in September 2005, to which the U.K. government has pledged $1 billion.

This development clearly has far-reaching implications for pharmaceutical companies: it resolves the dilemma they were facing in the third world—lose money or appear irresponsible. Now, they can play a constructive role and bring their strengths to bear on critical human problems, at a cost to profits that is real but nonetheless acceptable.

Conclusion

The pharmaceutical industry has done well and done good—but it has also behaved badly and stupidly. It has not understood that you cannot price life-saving medicines like you price autos or air travel: too much is at stake and it is politically unacceptable that people should die or suffer only because of their income levels. It has also not understood that the public expects to be told the whole truth about the safety of medicines to which they trust their lives and those of their loved ones, a point that should have been obvious.

In many industrial countries, the inherent conflict between access to medicines and profits for their producers is resolved by state control of the distribution of medicines. In such systems, pharmaceutical companies can bargain as hard as they wish with the government procurement agencies and yet have no responsibility for deciding who does and does not have access to medicines. So they are not in the political firing line. In the United States, with of the order of fifty million without health insurance, the conflict between access and profits is particularly acute and is a source of immense political conflict, with the pharmaceutical companies inevitably buffeted by this.

The international arena resembles the United States in that there is again an acute conflict between access to medicines by the poor and profits from their provision. In this context we can see progress: foundations and international agencies are stepping in to create a demand on behalf of the poor, allowing the market mechanism to work on their behalf and reducing the conflicts that the pharmaceutical industry faces.

In such circumstances, what is the socially responsible policy for the pharmaceutical industry? Unquestionably, the industry has to put patient welfare clearly above profits, as George W. Merck suggested, and has to be seen to be doing so very clearly. Without this, it will lose the support of the public and governments, which will cost it and its shareholders very dearly in the long run. Putting patient welfare first has implications in several areas, including drug testing and drug pricing. In testing, the industry must clearly operate at the highest level of transparency, making all safety-related information publicly available. In pricing, the industry must recall that society expects all who need them to have access to its products and price accordingly. In the United States, in the absence of radical changes in the health insurance system, this will mean a great extension of operations such as Together Rx Access, but again in a more transparent way and with as much effort put into advertising these as now goes into DTC advertising of some proprietary drugs. Using differential pricing for different income groups, as in access systems such as Together Rx Access, is in fact a natural and potentially profitable response on the part of sellers to a situation where buyers differ widely in income levels and the ability to pay.

6

Wal-Mart and Starbucks

Wal-Mart

Wal-Mart presents us with a paradox. It is one of the most admired companies in America, indeed in the world. It has been on *Fortune Magazine*'s list of the most admired for many years, and in 2003 and 2004 was top of that list, the most admired company in America two years running. Still regarded as one of the best companies in America to work for, it has morphed into one of the most hated even while continuing as one of the most admired. Wal-Mart even has its own NGOs devoted to harassing it and exposing its alleged failure. (See www.walmartwatch.com, a Web site devoted to rallying people against Wal-Mart and cataloging its failures, and www.wakeupwalmart.com, a site maintained by the United Food and Commercial Workers Union.)

How can a company be so hated and so admired? In part by being brilliant at the logistics and strategy of retailing, yet weak at thinking of the social implications of what it is doing. Wal-Mart has much in common with the pharmaceutical industry, which has contributions to human welfare to be proud of, yet is, nevertheless, widely distrusted. Both are brilliant in the technical aspects of their fields, yet tone-deaf to some of the wider social and political ramifications of their activities. At the same time, a part of Wal-Mart's problem is that it has become a lightening rod for a whole range of discontents with contemporary society, many focused on features that Wal-Mart exemplifies, but for which its overall responsibility is limited—globalization, the move from manufacturing to services in rich countries, suburbanization, and the dominance of chains in retailing.

Wal-Mart certainly earned its position as an iconic company. Founded in Arkansas in 1962, it spread by a strategy so clever that it is still discussed in business strategy textbooks over forty years later.[1] Before Wal-Mart's growth, accepted wisdom was that discount stores could only be profitable in large towns with populations in the hundreds of thousands. Sam Walton, Wal-Mart's founder, bet otherwise: he bet that a discount store could be profitable in a town of less than one hundred thousand people, perhaps as low as twenty-five thousand. If so, location in such a town had one over-whelming advantage: although there might be room for one discount store, there was certainly not room for two. So if he could establish Wal-Mart in such a town, there was a guarantee that competitors would not enter the same market. Walton's bet paid off: he had found a way to enter the grow-ing market for discount stores that more or less guaranteed no immediate competitors. He established a series of local monopolies in small towns in the South and southern Midwest of the United States After a few years, his competitors realized what he was doing and from then on Wal-Mart and its competitors were in a race to open stores in small-town America and make this their market. Wal-Mart moved fast and won: the number of Wal-Mart stores increased from 153 in 1976 to 859 a decade later in 1985.[2] Today, it has over five thousand stores worldwide. As it expanded, Wal-Mart grouped its stores together so that they could all be supplied from existing warehouses, keeping distribution costs low.[3]

After saturating the small-town market, Wal-Mart moved on to estab-lishing stores in larger cities and in metropolitan areas. It is far along this route: by now, Wal-Mart is the largest company in the world in terms of annual sales, with a turnover of $312 billion in 2005. With 1.3 million employees, it is also one of the largest companies in terms of employment, and is a dominant force in U.S. retailing: it accounts for about 8 percent of all U.S. consumer spending, excluding cars and white goods,[4] and over 140 million people shop at Wal-Mart each year. Wal-Mart is the biggest food seller in the United States.

Now a global phenomenon far from its small-town roots, Wal-Mart thrives by virtue of its extraordinarily efficient logistics and its cost-conscious management. It sells more per square foot of store space than any of its competitors, keeps lower inventories than its competitors, and routinely undercuts their prices by the order of 5 percent, often more, yet is still very profitable.

Wal-Mart's logistic skills are legendary. The computer that controls its logistics is the biggest in the country outside the Pentagon.[5] Wal-Mart was the first large retailer to introduce bar-code scanners at checkouts and pioneered real-time links from stores to suppliers that enable suppliers to see which of their goods are selling and at what stores, and so move to replenish stocks at those stores without instructions from Wal-Mart's management. They have invested more heavily than any competitor in information technology and remain on the forefront in the use of IT in managing their worldwide logistics.

Also legendary is Wal-Mart's cost-consciousness. Top executives travel coach, rent compact cars, and share hotel rooms to keep costs down when they travel. Their offices are sparse and furnished with samples from suppliers. They call suppliers collect, and bargain hard for good terms. Under the agreements they have with many suppliers, Wal-Mart only takes legal possession of a good from the supplier when it is scanned at the checkout, so their obligation to pay for it is only activated then—after they have been paid for it. Together with cutting-edge inventory management, this keeps their need for working capital low.

Wal-Mart is indisputably controversial: what is the source of the controversy? For one thing, Wal-Mart stands accused of outsourcing production of many of the goods it sells. It is one of the U.S.'s biggest importers from China, importing $7.5 billion directly from China and the same amount again through its suppliers.[6] Outsourcing, as we shall see, is controversial and is prone to be criticized by organized labor, which is indeed one of Wal-Mart's most vocal critics. Organized labor often represents precisely the groups who may lose from outsourcing—unskilled labor. But overall, outsourcing can bring gains to both countries involved in the transaction, and Wal-Mart is a good illustration of this point. It has used the cost savings from outsourcing to bring its famous "everyday low prices" to its customers and as a result has cut costs for them significantly.

A firm that outsources is responsible for monitoring the conditions under which its goods are produced and for ensuring that there is no abuse of labor in the process of production. It appears that Wal-Mart has not been as active as many other outsourcers in this respect—and as we note in Chapter 10, monitoring employment conditions in China, a major Wal-Mart source, is notoriously difficult. So there may be some genuine grounds for complaint against Wal-Mart for not being sufficiently attentive to employment conditions of its suppliers. But this is not a grave enough offence to explain the massive animosity to Wal-Mart manifest in some parts of society.

The biggest issues for Wal-Mart's critics are domestic, not foreign. A brief summary of the accusations against Wal-Mart must include at least the following:

- Gender discrimination
- Low wages and benefits
- Excessive use of part-time labor
- Forcing down both wages and employment in the retail sector wherever it operates
- Harsh working conditions, including failure to provide work breaks and forced and unpaid overtime
- A strongly antiunion stance
- Encouraging urban sprawl and the resulting environmental damage.

As a consequence, Wal-Mart currently faces over eight thousand lawsuits. Perhaps more important in the long run, it has faced determined and effective political opposition when trying to open new stores, largely in metropolitan areas. If this continues, it could be an important obstacle to the company's growth, which will increasingly have to be in metropolitan areas as it has saturated its traditional small and medium town markets.

Of the thousands of lawsuits against Wal-Mart, many are small and not important in the overall scheme of things: undoubtedly, the most important is a class action alleging gender discrimination in pay and promotion. In San Francisco, the company faces what could be the biggest class action lawsuit in history, which potentially allows 1.6 million past and present female employees to sue as a single class. According to a press release by the plaintiffs,

Although more than two thirds of its hourly employees are female, they hold only one third of store management jobs, and less than 15% of store manager positions. In addition, as Wal-Mart's own workforce data reveals, women in every major job category at Wal-Mart have been paid less than men with the same seniority in every year since 1997, even though female employees on average have higher performance ratings and less turnover than men. Internal Wal-Mart document acknowledge that it is "behind the rest of the world" in the promotion of women to management ranks.[7]

Wal-Mart is in a bind with this lawsuit: to settle would be expensive, probably several billion dollars, whereas to fight it in court would generate negative publicity and risk, damaging the company's reputation among women, who are its main clients. Having got into this position, in the first place, was a serious strategic error. Among the other lawsuits against Wal-Mart are thirty-three possible class action suits alleging that the company violated the Fair Labor Standards Act by such actions as failing to provide work breaks, forcing workers to work without pay, and failing to pay overtime.

Shortly after the gender discrimination class action was certified by a federal judge in San Francisco, Wal-Mart faced more bad news: federal immigration agents raided Wal-Mart's headquarters and sixty stores, arresting illegal workers who were working for a contractor used by Wal-Mart to clean the stores.[8] More legal action may arise from this.

If there is any merit at all in the various class actions against Wal-Mart, it has clearly behaved badly and indeed stupidly on distributional issues, identified in Chapter 1 as a potent source of conflict between the corporate world and society more broadly. Neither gender discrimination nor unfair and illegal treatment of employees is socially acceptable in the United States, and both can generate hostile responses from civil society and also costly legal and regulatory responses.

So what actually are the facts concerning Wal-Mart's treatment of its U.S. employees, and its impacts on the retail sector in general? Do the many allegations stand up on close examination? Not surprisingly, in a number of cases the answer depends on one's point of view, but there are some controversies that can be resolved by a careful look at the facts.

Wal-Mart's terms of employment: are wages low, are benefits poor, and does the company rely excessively on part-time workers who are not entitled to benefits or to seniority in their pay rates? These are hard questions to answer: neither Wal-Mart nor its competitors publish the wages that they pay nor details of their benefit plans, so we cannot just go and look up the answers.

TABLE 6.1 MSA Job Position Averages: Wal-Mart versus Wal-Mart-Weighted BLS

	Wal-Mart	BLS
Sales Person	9.22	10.85
Cashier	8.78	8.06
Fast Food Worker	8.95	7.27
Stocker	9.76	10.14
Baker	9.81	9.97
Maintenance	9.95	9.29
Tire Repairer	8.97	10.25
National Average for the Above Job Categories	9.17	8.46

Wal-Mart recently made data on employee earnings available to an economic consultancy firm, Global Insight, who used this to compare Wal-Mart wages with the average wages in the retail sector.[9] The data on averages is made available by the U.S. government's Bureau of Labor Statistics (BLS). Global Insight found no evidence that Wal-Mart was paying below-average wages: indeed, they found that to a limited extent the opposite was true. The following table summarizes their findings (Table 6.1).

For seven categories of retail employees, it shows the average hourly wage at Wal-Mart and the average for the retail trade overall as extracted from the BLS data. Rather than being national averages, the data were collected and compared for a number of metropolitan statistical areas (MSAs), typically large urban and suburban regions. This point is important, as there is considerable regional variation in wages: Wal-Mart's wages have to be compared with those in the retail trade in the same area and for the same job specification. Wal-Mart's wages are on average higher in three categories and lower in four, and over the United States as a whole they are slightly higher.[10] On the basis of this data, it is hard to argue that Wal-Mart pays significantly lower wages than its competitors in the retail trade: they appear to pay the going retail rate, perhaps slightly more. What this data does make clear is that the retail trade pays low wages: a wage of about

$10 per hour, at the high end of the number above, implies about $20,000 per year for a forty-hour week. This could place a family with several children below the U.S. government's poverty line (see Chapter 5).

Is Wal-Mart in any way responsible for the low wages in the retail trade? Has competition from Wal-Mart forced down wages of competitors? From an economic perspective, this is unlikely: wages are determined by demand and supply, and when Wal-Mart moves into a new area its first impact will be to raise the demand for labor, tending if anything to raise the wage rate. Global Insight argues that Wal-Mart increases overall employment in the United States: their claim is that through its efficiency it raises productivity, and by lowering prices it raises real wages and consumer purchasing power. To evaluate this and related claims, we need to see how Wal-Mart affects prices and employment. A study by the McKinsey Global Institute came to a similar conclusion on productivity: in studying the rise in labor productivity in the United States between 1995 and 2000, they found that "by far the most important factor in that [acceleration] is Wal-Mart."[11]

On the issue of Wal-Mart's impact on prices, there is unanimity among all who have looked into this: Wal-Mart has had a remarkable impact on retail prices in the United States. Global Insight, for example, estimated that over the two decades from 1985 to 2004, Wal-Mart was responsible for a 9.1 percent decline in the average cost of food prepared at home, and a 3.1 percent decline in the overall Consumer Price Index, an extraordinary impact for a single firm. By lowering prices in this way, the company has saved consumers $236 billion, or $2,329 per household, and has raised the value of consumer income. According to a separate study by Hausman and Liebtag, poor consumers have benefited most from these savings: they estimate that consumers earning less than $10,000 per year gained almost 30 percent in purchasing power over food because of Wal-Mart, whereas those earning $100,000 gained a 20 percent rise in their ability to purchase food.[12] These, clearly, are substantial effects.

How has Wal-Mart been able to affect prices so dramatically? Clearly, its technological and logistical excellence has played a large role. It is also credited with using its bargaining power to reduce the prices of imports from China and, of course, its legendary cost-consciousness is a major factor. Another interesting point emphasized by Hausman and Liebtag is its impact on profit margins in the retail food business. They note that from

FIGURE 6.1 Food CPI and PPI (1990–2004)

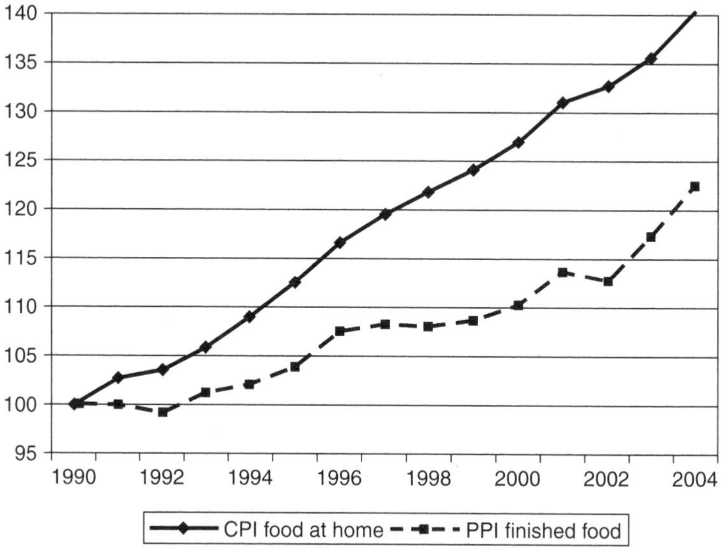

Source: Bureau of Labor Statistics (www.bls.org). Taken from Hausman and Liebtag as cited in note 7.

1990 to 2004, the Consumer Price Index for food rose far more than the food Producer Price Index: this means that what consumers were paying for food went up faster than the cost of producing food or of buying it wholesale—their figure (Figure 6.1) shows this clearly. Over this period, the Consumer Price Index for food rose 27.7 percent, whereas the equivalent Producer Price Index rose only 13.9 percent. This excess rise in the consumer prices of food is reflected in increases in the profit margins of two major supermarket chains, Safeway and Kroger. Up to 2001, Kroger's margins rose from 3.3 percent to 4.7 percent and Safeway's from 3.6 percent to 7.9 percent, more than doubling. This rise in profit margins for the established food outlets presented Wal-Mart with an opportunity, and their entry into and expansion in this area led to lower margins for the established sellers and, as we have seen, to much lower prices for consumers (Figures 6.1 and 6.2).

One aspect of Wal-Mart's performance for which it has been widely criticized is its impact on employment. It has been described as destroying jobs by driving competitors out of business, and by forcing them to cut back their labor forces to remain competitive. On the issue of Wal-Mart's impact

FIGURE 6.2 Grocery Store Operating Margins (1991–2004)

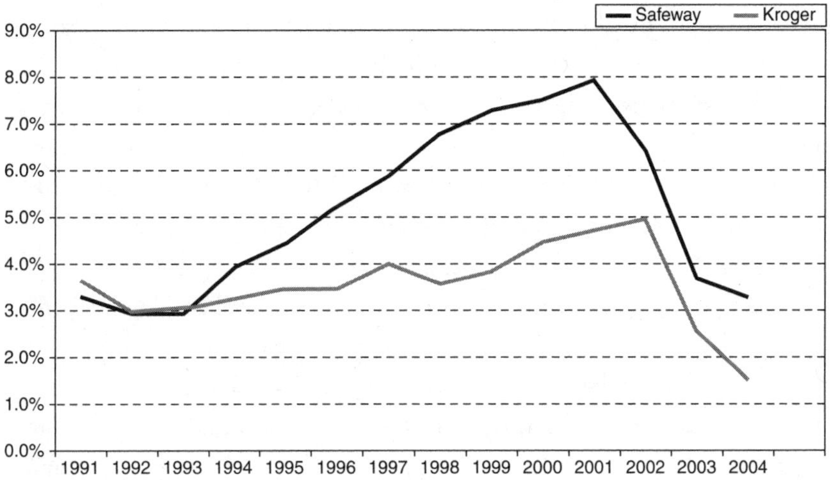

Safeway operating profit is defined as sales less operating and administrative expenses. Kroger operating profit is defined as sales less costs and expenses, excluding net interest expense. The strike in Southern California also contributed to the decline in Safeway's operating profit in 2003 and 2004
Source: SEC 10-K filings. Taken from Hausman and Liebtag as cited in note 7.

on jobs, there is disagreement among those who have conducted detailed statistical studies, though the disagreement is relatively mild. Global Insight in its analysis of the economic impact of Wal-Mart argues that

> With the opening of a typical 150–350 person store in a county, retail employment tends to increase by 137 jobs over the short term and levels off to a 97 job increase over the longer term. It also leads to net job declines in food stores and apparel & accessory stores, but to net job increases in building materials & garden supplies stores and general merchandise stores. This indicates that Wal-Mart seems to displace other retail establishments, but also serves to stimulate the overall development of the retail sector that leads to an overall positive impact (in terms of retail employment) for the counties in which Wal-Mart has expanded.

So the claim here is that a new Wal-Mart store in a town will raise retail employment by about one hundred jobs in the long run. This is less than the 150–350 people employed at the new Wal-Mart, so clearly between 50 and 250 people who were employed in the retail trade previously will lose their jobs. But taking into account the new jobs at Wal-Mart, there will be a net increase. Global Insight goes on to argue that there is additional job creation in the economy as a whole because of the increase in efficiency brought about by Wal-Mart driving productivity increases in the retail sector, and also because the decrease in prices brought about by Wal-Mart's activity leads to higher purchasing power and consequently increased consumer purchasing. They put this increase at 210,000 jobs in total by 2004.

Very similar results are obtained in a study by Basker, a study that is perhaps slightly more careful statistically than Global Insight's.[13] Basker looks at the impact of a new Wal-Mart store on county-level employment in the retail and wholesale trades, and on the number of retail establishments. Basker finds that when a new Wal-Mart store is opened, employment in the retail trade in that county rises by about one hundred immediately, but that this increase drops off by about half over the next five years, as some small retail firms close. Basker is therefore giving an estimate of Wal-Mart's county-level effect on employment that is about fifty as opposed to Global Insight's estimate of one hundred. These two estimates are of the same order of magnitude: Basker adds that some small retail outlets close and also notes that there is typically a small drop in wholesale employment in a county when a Wal-Mart store opens. She finds that a new Wal-Mart has no impact on parts of the retail trade with which Wal-Mart does not compete directly.

An alternative study of Wal-Mart's employment impact comes to a different conclusion. Neumark, Zhang, and Ciccarella (NZC)[14] also look at the employment impact of the opening of another Wal-Mart store: unlike Global Insight, they do not look into the economy-wide effects of Wal-Mart on employment as a result of its impact on productivity and prices. Nor do they replicate Basker's study of wholesale employment or of impacts on noncompeting aspects of the retail trade. But unlike the other studies, they also look at payroll data in an attempt to estimate Wal-Mart's impact on wages when it opens in a county in which it has not previously operated. NZC conclude that when a new Wal-Mart store opens, it reduces retail employment in the county by between 2 and 4 percent: for an average county this means by between one and two hundred jobs. This impact is spread over about five years, with the initial impact possibly being positive.

This conclusion is more or less the opposite of Global Insight's: why the difference?

One possibility is different data sets: Global Insight uses data from 1985 to 2004, whereas NZC use a shorter data set, covering the period from 1977 to 1995. Their data begins and ends earlier, so it is in principle possible that Wal-Mart's behavior and impact over the period not covered by NZC but covered by Global Insight—from 1996 to 2004—is sufficiently different from the earlier period to explain this contrast. In short, perhaps Wal-Mart became more employment-friendly in the late 1990s and in the new century. We cannot rule this out, as the company was under great pressure because of its alleged negative impact on employment over this period. But sadly, this is probably not the real explanation.

Although we cannot be sure, the cause of this difference is more likely to lie in a complex statistical problem known as "endogeneity." Here is the key point: suppose that Wal-Mart tends to open stores in areas where demand, and hence employment, is growing faster than the average. This would make economic sense, as a retailer wants to be where the demand is, though we cannot be sure that they have done this. Then when we look at the connection between Wal-Mart opening a new store and a change in employment, because employment in the new location is growing anyway, we would tend to see a correlation between Wal-Mart entry and employment growth—even when Wal-Mart is contributing nothing to employment growth. Global Insight claims that this is not a problem, whereas both NZC and Basker claim that it is. Without replicating all of the studies it is hard to be sure who is right here, but if forced to guess I would put my money on NZC, whose study seems very thorough and careful. The implication of this judgment is that the effect of Wal-Mart entry into a county is a small drop in retail employment. However, NZC go on to study the effect of Wal-Mart entry on total employment—not just retail employment—in a county and find that this is positive: a Wal-Mart entry raises total employment, even if it lowers retail employment. The overall increase is small, in the range of one to three hundred jobs in an average county.

NZC also look into Wal-Mart's effect on earnings when a new store is opened. Rather than looking at wages, they look at the effect of the new store on the total payroll for the county—the total amount paid out in wages. They find that expressed per person in the county, this number falls by about 5 percent. This is a surprising result, given their finding that total employment rises, and suggests a move to lower-paid jobs or to more part-time employment. None of the other studies report a similar impact: indeed this finding runs counter to Global Impact's conclusions, which are that Wal-Mart pays wages that are very much in line with the rest of the retail sector or perhaps slightly above.

There is one final issue on which Wal-Mart stands accused—it provides poor benefits and its employees are forced to use Medicaid and other social security programs to make ends meet. This accusation is again hard to evaluate, as good data are not available. Investigators have resorted to indirect ways of getting a perspective on this issue. The most persuasive evidence comes from studies by Michael Hicks, who looks at the effect of Wal-Mart stores on expenditure on various welfare programs—Aid to Families with Dependent Children (AFDC), its successor Temporary Assistance for Needy Families (TANF), and Medicaid. If Wal-Mart really provides inadequate benefits, then the presence of Wal-Mart stores in a state should increase the state's expenditures on these programs, and this is the connection that Hicks studies. He finds that for the first two programs—AFDC and TANF—the presence of Wal-Mart stores actually seems to reduce a state's expenditures slightly. So certainly there is no evidence here that Wal-Mart employees are so poor or lack benefits that they are forced to rely on antipoverty programs. With Medicaid, however, the conclusion is different. Each extra Wal-Mart employee appears to raise a state's Medicaid costs by $898. Wal-Mart employees use Medicaid and this imposes a cost on states. To understand the implications of this, first note that since 1996 people in full-time employment have been eligible for Medicaid if their incomes are sufficiently low: this change in eligibility conditions led to a rapid increase in Medicaid expenditures in the late 1990s.

A Wal-Mart employee who is eligible for both Medicaid and also for Wal-Mart's own medical benefits might reasonably be expected to choose Medicaid: it is free, whereas the Wal-Mart plan requires monthly payments and significant co-payments (employees are responsible for about one-third of the costs of medical treatment under the Wal-Mart health plan,[15] a figure higher than at competitors such as Giant and Safeway). The mere fact that some Wal-Mart employees are using Medicaid is not proof that Wal-Mart is providing no benefits, or is providing inadequate benefits. Furthermore, if some Wal-Mart employees are eligible for Medicaid, then it is reasonable for Wal-Mart to provide them with information about how to take advantage of this: this need not indicate, as some commentators have suggested, a devious plan on Wal-Mart's part to impose its employees' medical costs on the state. Hicks notes that $898 in annual Medicaid costs per Wal-Mart employee is similar to figures for other industries employing low-wage workers and similar to those for other nonunion retail stores. It is not surprising and shows, once again, that Wal-Mart is in a low-wage industry: it is not evidence that Wal-Mart is worse than its competitors in terms of wages or benefits (although as noted above it is less generous than some with respect to health benefits). Wal-Mart claims that 638,000 of its employees have joined its health care program (though other sources cite a rather lower figure[16]), that 5 percent use Medicaid, and that 19 percent are uninsured. Wal-Mart's health program costs $23 per month, covering three doctor visits each year after which there is a $1,000 deductible before coverage starts again.

Commentators in the press tend to see the difference between Wal-Mart's wages and benefits and those of competitors as rather starker than revealed in the studies just summarized. In 2005, *The Washington Post* commented that[17]

> Wal-Mart's hourly wage in the Washington region is $10.08, while Giant's and Safeway's is $13.19, the companies said. With overtime, the figure rises to $16 an hour for the union chains. Giant's and Safeway's health care plans cost the chains $12,249 for every full-time employee, nearly twice what Wal-Mart pays for a typical family plan, the companies said. Wal-Mart's cost for health benefits depend on the plan and deductible chosen by employees. While Wal-Mart workers have a 401(k) plan, with the chain matching up to 4 percent of employee contributions, depending on annual profit, Giant and Safeway are required by the union contract to pay into a more expensive pension plan.

There are several problems with this type of statement. Note, for example, the phrase "the companies said," which qualifies the statements about Wal-Mart wages and benefits relative to its two competitors. We have here Giant and Safeway's statements about their wages and benefits relative to

Wal-Mart, certainly not objective evidence. They have every interest in overstating their generosity as employers. In fact, competitors are probably poorly placed to know what Wal-Mart is paying, and there is no assurance here, even if the wage figures are accurate, that they refer to comparable jobs. Recall that there are many different types of position at a retail store and they pay different wages, as indicated in Table 6.1. It probably is true that unionized firms provide more generous pensions than Wal-Mart, and although they may provide better benefits, the statements in *The Washington Post* certainly do not prove this. The detailed studies that I have summarized here are the only ones that are based on systematic study of carefully collected data over many different areas.

In light of the studies reviewed, is Wal-Mart a responsible firm? One fact that emerges very clearly is that Wal-Mart has reduced prices, and that a substantial fraction of the population of the United States has benefited—probably over one hundred million people are somewhat better off because of Wal-Mart. Others, however, have lost their jobs as Wal-Mart has competed with their erstwhile employers, but on balance the company has led to an increase in jobs in the United States. And it has certainly led to an increase in jobs in China, a very poor country. Wal-Mart does pay low wages, though no lower than comparable firms, and indeed perhaps slightly higher than the average for the retail trade. People earning low wages are eligible for, and often take advantage of, Medicaid, and some Wal-Mart employees are in this category, about 5 percent according to Wal-Mart. One fact the debate about Wal-Mart's wages and benefits serves to highlight is that the retail trade as a whole is a source of "working poor." This trade employs many people who are unskilled and seek part-time work, and the abundance of people like this will drive wages down.

It does seem legitimate to criticize Wal-Mart for being less conscientious than many other Western firms about monitoring working conditions of its suppliers in China, and this is an area in which it could well learn from the experience of the apparel and footwear companies. The lawsuits outstanding against Wal-Mart also give cause for concern: allegations of violation of legally mandated working conditions are serious. They generate a strong response from the public—Wal-Mart's customers—and from regulators. Vindication of these claims against Wal-Mart could damage the firm's market position. Another issue that they certainly have to deal with is the gender discrimination class action suit action against them: if any of the allegations made in that are true, they suggest at the least very poor management of hiring policies and a great insensitivity to one of the major social currents of the era in which the company has evolved—the social and economic emancipation of women.

Somehow, the verifiable failings of Wal-Mart do not seem commensurate with the level of vilification that the company has faced, particularly when one takes into account the good that the company has done in holding down prices and generating employment. Wal-Mart pays wages that are low but typical of the retail sector, perhaps slightly better. It offers medical benefits that are again limited but are comparable to or better than those of competitors, many of whom offer no health insurance. Some of its employees use Medicaid, but then so do those of many firms in the retail sector, and Medicaid is intended to be available to the working poor, many of whom work in the retail trade. It tends to raise total employment locally when it opens a new store, but may reduce retail employment, and may also lower wages by of the order of 5 percent. It imports many of its products from China, but then so do most apparel, footwear, and electronics firms. Possibly, it is less conscientious than some other Western firms in monitoring the labor conditions of its suppliers. It may be guilty of gender discrimination in employment, though probably again no more than many other large corporations. Wal-Mart is also accused of stamping out "Mom and Pop" stores and thereby dehumanizing the retail trade. Although it has certainly been a part of this process, it began before Wal-Mart appeared on the scene, with the development of supermarkets, and has been going on apace ever since. Wal-Mart represents just one stage of this process. Incidentally, "Mom and Pop" stores typically pay very low wages and provide little if anything in the way of benefits: they are romanticized by some of the critics of modernization. To set against all these factors, Wal-Mart has played a major role in holding down prices in the United States, in the process raising the real incomes of most consumers and making proportionally the biggest contribution to the purchasing power of the low-paid, precisely the people whom it stands accused of exploiting.

It is difficult to reconcile the facts with the intensity of the campaigns against Wal-Mart. The strength of its antiunion campaign is possibly one factor in explaining the reaction against Wal-Mart: labor unions have played leading roles in the anti–Wal-Mart movement, retaliating for a very effective and resolute strategy to prevent unionization in its stores. Several of Wal-Mart's competitors are unionized, so that as Wal-Mart replaces them as the dominant player in the retail business, there is a reduction in unionization. But again, there are other visible companies that have been equally resolute in preventing unionization, Toyota being an example: Toyota's U.S. plants are all nonunion in spite of many attempts by the United Auto Workers Union to change this. The gender discrimination suit has certainly hurt too. But one cannot help surmising that overall Wal-Mart was as much as anything guilty of being in the wrong place at the wrong time and was targeted in part because it was a convenient symbol for a range of changes with which it is associated and to which a variety of groups object. With its international expansion and its trade with China, it is a symbol of globalization. It is also a symbol of postindustrial capitalism and of the developing service sector, substantially nonunion, that has replaced manufacturing as the primary employer in the United States and is beginning to do so in many other countries.

Since 2005, Wal-Mart has begun to change its image, and possibly its reality, in interesting ways. In 2006, it announced that it would seek to sell only fish certified as sustainably caught by the Marine Stewardship Council. As Wal-Mart is the largest food retailer in the United States, this is an important move. Many commercial fisheries are grossly overfished, with the fish populations reduced to 10 percent or less of what they were only half a century ago and in danger of effective extinction by modern high-technology fishing fleets.[18] Moving to reliance on sustainable fisheries could help avoid the looming extinction of many important fisheries and the wholesale destruction of marine ecosystems and the fish, birds, and mammals that depend on them. In addition to these moves, Wal-Mart is entering the organic food market, planning to become one of the largest retailers of organic food in the United States.

As another element of this environmental drive, Wal-Mart is also seeking to use renewable energy to power its stores and to improve dramatically the fuel efficiency of its truck fleet. At one of its stores in Plano, Texas, it even has a large working windmill generating electric power for the store in its parking lot. Commenting on the evolution of climate change as an issue in U.S. politics, *The Washington Post* recently commented that:[19]

> Washington is finally talking about climate. But for action, try Bentonville, Ark., where Wal-Mart chief executive H. Lee Scott Jr. announced this month that his company would double the energy efficiency of its 7,000-truck fleet in a decade, reduce waste from its U.S. stores by 25 percent in three years and design a new prototype store that will reduce greenhouse emissions by 30 percent. "Have you ever known Wal-Mart not to follow through on a commitment of this kind?" one speaker asked. "I have not."
>
> The speaker was Al Gore.
>
> Indeed, Wal-Mart is already cutting emissions, which is a big deal, because the company is the largest private consumer of electricity on the planet.
>
> Wal-Mart has reduced its fuel use 8 percent by preventing its trucks from idling, saving $25 million over the past year while cutting 100,000 metric tons of emissions. It recently began buying organic cotton, and all 3,700 of its U.S. stores are using energy-efficient light bulbs. Wal-Mart is so big that a slight reduction in the packaging of one of its toy lines saved the company $2.4 million last year by cutting trucking costs, while saving 1,000 barrels of oil and 3,800 trees.
>
> Scott thinks waste reduction and energy efficiency are good for business as well as the Earth; he eventually wants his company to generate zero waste and use only renewable energy, and he wants his 60,000 suppliers to follow suit. That could drive the climate debate faster than years of congressional bloviation.

These moves represent a major change in Wal-Mart's image, and if implemented fully would make it one of the "greenest" companies in the retail trade, indeed possibly one of the greenest in the United States in any business. In this as in all other areas, Wal-Mart's massive size and bargaining power really matter: if they pressure their suppliers to find organic foods and sustainably caught fish, the result will be a huge expansion of these sectors, bringing them from boutique scale to the mainstream.

Wal-Mart's environmental moves do not address the criticisms raised by its enemies, which almost all focus on issues related to labor. So the greening of Wal-Mart is not a direct response to its critics, although it could be an attempt to outmaneuver them by building support from the predominantly liberal environmental community as a way of outflanking its also predominantly liberal critics. But there is no question that a massive retail operation like Wal-Mart has a huge environmental impact, through electricity consumption, gasoline consumption, and the conditions under which its products are made or grown. The policies that Wal-Mart is now espousing are all appropriate reactions to the external costs of its actions, clear attempts to reduce or internalize these and are therefore very legitimate as a corporate responsibility strategy. But they leave unaddressed the subjects of the various lawsuits against Wal-Mart, especially the one claiming gender discrimination.

Another interesting question is whether the campaigns against it matter to Wal-Mart. It has, after all, continued to thrive in the face of hostility from activists for several years now. Does it really need to address their concerns? Wal-Mart's standing with the public is still generally high and there have been no significant moves to boycott it. There is one area in which these attacks are beginning to hurt, and that is in its plans for expansion into major metropolitan areas. On several occasions in recent years, Wal-Mart's plans to open new stores in metropolitan areas have been blocked by the campaigns of activists. In 2003 and 2004, Wal-Mart attempted to gain permission to open a new store in the Inglewood suburb of Los Angeles: its application was rejected by the city planning authorities and the company then moved to bypass this rejection by putting the issue on a community ballot, where it was again soundly rejected.[20] *The Washington Post* recently commented on the growing opposition to Wal-Mart's expansion into urban areas in the following terms:[21]

Legislation before the D.C. Council would ban new stores with more than 80,000 square feet that devote 15 percent of their space to food and other nontaxable merchandise.

A bill passed by the Maryland General Assembly would require companies with more than 10,000 employees to spend 8 percent of payroll on health care.

A zoning rule approved in Montgomery County restricts the location of outlets larger than 120,000 square feet with a full-service grocery and pharmacy.

But behind the hodgepodge of figures is a very specific goal: Keeping out Wal-Mart Stores Inc. As the discount giant shifts its focus from the Washington region's fast-growing fringes to its dense urban center, it has become locked in a bitter behind-the-scenes struggle with the local unionized grocery industry, which is scrambling to erect legislative barriers to the chain's growth.

The fight is taking on national significance. Wal-Mart, which has conquered rural America with more than 3,000 stores, desperately needs to break into the urban market to maintain its phenomenal growth. So far, it has been rebuffed in Chicago, New York, and Los Angeles, and the retailer views Washington as an important frontier for expansion.

This report has a valid point: for Wal-Mart to continue growth in the United States, it needs to gain market share in the large urban markets, where it has not so far penetrated. This is precisely where its expansion plans are now meeting effective opposition, largely from coalitions led by labor unions. This has the potential to be costly to Wal-Mart; it is a liability that was generated by Wal-Mart's aggressive stance on unionization that may eventually act to derail an important element of its strategy.

Starbucks

Starbucks is another iconic company, successful beyond the wildest dreams of its founders. Like Wal-Mart, it has come to symbolize globalization and the spread of American institutions around the world. And they both symbolize the growth of the service sector as a source of employment. Starbucks could easily have followed Wal-Mart along the road to controversy and ill-repute, but some early strategic choices took it in a totally different direction.

Whether this was by luck or judgment it is hard to tell, but Starbucks seems to have anticipated the three areas in which it could run afoul of conflicts with NGOs and the body politic. Growing coffee can be very hard on the environment: there is a real external environmental cost to this activity, which typically leads to a response by civil society. Growing coffee is also very unrewarding financially, with many coffee growers in the same financial bracket as the laborers in Chinese assembly plants. Finally, it is easy in a labor-intensive service business to skimp and save on wages and benefits, producing a cadre of poorly paid and discontented employees whose plight attracts public sympathy. By aggressively pro-environment and prolabor policies, Starbucks avoided all of these risks almost from the outset. But before discussing these aspects of its strategy, we need some more background on the company.

What is most remarkable about Starbucks is that a chain of cafes can be worth $28 billion[22]—that is, $28,000,000,000. With about eleven thousand stores worldwide, this works out to nearly $2,500,000 per cafe. This seems almost a preposterous idea at first. Yet the earnings are there to justify this value—Starbucks' earnings increased from $93 million in 2000 to almost $500 million in 2005. Although Starbucks was founded in 1971, for its first eleven years it was run by different and altogether less ambitious management: Howard Schultz, the present chief executive officer, bought the company in 1987 and took it public in 1992. Schultz always wanted to create an employee-oriented company, and in line with this their Web site comments that

> We always figured that putting people before products just made good common sense. So far, it's been working out for us. Our relationships with farmers yield the highest quality coffees. The connections we make in communities create a loyal following. And the support we provide our baristas pays off everyday.[23]

In fact, in their Corporate Social Responsibility Report for 2005,[24] Starbucks is quite articulate about the role of CSR in their success and has the following to say:

> Starbucks defines CSR as conducting business in ways that produce social, environmental and economic benefits for the communities in which we operate. We believe our strong commitment to CSR benefits both Starbucks and our stakeholders, including shareholders. A few of the tangible benefits are:
>
> - Attracting and retaining our partners (refers to employees—GMH)— We believe Starbucks commitment to CSR leads to higher than usual levels of satisfaction and engagement among our partners.

- Customer loyalty—Studies have revealed that customers prefer to do business with a company they believe to be socially responsible, when their other key buying criteria are met. We believe customer loyalty has been a driving force behind Starbucks phenomenal growth and long-term success.
- Reducing operating costs—Many environmental measures, such as energy-efficient equipment or lighting, involve initial investments but deliver long-term environmental and cost-saving benefits.
- Strengthening our supply chain—To have a sustainable business, we need a reliable and responsible supplier base that can keep pace with our growth. Starbucks invests in measures to ensure our suppliers have the opportunity to do so.
- License to operate—Having a strong reputation as a socially responsible company makes it more likely we will be welcomed into a local community.

This sharp focus on CSR is manifested in several ways. Wages paid to Starbucks employees ("baristas") are high relative to the service sector, and health benefits are available on very reasonable terms to all employees who work more than twenty hours per week. In 1991, the year before it went public, it became the first privately owned company in the United States to offer its employees a stock-ownership plan. Treating employees generously may in the long run make money for Starbucks. They estimate that training a new employee costs $500.[25] Turnover in businesses such as Starbucks' is notoriously high, whereas Starbucks employee turnover is way below the industry average. If generous treatment of employees was responsible for reducing it from the industry average of 200 percent per year to its actual level of 65 percent, then it could save training costs of the order of $60 million annually, in addition to the intangible but important benefit of having customers served by enthusiastic and committed staff.

Through a partnership with the environmental group Conservation International, Starbucks has made impressive efforts to reduce the environmental impact of the coffee farms in its supply chain. Coffee is grown in tropical and subtropical regions and often on land covered by forests. This land can be used in two different ways—to produce shade-grown or plantation-grown coffee. Shade-grown coffee comes from coffee bushes that are planted among other forest trees and are, as the name indicates, shaded from the full intensity of the sun by these other trees. Shade-growing does not require that the forest be cleared: it is thinned, but to a degree that is compatible with the continued existence of a significant part of the initial biodiversity in the forest. Shade-grown coffee is "green" coffee, with a limited environmental footprint. Plantation-grown coffee, on the other hand, is grown on land from which the forest has been cleared completely. Coffee bushes grown on plantations require heavy use of fertilizers and pesticides and so have a double environmental impact—through the destruction of forest cover and the application of agricultural chemicals. Yields per hectare are greater with plantation growth, but so are costs because of the chemicals needed.

Beginning in 2000, Starbucks worked with Conservation International (CI) and a group of coffee growers near the El Triunfo Biosphere Reserve in Chiapas, Mexico, teaching the growers how to grow coffee in ways that were relatively environmentally benign and also met Starbucks' quality standards. Coffee had to be shade-grown, no coffee pulp was to be thrown into the rivers, and hired laborers had to be given shelter, in addition of course to the coffee being good enough to be acceptable to Starbucks clients.[26] CI had several employees working full time with the growers, explaining the changes that were needed and giving advice on the new techniques. The payoff to farmers from adopting the new standards was that they would win the right to sell beans to Starbucks at prices representing a considerable premium over what they would otherwise be paid. The CI employees working with the growers quickly found that shortage of cash was a real problem for them, forcing them to sell crops early in the production cycle on bad terms, or to borrow at outrageous interest rates from local moneylenders (see Chapter 9). Starbucks and CI contributed to resolving this problem: Starbucks by guaranteeing loans to the growers and CI by arranging loans for them from the International Finance Corporation (see Chapter 4).

The Starbucks–CI project was successful: within three years, by 2003, growers were getting an average of 87 percent more than the local price for their beans and production of green coffee had increased by about

300 percent. Both the environment and the local growers were better off as a result. Starbucks then moved to generalize what had been achieved here, by introducing new coffee-purchasing guidelines incorporating the standards that had been achieved in Chiapas. These guidelines committed Starbucks to paying premium prices for any coffee that could be shown by independent verifiers to meet some or all of its standards, with the amount of the premium depending on the number of standards met.

Separately, Starbucks moved on the front of providing better terms to coffee growers by purchasing "fair trade" coffee, coffee from sources that guaranteed that growers and their employees were adequately remunerated. There was no guarantee that this was shade grown, and in some cases the quality of the product was below what Starbucks normally required. But Starbucks labeled this coffee as "fair trade" and sold it in its stores, believing that customers should be given the choice of buying coffee from sources that treated employees well.

In fact, from 2000 onward Starbucks shifted more and more of its coffee purchases to channels that ensured that a relatively large fraction of the final purchase price reached the growers, by purchasing directly from growers or their cooperatives, rather than from wholesalers and importers. Cutting out several layers of intermediaries gave Starbucks more control over product quality and made more money available to the originator of the product. In 2002 they bought 26 percent of all their coffee directly from growers, whereas in 2005 this figure reached 32 percent. At the same time, the amount purchased under long-term contracts with growers, assuring growers of prices and purchase volumes and removing the risks associated with price fluctuations, grew from 3 to 36 percent over these same two years.

Summarizing, Starbucks faced three potential sources of conflict with civil society and its consumers—the environmental impact of coffee farming, the poor earnings of coffee farmers, and the low wages of its employees in the retail food business. Acting decisively on each of these has kept them out of conflicts so far. It may well have saved money by reducing labor turnover and training costs too. Beyond these effects, it has contributed to building an image of a company that shares the values and concerns of its target market of young, educated, and relatively affluent professionals.

This is a prerequisite for the success of their strategy of making Starbucks a "third place" away from home and office that is integral to the lives of their clients. An image like Wal-Mart's would not work for Starbucks. As Wal-Mart seeks to maintain its growth by moving into metropolitan areas and moving upmarket, it is adopting some of the same strategies as Starbucks, emphasizing its environmental credentials.

7

Interface and Monsanto

Interface

Interface is a carpet company. In fact, it is the largest such company in the world, selling 40 percent of all the carpet tiles used in commercial buildings in 110 countries around the world, with sales of about $900 million in 2004.[1] For a company founded only in 1974, this is an impressive achievement. The current CEO, Ray Anderson, was the founder: he established Interface as a joint venture between Carpets International Plc, a British company, and a group of American investors. Carpet tiles, Interface's main product, are attractive to commercial users because they allow selective replacement: you can replace the worn parts of a floor cover without changing the ones that are still in good condition. As corridor areas wear much faster than, for example, areas under desks, this can lead to substantial long-run savings in the cost of floor coverings. The manufacture and use of carpets have an environmental impact: their main feedstocks are man-made fibers, principally nylon and rayon, made from oil. This means that carpet is very durable and hard to break down, and when scrapped at the end of its useful life may remain in a landfill for as long as twenty thousand years. As much as 4.5 billion pounds of carpets go into landfills annually in the United States. Over twenty years as much as 100 billion pounds of carpet could therefore end up in landfills and remain there more or less for the rest of human history.

During the early 1990s, Interface customers started inquiring about Interface's environmental impact, an issue to which the company had previously given little thought. Anderson read and was greatly influenced by *The Ecology of Commerce* by Paul Hawken, an environmental writer and entrepreneur. Hawken's book argued that business is the main driver of environmental destruction, and that conservation of the environment will only be possible when businesses are transformed by focusing on and minimizing their environmental impacts. This, he suggested, will require reinventing business models.

Anderson and the executives of Interface were quickly moved by Hawken's book to reduce Interface's environmental impacts and set themselves ambitious goals. These were: eliminating waste, reducing toxic emissions, using renewable energy, more efficient transportation, educating customers and suppliers that "environmental sustainability is not only the right thing to do, it is also the smart thing," and finally "closing the loop" and redesigning commerce to focus on providing value and services, rather than on physical materials. The idea here was to avoid disposing of carpets into landfills at the end of their lives and to find ways of recycling them instead.

These goals were adopted in 1994, and within three years Interface had made real progress on several of them. They cut the disposal of waste from their factories by about 60 percent, in the process saving money and improving their bottom line. During this period, the company also prospered, doubling revenues and employment and tripling profits. But in spite of these achievements, it remained the case that billions of pounds of carpet still went to landfills each year. Anderson was captivated by a concept from Hawken's book that seemed to offer the potential to address this problem, the concept of selling services rather than physical products. Hawken presented the idea in these terms:

> What we want from products is not ownership per se, but the service the product provides: transportation from our car, cold beer from the refrigerator, news or entertainment from the television. Under the intelligent product system, these products would not be sold, but would be licensed to the purchaser, with ownership retained by the manufacturer. When you bought a refrigerator, a VCR, or car, you would buy the license to use and operate it.... But the product could not be thrown away or disposed of. It must be returned by the final user, or in the case of larger appliances, picked up by the manufacturer or retailer.

Based on this vision of a product that recycles between producer and consumer, Interface developed what its executives saw as the pinnacle of its environmental achievement, its Evergreen Services Agreement (ESA). The idea was to lease carpet covering to customers, rather than sell it, and take it back at the end of its life. The reasoning behind this was Hawken's: clients want floor covering not carpet, so Interface would provide the services of floor covering and retain ownership of the carpet. As ownership of the carpet would remain with Interface, they would assume responsibility for maintaining it—vacuuming it and replacing tiles that were badly worn or stained—and would offer their clients a deal consisting of a bundle of services including carpet rental, carpet maintenance, and carpet replacement. Clients would buy floor-covering services from Interface, not carpet: they would never own the carpet.

Interface saw this as an attractive business model for them: it would take them into the service business, which they believed to be a more stable and high-margin business than the sale of carpets. Companies continue to clean and service their carpets even when they are not buying new ones, even through recessions, Interface thought, whereas carpet sales are notoriously cyclical and can fall off sharply when profits are down. Replacing carpets is an investment that a company in financial difficulties can easily postpone. Interface also believed that they could make this an attractive proposition for their customers: by replacing only the small fraction of a carpet that it was worn or dirty, they could offer a continuing high-quality service at low cost. And by offering a lease they allowed customers to avoid the large up-front investments needed to carpet a large office building, which could easily exceed $1 million. This meant more efficient use of money for the clients, with less tied up in carpets and more in productive business assets. It all seemed like a very compelling case indeed.

Interface started marketing the ESA in 1995 and found its first customer for this approach in the Southern California Gas Company. Optimistic that the idea would take off among large clients, Interface's top management spent considerable time and energy marketing the ESA concept. Anderson, Interface's CEO, gave as many as one hundred presentations per year on the ESA concept and gained rock-star status on the corporate environmental circuit, with Interface receiving widespread acclaim for their environmentally sensitive business strategy. Their chief financial officer spent time fine-tuning the lease, because Interface wanted the lease to meet the accounting criteria set by the U.S. Financial Accounting Standards Board (FASB) for an operating lease. If the ESA lease met these standards, the customers would not have to report any aspect of it on their balance sheets and would have no capital tied up in their carpets, leading potentially to more efficient use of capital and a higher return on assets. In doing this Interface encountered a difficulty, as the FASB requirements for a lease to be an operating lease were rather stringent. Interface's senior vice president for finance put the criteria for meeting FASB requirements as follows:

> According to the first test, Interface could not transfer title; FASB wants to be sure that there is no transfer of ownership. Second, we cannot give the customer a bargain purchase offer, so that they can just buy cheap at the end of the lease. Third, we have to look at the term of the lease compared to the life of the product; in this case, the life of the carpet is about 10 years. The term of the lease cannot exceed 75% of the life of the product, which is why we arrived at a seven-year lease. And fourth, we have to do a calculation of the present value of all future lease payments at an assumed cost of capital.... The sum of the present value, under rule four, cannot exceed 90% of the fair market value of the product; otherwise the customer is actually paying for it.[2]

These terms limited the deal that Interface could offer: even more important as a limitation was the fact that carpets could not profitably be recycled, so that the value of the carpet to Interface at the end of its life was zero. Indeed, it might even be worse than this: Interface would have to pay tipping fees to dispose of the carpets it took back from clients. Because of the FASB regulations—in particular the requirement that the present value of payments not exceed 90 percent of the value of the carpet—and the zero scrap value of the carpet, offering a seven-year operating lease amounted to selling the carpet at a substantial discount to the regular price. As Interface was going to lose money on the lease relative to a regular sale, they had to compensate for this in the terms of the maintenance and selective replacement agreements and make enough profits from these to make the entire deal profitable for them. In order to be able to provide maintenance and selective replacement services to clients all over the United States, Interface built a chain of carpet dealers throughout the United States, a significant investment.

In spite of their initial success with the Southern California Gas Company, Interface found that the Evergreen Services Lease was not selling: between 1995 and 2001 only six customers signed ESAs. One sale that Interface had hoped to close, but did not, was to the University of Texas at Houston, who in 1999 expressed interest in the ESA lease. UT Houston was already an Interface client and was known to be environmentally sensitive. After long negotiations, UT Houston rejected the ESA lease, which disappointed Interface greatly, as this was a prestigious client with a known environmental orientation.

Through to the present, Interface has continued to have little success with its ESA. It has made great progress with many of its other environmental goals, but success with the ESA concept has eluded it, in spite of the acclaim with which the concept was greeted.

Why has Interface's ESA not sold, and why has the attainment of their much-vaunted goal of moving to a rental rather than an ownership model for carpets eluded them? The terms that Interface offered to UT Houston give some insights into this. UT needed 40,000 square yards of carpet, which they could buy for $25.50 per square yard plus installation costs or a total of about $1.2 million. Interface offered to lease this to them for $16,411 per month, plus $7.95 per square yard per year for maintenance and replacement. Over the full seven years of the proposed lease, these terms would amount to a payment of about $2.6 million in present value terms, more than twice the cost of buying outright. Of course outright purchase would require separate payments for cleaning and selective replacements, but UT's facilities manager clearly felt that he could meet these requirements for less than the cost of buying the carpet. Another perspective on this offer is that for maintenance and replacement payments of $7.95 per square yard per year, UT could replace the entire carpet roughly every four years. Obviously this was not an attractive deal to the potential client, and looking from the outside and with the admitted advantage of hindsight it is difficult to see why Interface ever thought that it would be attractive. Buying outright and using inexpensive janitorial labor, probably poorly paid immigrants, to clean and maintain the carpet were clearly a winning strategy for the client.

Why did Interface make such an unattractive offer? In part, as we saw above, this was because of the limitations imposed by FASB requirements on operating leases. But in the case of the UT, FASB requirements were irrelevant, as UT like all universities is a tax-exempt institution. Interface could certainly have offered a longer lease and varied other aspects of the lease conditions in this case. Another aspect of the problem was undoubt-edly that Interface's costs for cleaning and maintaining the carpets were higher than UT's: Interface had to buy and build out a national network of carpet dealers who could both sell and maintain their products. The overhead costs associated with this were certainly enough to make Inter-face's costs uncompetitive even if its labor costs were comparable to those of UT's janitors. But Interface had to charge enough on its cleaning and maintenance costs to recover the losses that it was making on the lease of the carpet because of its insistence on meeting FASB requirements for an operating lease. Interface's maintenance payments were bound to seem outrageous.

There is another perhaps more important reason for Interface being unable to offer attractive terms on the Evergreen Services Lease. Remem-ber the motivation for the lease approach: Interface wanted to be in the business of leasing rather than selling carpet, because—it believed—clients wanted floor-covering services and not carpets per se. But switching from an ownership to a leasing model was not an end in itself: this was motivated by Hawken's idea that products should not be thrown away at the end of their lives, but should be returned to, or collected by, the manufacturer. Hawken's vision was that the manufacturer would then be able to reuse many parts of the product in making new ones, so that recycling would be increased and waste reduced. Whether this was in fact a plausible vision I shall discuss later.

For the time being, let us accept it as a good idea and see what that means for Interface's ESA. If a discarded product, or some part of it, can indeed be used by the manufacturer as an input to the production process, then that product has value to the manufacturer. It saves him the cost of buying some components and he can afford to pay for it up to the costs that it allows him to avoid. If carpet could be recycled, then the discarded carpet would have real value to Interface, and this would allow them to make the lease deal more attractive. They could give an allowance for the value of the carpet when taken back, and the more useful the carpet to them, the more it could be recycled, the sweeter they could make their offer in this respect. But Interface was not going to reuse the carpet or recycle it in any way: they were going to send it to the landfill just as their clients would if they owned it rather than leased it. In other words, leasing rather than owning generated no economic value in this case, and elementary economic logic tells us that if a deal structure generates no economic value relative to alternatives, then it can never be made more attractive to both parties than the alternatives. This fundamental economic truth Interface failed to see, and this is really why they could never make their lease deals attractive enough to sell. Had they found a way of making recyclable carpets, then they would have been able to offer great lease deals and we would now see most commercial carpets being leased not owned. And in fact this may still happen: if the price of oil is high enough, recycling old carpets becomes competitive with using oil to make new nylon and rayon, and oil prices at about $90 per barrel are in the region where recycling could be competitive. It, however, is probably too late for Interface to get back into the leasing business: for the last three years they have made losses and have now sold their carpet distribution and maintenance business at a loss.

What do we conclude from this story? Interface's ESA model never really had any environmental advantage, because it was never going to lead to more recycling and less waste, which was the putative aim of the project. Not all environmental advantages can be translated into business advantages, but many can. And nonexistent environmental advantages certainly cannot be translated into business gains, however skilled the marketing and however carefully crafted are the terms of the lease.

It is worth going back to Interface CEO Anderson's inspiration for the ESA, the vision of Paul Hawken quoted earlier. He wrote, "What we want from products is not ownership per se, but the service the product provides: transportation from our car, cold beer from the refrigerator, news or entertainment from the television."

It was this observation that motivated Anderson to devise the ESA: he was switching from selling to leasing in order to minimize waste and generate more recycling. Without the technology to recycle, the quest was always in vain—but what about the model underlying Hawken's influential vision? One can make an argument that it is also flawed. Certainly, we want to encourage recycling whenever it makes economic sense, which is far more often than we practice recycling now. But the manufacturer is not necessarily best placed to recycle a product. Think by way of illustration of a used washing machine, a difficult item to dispose of. Some parts can be recycled, mainly the steel panels on the front, back, sides, top, and bottom.

A steelmaker can use these in a furnace making steel and will be willing to pay for them. But the maker of the washing machine has no use for them: they will be dirty and scratched from many years of use and cannot be reused, and anyway new machines will be of a different design so that these parts would be of no value even if they were clean. So encouraging the maker to take the machine back is a mistake: it is not the maker to whom it is valuable, but rather a steel plant, and under the current waste-management system that is probably where it will end up, as the steelmaker will be willing to pay the most for it. It will go to a scrap metal merchant who will break it up and sell the steel to a steelmaker and likewise sell any other reusable parts to whoever finds them valuable. There is no sense in arguing that the maker of a product is "responsible" for it and has to take it back: when its useful life is through, it has to go to whoever can make best use of its components and materials. If that happens to be the maker, fine, but often it will not be.

Monsanto

Interface is a company that had good environmental press because of an idea about how to improve the environment, an idea that did not work out. It got more credit that it deserved. Monsanto is the opposite: it set out to do good for the environment and was vilified by environmentalists. In fact, in the late 1990s it was almost driven into bankruptcy, although now it is thriving. Monsanto invested billions of dollars genetically modifying crops to make them more productive and require less use of insecticides, rendering the growing process less environmentally harmful.[3] Their aim was to make agriculture sustainable while improving crop yields in poor countries.[4] With this aim and with proprietary technologies to implement it, Monsanto should have been a poster child for CSR; instead they were almost destroyed by opposition from environmental groups. Consumer opposition to genetically modified crops led to their being abandoned by farmers, financially weakening Monsanto, which was then taken over. Monsanto's problem was that it focused on one private–social cost gap—that associated with the use of insecticides on growing crops and the environmental damage that these insecticides cause—but in the process missed another more serious one: that associated with people's fears of genetically modified foods. From the consumer perspective, Monsanto was seeking to raise farm productivity and lower farm pollution, which was all for the good, but was seeking to do this by passing to consumers new and unknown risks, the risks of genetically modified foodstuffs that had never been extensively tested. Monsanto's failure was not a failure to take CSR seriously, but the failure to implement it thoroughly and follow through on all of its implications.

Monsanto's vision is captured in an interview that its then CEO Robert Shapiro gave to the *Harvard Business Review* in 1997. Shapiro emphasized the immense growth in world population that was inevitable over the coming decades and the growth in demand for food that would follow. Without dramatic changes in agricultural practices, this would lead to food shortages, as current agriculture was not sufficiently productive, and to environmental destruction, as agriculture is one of the main drivers of environmental damage. "We are entering a time of perhaps unprecedented discontinuity," he comments, "Businesses grounded in the old model will become obsolete and die." He then goes on to argue that

> In the twentieth century we have been able to feed people by bringing more acreage into production and by increasing productivity through fertilizers, pesticides, and irrigation. But current agricultural practice isn't sustainable: we've lost something on the order of 15% of our topsoil over the last 20 years or so, irrigation is increasing the salinity of the soil, and the petrochemicals we rely on are not renewable.

> Most arable land is already under cultivation. Attempts to open new farmland are causing severe ecological damage. So in the best case, we have the same amount of land to work with and twice as many people to feed. It comes down to resource productivity. You have to get twice the yield from every acre of land just to maintain current levels of poverty and malnutrition.... The conclusion is that new technology is the only alternative to one of two disasters: not feeding people—letting the Malthusian process work its magic on the population—or ecological catastrophe.

New technology, Shapiro goes on to argue, means genetic modification, using in more productive ways the information contained in the genome.

> Using information is one of the ways to increase productivity without abusing nature. A closed system like the earth's can't withstand a systematic increase of material things, but it can support exponential increases of information and knowledge. If economic development means using more stuff, then those who argue that growth and the environment are incompatible are right.... But sustainability and development might be compatible if you could create value and satisfy people's needs by increasing the information component of what's produced and diminishing the amount of stuff.... We can genetically code a plant, for example, to repel or destroy harmful insects. That means that we don't have to spray the plant with pesticides—with stuff. Up to 90% of what is sprayed on crops is wasted. Most of it ends up on the soil. If we put the right information in the plant, we waste less stuff and increase productivity.

This, then, was the vision that drove Shapiro to convert Monsanto from a chemical company to the world's first major life-sciences company: the vision of an overcrowded and polluted earth that could be saved by genetic technologies with the capacity to increase agriculture's productivity while reducing its environmental impact. It was a beguiling vision that drove Shapiro and his colleagues to look for associated business opportunities and to restructure Monsanto radically, emphasizing research on genetic technologies and spending $8 billion on acquiring seed companies whose products were the vehicles through which genetically modified crop technologies could be marketed.

From its founding in 1901 in St. Louis, Missouri, Monsanto was a chemical company, with products that included aspirin, saccharin, acrylic, plastics, fertilizers, and weed-killers. Its best-selling herbicide Roundup was developed in the 1970s, and in 1998 contributed $1 billion to Monsanto's operating earnings. It was about to go off patent, presaging a probable sharp drop in these earnings. From the early 1990s, Monsanto began the development of agricultural biotechnology, quickly becoming the leader in this field. In 1992, the U.S. Food and Drug Administration (FDA) approved the use of genetically modified (GM) foods on the grounds that they were "substantially similar" to the nonmodified versions of the same foods.

Because they were not perceived to pose any more risks to human health than the nonmodified varieties, the FDA did not require GM foods to be labeled so.

In 1995, the first products of Monsanto's agricultural biotechnology reached the market. One important product was soybeans that could withstand their Roundup herbicide ("Roundup-Ready" soybeans); another product line was potatoes and cotton whose genes had been modified to allow them to resist pests that commonly attacked those crops. Called Bt-potatoes and Bt-cotton, the genomes of these crops incorporated genes from the bacterium *Bacillus thuringiensis,* a microorganism that produces a compound toxic to these pests. The genetic modification allows the modified plants to produce this toxin too, so that they were also poisonous to their main insect pests. Hence, they could be grown without the application of insecticides.

Roundup-Ready soybeans were attractive to farmers because they would no longer need to weed fields of soybeans when growing: Roundup could be applied and it would kill everything in the field except the soybeans. Weeding large fields of growing soybeans was otherwise done by tilling between the rows of beans and besides being costly often led to soil erosion, a major environmental problem in most intensively farmed areas.

Bt-crops were attractive because they did not need to be sprayed with pesticides, saving money: there was also an environmental gain here too, as not spraying with pesticides reduced poisonous runoff into groundwater and streams and also reduced agriculture's impact on insect populations, many of which, such as bees, were benign and indeed helpful as they play a key role in pollination. (The destruction of pollinators by herbicides is a sad and little-known story.[5])

Monsanto imposed some quite stringent conditions on farmers who used their GM crops. For example, those using Roundup-Ready crops had to use Roundup as a herbicide, even though the same active ingredient was available in other products now that Roundup was off patent—a clever way of effectively extending the patent life of Roundup. Also farmers had to agree not to resell GM seeds, not to retain them for planting later, and not to retain seeds from this year's crop to plant for next year. Monsanto claimed that these provisions protected their intellectual property, but as they also protected Monsanto's market position this claim could seem disingenuous.

Most farmers in industrial countries had long since given up using seeds from this year's crop for next year, and the hybrid species being used were not productive when used like this. But in developing countries, "brown bagging," using this year's crop seeds to plant next year, was and still is common.

The late 1990s saw the emergence of concerns about the environmental impacts of GM crops. Two events in particular were influential: Roundup-Ready canola plants in Canada cross-pollinated with a weed growing off the field, leading to a weed that was also Roundup-Ready, that is, immune to herbicides. Immediately labeled a "superweed" by the press, this led to concerns about the impact of GM crops on weeds and other naturally occurring plant species. And in 1999, a scientist at Cornell University fed Monarch butterflies with plants that had been dusted with pollen from Bt-corn and found that a large proportion of their larvae died. This immediately led to concerns about the effects of GM crops on insect populations, although most scientists, including those in the Cornell lab that conducted the experiment, emphasized that the conditions experienced by the butterflies in the lab were most unlike any that would be experienced in the field. Nevertheless, these events began to turn environmental groups against Monsanto's GM crops. This opposition was heightened when Monsanto bought Delta & Pine Land Company, a cottonseed producer that owned the patents to "terminator genes," genes that when inserted into a plant's genome could be used to turn on or off the expression of selected characteristics. These genes could turn on or off the ability to resist salt, or pests, and could also turn on or off the ability to produce fertile seeds—in other words, they could render a plant sterile. This could have become an interesting technology for protecting Monsanto's intellectual property— Monsanto could have used these genes to make sure that farmers could not keep seeds from this year's crop to plant next year by making the seeds sterile. Some groups were concerned about sterility spreading through cross-pollination, and others saw this as a blow to the economic prospects of poor farmers in the third world—even though such farmers were most unlikely to be using Monsanto's expensive GM seeds. None seemed to take into consideration the fact that GM crops could have beneficial environmental impacts through less use of pesticides and less soil erosion.

While the environmental groups were developing hostility to GM foods, consumers in Europe were doing likewise. In 1996, the European Union approved the use of GM soybeans on the grounds that they were "substantially equivalent" to non-GM soybeans, and in the fall of that year the first imports of American GM soybeans began to arrive in Europe. This timing was incredibly inauspicious: for reasons that had nothing to do with Monsanto, European consumers were in no mood to trust governmental assurances about the safety of GM food. British consumers were reeling from the shock of discovering that, contrary to many firm governmental and scientific assurances, bovine spongiform encephalopathy (BSE) had crossed from cattle to the humans who ate them. BSE is a degenerative brain disease leading to a prolonged death, and in humans it lead to a condition known as new variant Creutzfeldt–Jakob disease (nvCJD) that was inevitably fatal. There had been rumors in the press that this might be happening, but these were discounted as alarmist by governmental agencies, which subsequently had to admit to being seriously in error on this matter. Overall, consumers were left with the impression that government assurances of the safety of food were worth little and that the government was more interested in protecting the financial interests of the food industry than the health of consumers. At almost the same time, there were other unrelated food-safety scandals in other European countries, also involving attempted cover-ups by governments.

As a result of this fateful coincidence, Monsanto ran into an amazing storm of opposition when they attempted to sell their GM soybeans in Europe. Many large NGOs, and especially Greenpeace, threw all of their resources into opposing GM foods, and consumers were in a mood to listen and believe. Before long, prominent retail food chains were promising not to sell GM foods, and U.S. farmers found that their exports to Europe were dropping fast. (U.S. corn exports to the EU dropped 96 percent in one year.[6]) Monsanto's sales dropped rapidly as its farmer customers saw consumer reactions to GM food, and with high levels of debt from the acquisition of seed companies as part of its strategy of expanding into the agricultural market, Monsanto was in financial trouble. Its pharmaceutical arm was profitable, but losses from the agribusiness operations offset this and drove the firm as a whole into the red. Monsanto's best hope was a new infusion of capital, and in 1998 it negotiated a merger with American Home Products, a profitable but second-tier pharmaceutical company. This deal fell apart, and in April 2000 Monsanto and Pharmacia and Upjohn merged to form Pharmacia. Although billed as a merger of equals, this was really a takeover by Pharmacia, who merged Monsanto's profitable pharmaceutical operations with its own and structured the agribusiness as a separate company 85 percent of which was owned by Pharmacia. Driving Pharmacia's acquisition of Monsanto was Monsanto's blockbuster drug Celebrex, a Cox-2 inhibiting antiarthritis drug that was generating revenue of about $3 billion annually. Monsanto also had another similar drug in the pipeline, Bextra, and both have been highly profitable for Pharmacia. (Both are competitors of Vioxx, discussed at length in Chapter 5.) The story went full circle when in the fall of 2002 Pharmacia spun off its 85 percent of Monsanto in an initial public offering, establishing Monsanto once again as an independent agribusiness company.

As an again-independent company, Monsanto has performed well financially, with its stock price moving from the teens to over 80 (although at 80 some analysts consider it overvalued with a price-earnings ratio of about 40). Driving this growth was the growing use of GM crops: from 1996 to 2003, the global area of transgenic crops increased forty times, from 1.7 million hectares to 67.7 million. In 2003, the United States was the largest grower of GM crops in the world, with 84 percent of the acreage: next were Canada, Brazil, and China. Two crops, cotton and maize/corn, accounted for 84 percent of GM acreage and adding in rapeseed/canola brought this up to 99 percent.[7] All of the GM crops used commercially are either herbicide-resistant or Bt-variants engineered to resist pests: there has been no innovation in the product line since the early 1990s.

Although it has earned great returns for its shareholders since its flotation, Monsanto's future is far from assured. After years of heavy Roundup use, weeds are developing resistance to Roundup, and in consequence farmers are using more herbicides with Roundup-Ready products, greatly reducing their economic appeal.[8] There is also some evidence that although Roundup does not kill Roundup-Ready crops, it reduces their yield, again cutting into the competitive edge of a major part of Monsanto's product line. Furthermore, consumers are still uneasy about GM foods, with evidence that the unease that originated in Europe is spreading to the United

States. Monsanto's main market is in fact not food for direct human consumption, but soybeans for cattle, cotton for textile uses, and canola for producing canola oil, but consumer unease about the product tightly limits its market potential.

Overall, what does the Monsanto story tell us about the connection between doing well and doing good? As it moved into GM crops, Monsanto was a company with a vision: a vision with which many environmentalists agreed. It was a vision of a sustainable agriculture able to feed a growing population through less destructive practices. With the immense benefits of hindsight, it seems that there were two flaws in that vision. One, it was inaccurate. It is not clear that GM foods, at least as available today, are as environmentally benign as Monsanto believed in the 1990s. Second, Monsanto focused on *its* consumer, the farmer, and not on the ultimate user upon whom the entire value chain depends, the end consumer. By not anticipating consumers' reactions to novel foodstuffs with science fiction overtones, and not offering any real benefit to these consumers, Monsanto failed to anticipate the single most salient obstacle to its business plan. More consumer research early on could surely have uncovered this and helped the Titanic of the GM world avoid its iceberg. It is also probably true, though inevitably speculative, that if Monsanto really had been able to find a way of increasing agricultural productivity that was environmentally benign and was acceptable to consumers, then it would have reached financial nirvana. And it is also probably true, and again speculative, that GM crops will one day play an important role in meeting the food needs of a world of ten billion people. But, Monsanto may not be the firm to sell those crops.

8

Outsourcing

Outsourcing is one of the most controversial and divisive topics on the contemporary political scene. American and European manufacturing companies commonly carry out much of their production in low-wage countries, through local subsidiaries or through independent companies specializing in products to be sold under Western brand names. In the press this practice is often referred to disparagingly as "exporting jobs."

Most garment and footwear manufacturers use overseas subcontractors to produce their goods, as do many makers of electronic devices. Indeed, in industries where labor costs are important, outsourcing is now virtually ubiquitous: for example, in the low- and medium-price categories, very few items of apparel sold in the United States are made there whatever the nationality of the company under whose brand they are sold, and electronic appliances—computers, cell phones, TVs, and DVD players—are again almost universally made outside the United States, even if sold under a U.S. brand. An interesting aspect of this trend is that even though it began with labor-intensive products and unskilled labor, it has now moved upscale to the point where some information technology jobs requiring considerable sophistication are moving to countries where wages are lower, most notably India.

It is easy to see what is driving this process—huge wage differentials between industrial and developing countries. In many poor countries, a few dollars a day is considered a reasonable wage, and a day probably means working for ten hours or more. In the United States, $48 is the minimum wage for an eight-hour day, and in industries requiring significant skills and having some degree of unionization, daily wages and benefits exceed $100 and may even approach $200. So we see labor cost differentials of the order of 100 to 1—very suggestive of relocation for labor-intensive operations.

Fifty years ago the wage differentials were just as big as they are now, yet outsourcing was not an issue. Part of the explanation is that this cost differentials only translates into an equivalent cost saving if foreign labor is as productive as Western labor. Today many poor countries have good educational systems and plant and equipment as modern as that in the West, so their productivity is comparable to ours and wage differences translate into equivalent cost differences. This was not always so: educational standards in poor countries have risen, and reduction of trade barriers and the growth of cross-border investment have made it easy for them to get the latest plant and equipment.

Another important factor in the growth of outsourcing is that it is far easier now than in the past to import the finished outsourced goods back to the home market: transport costs have fallen, tariffs have fallen, and information technologies make managing the logistics far easier. Companies such as Federal Express and United Parcel Service specialize in managing international logistics and will take care of transportation, customs, and all other aspects of moving goods. Also very important is the decline in tariff rates over the last half-century: U.S. companies importing goods made in poor countries now have to pay much lower tariffs than was the case even twenty years ago. These factors that drive outsourcing are major features of the contemporary world economy and are not going to change in the near future.

Does outsourcing raise questions about a corporation's responsibilities to society? Undoubtedly it does, although they are not easy to answer. What makes outsourcing controversial in the developed world, of course, is that it appears to create jobs in poor countries and not in the United States or Europe. There are allegations, furthermore, that it takes jobs from the United States and Europe—political debate in the United States is replete with references to the "sucking sound" of jobs being moved to Mexico as a result of the North American Free Trade Area (NAFTA). In the United States, Democrats and the labor unions opposed the recent signing of the Central American Free Trade Area Agreement (CAFTA) for the same reason, a fear that U.S. jobs would be lost to low-wage countries.

An important background fact is that in the United States, and also in several other industrial countries—the United Kingdom and Germany included—the period from the 1960s to the 1980s saw a sharp drop in the employment of unskilled workers and in their wages. The wages of unskilled workers fell both relative to the wages of more skilled workers and also in real terms: a drop in wages for such a large group was a phenomenon unprecedented in recent economic history. In the United States, this took the form of a widely noted increase in the "College Premium"—the difference between the earnings of college graduates and those whose highest qualification is a high-school diploma. What are the possible explanations for this divergence between the economic fortunes of the skilled and unskilled?

Many studies have analyzed the impact of outsourcing on wages and employment in Western countries, and in general their conclusions are far more nuanced than those suggested in the press and in political debate. Most researchers have given pride of place to technological change rather than outsourcing as the driver of the increasing gap between skilled and unskilled. The growth of automation and computerization led to a drop in job opportunities for the unskilled, because their jobs were replaced by automatic systems. The other side of this coin was an increase in demand for highly trained workers to design, make, and manage the automated systems. For example, unskilled or semiskilled assembly line jobs, a major source of employment in the 1950s and 1960s, have been replaced because of a transition to assembly lines "manned" by computerized robots. This process has displaced many semiskilled manual jobs. A natural consequence of a drop in demand for unskilled labor was a drop in the wages it could earn. Other minor contributory factors could include (in the United States) a drop in the real value of the minimum wage, which failed to keep pace with inflation, a drop in unionization, and to some degree an increase in the supply of unskilled workers through immigration. Outsourcing also contributed to this drop in the wages of the unskilled, as it, like automation, reduced the demand for unskilled labor in the industrial countries. Unskilled labor in rich countries was replaced by much cheaper unskilled labor in poor countries. The general sense, however, is that outsourcing was not the primary reason for the decline in the wages of the unskilled, but played a role secondary to technical change. Consequently, even if outsourcing were reversed, we would not roll back the drop in wages of the unskilled.

Some analysts suggest that even this secondary role is overstating the impact of outsourcing. By cutting costs and making firms more competitive and profitable, outsourcing may have enabled them to expand output and increase jobs in areas other than labor-intensive manufacturing. By this mechanism, outsourcing may have supported the creation of new jobs to replace those lost abroad, though these were generally not jobs for unskilled manual workers. According to a recent study by Harrison and Scorse,[1] most U.S. companies that expand employment overseas also expand domestic employment. This correlation between the expansion of domestic and overseas employment supports the idea that outsourcing allows companies to create more domestic jobs along with the low-wage overseas jobs. These authors do, however, find some exceptions, one being the textile industry, where there has been a clear flow of jobs away from high-wage countries.

This discussion touches on a more basic strategic factor that we need to consider in evaluating outsourcing's overall impact on the economy. Countries such as the United States will never prosper on the basis of using cheap labor to make labor-intensive products: poor countries will always beat the rich countries at this type of activity, just because of their poverty, which gives a huge competitive advantage in labor-intensive operations. The route ahead for rich countries, if they are to stay rich, is via products that use the skills in which they as rich countries are competitive—skills related to high technology, design, fashion, and intellectual property. Defending industries such as textiles and shoemaking from competition from the developing world is a forlorn venture, one that will never succeed. One can argue that there is a degree of inevitability about outsourcing that makes resisting it like resisting the tides and that the right strategy is to use it to our advantage and adopt policies that mitigate the damage it does to unskilled workers.

It is clear that outsourcing is in many respects to our economic advantage. By lowering costs, it keeps prices down and raises profits, helping both consumers and shareholders. And by raising a firm's profits, it also helps employees who are not involved in labor-intensive operations—clerical workers, IT workers, and designers. Most companies have many more customers and shareholders than unskilled employees, so that the balance of advantage in total may be positive even when there is a loss of unskilled jobs. And the creation of jobs in poor countries, as I shall argue in more detail in this chapter, is in itself a good outcome: it reduces poverty in some of the poorest places in the world and helps poor countries take the first step on the road to industrialization. Ultimately, this will lead to them being customers for our more expensive goods and services.

The Ethics of Outsourcing

What are a Western company's obligations if it decides to outsource some of its production to a low-wage country? Should it, for example, be concerned about the issues just discussed—about the possibility that in outsourcing it might contribute to a widening gap between skilled and unskilled workers in its home country? This is certainly a legitimate question, but is only a small part of the picture. Customers and shareholders, and some employees, will gain from outsourcing. The company will be more competitive and efficient, and its jobs will be safer. Low-wage employees in poor countries will gain. These positive effects have to be offset against any worsening of the domestic income distribution as a result of outsourcing. Like many other decisions in the outsourcing area that we shall see here, this could be a tough call. In most cases, commercial imperatives to outsource will be strong, perhaps even a matter of the survival of the company, leaving its executives with little choice. Even if they feel that they have a choice and could survive without outsourcing, it is still possible that the ethical balance will tilt them toward outsourcing: the gains, in terms of employment in poor countries, profits, lower prices, and more stable jobs, may well seem to outweigh the loss of unskilled jobs in the home country.

Once a decision has been made to outsource, many other issues arise. As we noted in the first chapter, wages in poor countries are incredibly low. This should not be surprising—this is what it means to be a poor country. A few dollars a day for a long, hard day is not uncommon. Employment conditions may be shocking too, reminiscent of the nineteenth century in the United States and Europe. And it is not uncommon to find children working in factories, again reminiscent of the now-rich countries a century or less ago. Under these circumstances, is it exploitative to outsource to poor countries? What are a Western company's obligations once operating in a poor country—should it pay wages and provide working conditions that would be acceptable at home, as some in the labor movement claim, or is it acceptable to provide employment on conditions that although far poorer than those at home are, nonetheless, agreeable to local people?

Case Studies

A good way to start this discussion is to look at some outsourcing cases, in order to understand better how the issues appear to managers setting up and running an outsourcing operation. "Sweatshops," to use popular parlance, started to make headlines in the 1980s and 1990s in the United States. One of the first companies to make the headlines because of outsourcing was Nike. A highly visible and successful U.S. maker of athletic shoes and clothing, Nike had always relied on sourcing its labor-intensive products from low-wage countries, principally in Asia. It chose not to own factories there but to subcontract to independently owned manufacturers, and during 1997 incidents at these factories made headlines. Employers were found to be paying less than the local minimum wages, and on several occasions supervisors physically abused employees whose work was substandard, hitting them or forcing them to run long distances as punishment. A male Taiwanese supervisor famously hit female Vietnamese workers in the face with allegedly substandard shoes. These instances of underpayment and physical violence shone a spotlight on outsourcing, bringing many more incidents to light and starting a public debate about pay and conditions in Asian factories supplying Western consumers. Nike initially dismissed the whole issue, arguing that conditions in subcontractors' factories were not its responsibility and that there were no serious problems in the factories anyway. In Michael Moore's 1997 documentary *The Big One,* Nike CEO Phil Knight is seen as saying that he is comfortable with fourteen-year-olds working in factories. But when Nike realized that this issue would not go away and had the capacity to damage their brand, they reacted sharply, insisting that the offending supervisors be fired, local minimum wage laws be respected, and empowering auditors Ernst and Young to randomly monitor conditions in subcontractors' plants and conduct confidential interviews with employees. Only a year after the interview with Michael Moore, Phil Knight said that "Nike is raising the minimum age of footwear factory workers to 18…Nike has zero tolerance for underage workers."[2] Knight defended Nike's role in developing countries with statements such as "[i]t sounds like a low wage and it is. But it's a wage that's greater than they used to make" and

> Whether you like Nike or don't like Nike, good companies are the ones that lead these countries out of poverty. When we started in Japan, factory labor there was making $4 a day, which is basically what is being paid in Indonesia and is being so strongly criticized today. Nobody today is saying "The poor old Japanese." We watched it happen all over again in Taiwan and Korea, and now it's going on in Southeast Asia.[3]

The public found these statements less than compelling, and Nike was widely accused of "ruthless exploitation" (by members of the U.S. congress[4]) and was subject to boycotts and protests at events in which it was involved. A defensive move by Nike that backfired and led to strong criticism was the appointment of Andrew Young, ex-U.S. ambassador to the United Nations and a civil rights leader, to conduct an independent analysis of labor conditions of Nike's suppliers. Young wrote a report lauding conditions in these factories, but his supposed independence was undermined by his admission that he spent only ten days visiting factories all over Southeast Asia, was always accompanied by management, and spoke to employees through translators provided by Nike. Critics seized this as an attempt by Nike to whitewash its operations and hide the issues.

Everyone from Nike's CEO Phil Knight down was clearly unhappy about the damaging publicity Nike received and believed it to be a threat to Nike's dominance of a market that depends strongly on positive image and consumer perceptions of a company. It is not possible to prove with certainty that Nike suffered financially because of accusations of exploitation and running sweatshops, but Nike's net income did drop from $795.8 million in fiscal 1997 to $399.6 in fiscal 1998, and its share price also dropped about 20 percent during the period of this controversy, with competitors taking market share. Subsequently, Nike has become a leader in the movement to improve labor conditions in poor countries, acting with all the fervor of a convert.

Levi Strauss has a very different record on overseas subcontracting. An iconic U.S. company dating from the days of the 1849 California gold rush,

Levi Strauss got its start in life selling to the famous '49ers who migrated west to search for gold. Outliving the event that gave it birth, Levi became the ranking supplier of denim clothes to the United States and much of the world. They expanded to a wide range of leisure clothes, sold mainly under the Levis and Dockers brands, and by 1993 were the world's largest brand name apparel manufacturer. All their manufacturing facilities were initially in the United States, where they had been since the nineteenth century, but their use of outsourcing expanded in the 1970s and 1980s, and by 1992, 54 percent of their garments sold in the United States were produced abroad.

From the late 1980s, Levi Strauss' management worried about wages and employment conditions at their suppliers. They felt they had an ethical obligation to the employees there, even if they were not legally Levi Strauss' employees, and were also concerned about the risk of a public-relations disaster, as indeed happened later for Nike and several others. "What would this look like if a 60 Minutes camera crew showed up at the [factory] door?" was a question they asked systematically of the factories that supplied them.[5] So from the start, Levi Strauss implemented a very strict code of conduct for its subcontractors and dealt only with those who complied with this. Levi Strauss argued that even if this imposed costs on its suppliers, they would benefit because other Western producers would want to do business with them once it became known that they met Levi's standards. And in extreme cases they were willing to provide financial assistance to a supplier whom they valued and who could not improve working conditions because of the lack of capital. Compliance with health and safety standards, for example, would require investment, and on occasions Levi Strauss provided loans, or agreed to higher prices for a period, to fund this. For Levi Strauss, confronting the issues raised by outsourcing was a central part of their strategy from the start and not something that they were forced into. Not surprisingly, they fared better than many other garment firms.

Another perspective is provided by the experience of Charles Veillon, a Swiss mail order company that in 1994 began offering handwoven carpets in its catalogue. Its CEO was disturbed by seeing a television documentary about child labor in carpet-making, in which the Swedish furniture giant IKEA was accused of being a major buyer of carpets made by children working under conditions of near-slavery. In order to avoid the same fate, he began researching Veillon's carpet suppliers.[6] As a medium-sized firm it bought from middlemen rather than the makers and found that most of its suppliers were either unable or unwilling to give details of their sources.

In order to try and get better control of its sources, Veillon moved to buying directly from carpet makers, and started working with NGOs to determine those that were free of child labor. As there were then over six hundred thousand carpet looms in India alone, determining those that complied with regulations about child labor was virtually impossible. Another possible route was via certification, in this case by Rugmark, an export licensing and labeling campaign started by a consortium of human rights NGOs operating under the name South Asia Coalition on Child Servitude (SACCS). Rugmark's aim was to certify large numbers of carpet makers as compliant with strict standards on the use of child labor. The operation was supported by a levy of 0.25 percent of the export price of a carpet paid by the maker and a voluntary contribution of 1 percent of the invoice price of the carpet by the importer. If importers were worried about the use of child labor and wanted to be certain of avoiding this, makers would, Rugmark hoped, see the 0.25 percent levy as worth paying to get their business.

Charles Veillon's story is interesting in several respects. It shows clearly how difficult it is for a small firm to monitor the conditions under which its products are made in the developing world. They had neither the resources nor the influence of Nike or Levi Strauss, two household names, and could not on their own verify employment conditions of their suppliers. The role for a certification system like Rugmark, which had several competitors, is clear in such cases: small and medium companies can use this to get some assurance about their suppliers.

Facts About Outsourcing and Low-Wage Countries

What we know about the impact of outsourcing on the receiving economy suggests that it is an unambiguous benefit. Western firms usually pay higher wages and offer better conditions of employment than those that are locally owned, and when they operate through subcontractors they put pressure on them to do likewise. And whether outsourcing offers better terms of employment or not, it certainly increases job opportunities and generates income in the recipient economy. It probably also assists in the transfer of new technologies to the recipient economy and provides valuable training in industrial manufacturing. By way of example, making shoes for Nike will teach a company how to make athletic shoes—what materials to use, where to buy them, and how to work with them. Nike provides this information. These skills can then be used to supply other manufacturers, or even to set up a unit in competition with Nike. In China, subcontractors have often taken the skills they learned as agents for other companies and used these to manufacture the same goods in competition with their erstwhile client. All of these are clear gains for the local population. When we first encountered Nike CEO Phil Knight's comment on wages of Nike suppliers in Asia—"it sounds like a low wage and it is. But it's a wage that's greater than they used to make"—it may have sounded a weak defense. But in fact this is true and it highlights an important point: $5 a day, though low by our standards, is better than $2.

To give a sense of the magnitude of the effects of outsourcing on wages, I quote some data on Indonesia. Ann Harrison and Jason Scorse[7] of the University of California at Berkeley studied wages at domestic and foreign firms in Indonesia between 1990 and 1996 and found that the latter pay more. But this does not necessarily establish the point that interests us, as the higher pay could be due to the fact that foreign factories have employees who are better educated or have more work experience. The authors control for this with data from the Indonesian census, which gives the characteristics of the workers at each plant. Using this detailed data, they find that after allowing for possible differences in education and training, foreign firms pay between 5 and 10 percent more for unskilled workers and between 20 and 35 percent more for skilled workers. They conclude by asking why—"Do foreign firms pay higher wages in order to deflect criticism from others? Do they pay higher wages to prevent their employees from leaving to set up their own enterprises? The evidence on this question is not clear."[8]

Several other relevant points emerge from the study by these authors. They compare wages in three classes of firms—domestic, foreign, and those that export. Domestic firms are those that are not foreign-owned and do not export: exporting firms may be owned by locals or foreigners. Foreign firms are those that are foreign-owned. They find that the highest wages are paid by foreign-owned firms: those that export come next, and those that are entirely domestic come last in terms of wages paid. The numbers are striking: in 1996, foreign firms paid on average wages of 3270.3 thousand Rupiahs per year, exporting firms paid 1831.8 thousand Rupiahs, and domestic firms paid 1123.3 thousand. (There are about 9000 Rupiahs to one dollar.) The difference between the domestic and foreign firms is almost three to one, with export-oriented but possibly domestic firms in between. Breaking out firms making textiles, apparel, and footwear (TFA), which is where most sweatshop allegations focus and where much outsourcing occurs, the numbers are similar but less dramatic. Foreign firms pay on average 1775.1 thousand Rupiahs, exporters 1462.4, and domestic 1078.2. So although the wages paid by outsourcers are low by our standards, they are clearly high by those of the economy in which they operate.

The other effects of outsourcing on the recipient economy are less easily quantified but probably also positive. These include an increase in the demand for labor and therefore in the number of jobs in the industrial sector, training workers to operate modern production equipment, and in some cases the transfer of technology to the recipient country. In addition, outsourcing generates revenues for the local government, through income taxes paid by employees, profits taxes and social security payments made by companies, and sales taxes levied on purchases by employees. And by increasing exports, outsourcing provides foreign exchange to pay for imports.

Why, then, is there so much unease about the impact of outsourcing on developing countries, if all the evidence suggests that this is positive? My colleague Jagdish Bhagwati[9] suggests this is self-serving: he notes that all the concern about outsourcing comes from people in rich countries, and suggests that it is a form of protectionism by the labor movement in industrial countries and its sympathizers, a way of trying to prevent the downward pressure on unskilled wages that we noted earlier. Bhagwati is adamant that people from poor countries never complain about the impact of outsourcing: they are well aware of its benefits, he suggests.

Another possibility is that people in Western countries are horrified to read of wages in the range of $1 to $6 per day and automatically think that these are unfair and exploitative, because they would be so in their own countries. They are lazy and don't make the mental translation into the circumstances of poor countries and don't realize that people earning $2 per day may jump at the opportunity to earn $5 per day. Perhaps they also fail to realize that in poor countries the alternative to a low-wage job is not social security or welfare: it is begging or starvation. In corroboration of this, innumerable reports in the Western press show that many of the poor in developing countries are enthusiastically seeking precisely the low-wage jobs with Western companies that many Western activists decry as exploitative. For example, on January 14, 2004, Nicholas Kristof wrote in *The New York Times:*

> Nhep Chanda is a 17-year-old girl who is one of hundreds of Cambodians who toil all day, every day, picking through the dump for plastic bags, metal cans and bits of food. The stench clogs the nostrils, and parts of the dump are burning, producing acrid smoke that blinds the eyes.
>
> The scavengers are chased by swarms of flies and biting insects, their hands are caked with filth, and those who are barefoot cut their feet on glass. Some are small children.
>
> Nhep Chanda averages 75 cents a day for her efforts. For her, the idea of being exploited in a garment factory—working only six days a week, inside instead of in the broiling sun, for up to $2 a day—is a dream.
>
> "I'd like to work in a factory, but I don't have any ID card, and you need one to show that you're old enough," she said wistfully. (Since the candidates [in the 2004 U.S. election] are unlikely to find the time to travel to the third world anytime soon, I put an audio slide show of the Cambodian realities on the Web for them at www.nytimes.com/kristof.)
>
> All the complaints about third world sweatshops are true and then some: factories sometimes dump effluent into rivers or otherwise ravage the environment. But they have raised the standard of living in Singapore, South Korea and southern China, and they offer a leg up for people in countries like Cambodia.
>
> "I want to work in a factory, but I'm in poor health and always feel dizzy," said Lay Eng, a 23-year-old woman. And no wonder: she has been picking through the filth, seven days a week, for six years. She has never been to a doctor.
>
> Here in Cambodia factory jobs are in such demand that workers usually have to bribe a factory insider with a month's salary just to get hired.

Along the Bassac River, construction workers told me they wanted factory jobs because the work would be so much safer than clambering up scaffolding without safety harnesses. Some also said sweatshop jobs would be preferable because they would mean a lot less sweat. (Westerners call them "sweatshops," but they offer one of the few third world jobs that doesn't involve constant sweat.)

In Asia, moreover, the factories tend to hire mostly girls and young women with few other job opportunities. The result has been to begin to give girls and women some status and power, some hint of social equality, some alternative to the sex industry.

This is a powerful illustration of how unattractive the alternatives to making goods for Western consumers are if you are an unskilled worker in a poor country. The *Economist* (November 28, 2002) has a similar comment on a recent decision by Reebok to stop using a subcontractor in Thailand:

How little the dangerous fashion for corporate social responsibility has to do with a truly responsible attitude by businesses is aptly shown by Reebok International. This American sports-goods supplier claims to have pioneered good corporate practice.

Doug Cahn, the company's head of human rights, talks about values, fairness and principles, with all the zeal of an anti-corporate lobbyist. He presents the news that Reebok has just decided to withdraw business from a subcontracted factory in Thailand as a proof of corporate caring. The reason: the 400 or so workers employed there to make shorts and shirts were working for more than 72 hours a week.

It is responsible to press for better standards, but the supply of good jobs matters too. Workers at this Bangkok factory were paid above the minimum wage, with health-and-safety rights that few local manufacturers would offer. Many factory employees in developing countries want to work more hours rather than fewer.

Although Mr. Cahn denies it, the company seems to have pulled out to avoid allegations that it was doing business with what critics call a sweatshop. "There are always people outside who want to talk with our factory workers to check our standards," he says. Reebok has been stung before. One troublesome former factory worker in Hong Kong, Han Dong-fang, hosts a radio show calling for workers to telephone with their complaints. "He is a lightning rod for criticism," says Mr. Cahn, before adding quickly that "criticism is one of Reebok's most valuable resources.

These examples, and the facts about wages in companies producing for Western markets, put a very different spin on the idea that Western companies operate through exploitative sweatshops. Some possibly do, but in many cases through their outsourcing they offer attractive opportunities that would not otherwise be available.

The contrast between off-the-cuff response and reality is perhaps sharpest in the field of child labor, a topic that quite naturally promotes a visceral reaction. In discussing the Charles Veillon case, we saw that many Western companies will go to great lengths to avoid products made with child labor, partly no doubt because their managers find the use of child labor repugnant, but also because they fear the reactions of their home press and their consumers to allegations of child exploitation. No one wants a TV or newspaper headline alleging that they exploit poor defenseless children in third-world countries.

Yet in fact an analysis of child labor is complex: parents anywhere, developing countries included, do not generally send their children to work unless this is really necessary and there are no alternatives. Obviously it would be better if the children were in school, but there may be no school, or the parents may be unable to afford the fees, or the child's labor may be critically needed in the family farm, upon whose yield the family's health will depend. If the child is working to produce goods for export to the West, then the income he or she earns may be critical to the family's survival. There is interesting evidence on just this point from Vietnam. Studies show clearly that as families' incomes rise, child labor drops. Specifically, as rice prices rise and the incomes of rice farmers rise too, there is a decline in child labor.[10] What this shows is that children are working because the family would starve if they did not, and when financial circumstances are no longer so pressing then they cease to work. This suggests that buying rice from Vietnam might be a better way of ending child labor than banning it outright. So without in any way defending child labor, we have to understand that there can be compelling reasons why this happens. In an ideal world there would be no child labor, there would be good schools, and families would be able to afford the school's fees and would not need the income that child labor can produce. But, in developing countries in particular, the world is far from ideal. Consequently, prohibitions on child labor, insensitively implemented, can do more harm than good. Bangladesh, a very poor country to which many textile and apparel companies outsource production, provides a shocking example. With a long record of child labor in Bangladesh, companies there were frightened that Western corporations would sever their relations because of child labor and so fired their child workers. Studies that followed the fortunes of the laid-off children showed that in the months that followed most of them lost weight and suffered a decline in their health. Some became prostitutes.[11] They were better off before when they were in the garment industry. But in an ideal world, people from rich Western countries would have taken them out of employment and paid for their education.

The complexities of child labor are well illustrated by the case of soccer balls: historically, top-grade soccer balls, as used in tournaments, have been made in the Sialkot region of Pakistan. They were made by women and children working at home: managers distributed materials and tools to their homes and collected the finished products. The discovery that child labor was involved led to a predictable uproar among activist groups in the West and pressure on the brands involved—including Nike—to stop this. As monitoring the use of child labor was impossible while work was done at home, the subcontractors changed working arrangements, constructing factories at which soccer-ball manufacturing would be centered. There, working conditions could be adequately monitored. This sounds like a good outcome, but in fact its social consequences were highly regressive. Pakistan is an Islamic country where Islamic law and custom, combined with some of the consequences of the caste system, imply that women cannot work outside the home: castes cannot mix, nor can the sexes, and women cannot travel away from their villages. So transferring the work to factories meant that soccer balls now had to be made by men. The loss of employment and income by women had a harmful effect on their social status, which, initially low in an Islamic country, had improved because of the income from making soccer balls. After some argument it was agreed that women could work in single-sex factories, restoring the opportunity of gainful employment. Yet even this concession was of little value, as many of the women had no means of transportation to the new single-sex factories and had no way of taking care of their children if they were not able to take them to work. The bottom line here is that a move to enforce Western-style labor standards in a poor Islamic country backfired: in the end, women and children, the poorest groups in affected region, were harmed by the loss of job opportunities. And the subcontractors who managed the manufacturing process were also harmed: their costs were raised and profits lowered, and they lost market share. It is worth noting that the form of child labor involved here—working at home with their mothers—was probably about as benign as child labor can be. There was no question of harsh factory labor in dangerous conditions.[12] The leader of a local Pakistani child welfare NGO made his position clear:

> If it were up to me, I would take child laborers out of the more hazardous professions and put them into the soccer ball industry—there are no chemicals, they are well paid, and the hours are flexible. The children can work at home in their spare time, mixing it with housework or after school. I am very worried that the children taken out will end up in more dangerous occupations. This is an easy sector when compared with carpets or leather tanneries.[13]

Another reason why Western activists are hostile to outsourcing could be its impact on inequality in developing countries: in many cases it increases inequality, by raising the wages of workers in fields such as apparel, footwear, and textiles, while leaving those in other businesses at their original low levels. The data on Indonesia presented by Harrison and Scorse shows this effect, with a difference of about three to one between the wages paid by foreign-owned firms and strictly domestic ones. This means that outsourcing can create a new and relatively privileged class of workers, with better wages, benefits, and working conditions. Of course, no one is being harmed by this: the point is just that some are gaining, whereas others are left where they always were. If you have really strong egalitarian instincts, you might find this unattractive, but most of us are probably happy to see at least some of the poor being lifted out of abject poverty, provided that no one else is harmed.

Corporate Responsibility and Outsourcing

Now that we have some understanding of outsourcing and its impacts on Western and developing countries, we can return to the questions posed initially: what are the responsibilities of a Western company outsourcing to a poor country? And what policies are in the best long-term interests of the company's shareholders?

It seems rather clear from the evidence presented that outsourcing is good for poor countries, and that even if the wages paid there are a small fraction of what would be acceptable at home, outsourcing offers enhanced economic opportunities to poor people. Wages that are low by Western standards are not a sign of exploitation, but rather a symptom of poverty and underdevelopment, and in general Western companies seem to pay wages that are a considerable improvement on those offered by domestic firms. But, one might ask, could Western companies not afford to be more generous still? Could they not pay five times local wages rather than only two or three times? Could they even pay wages that approach Western levels?

To address this question the chart shows an approximate cost breakdown for a pair of athletic shoes sold by Nike and made under subcontract to them, assumed to sell retail for $100. To many, the most striking fact will be the size of the retail margin, at 47 percent by far the largest element in the total of $100. This covers the retailer's distribution costs, staff costs, rent, heating and lighting, and store displays (Figure 8.1).

Nike's profits on the $100 shoes will be about $4, and the manufacturer's will be about $1.90. Labor costs in manufacturing are about $2.59 per pair. Suppose Nike was to double the wage rate, from say $3 daily to $6; this would increase labor costs per pair of shoes from $2.59 to $5.18, an increase big enough to reduce Nike's profits by more than half. As Nike's profits are not unusually high, this is a move that its executives could not even consider: it would reduce Nike's share price greatly and subtract billions of dollars from shareholders' portfolios. As an alternative, Nike might consider instructing its subcontractor to raise wages and then pass the extra costs on to the retailers by raising prices. But it is not clear that Nike has enough market power to do this: retailers might just refuse to pay the extra, especially if Nike's competitors made no changes in their prices. This is the type of move that would have to be made in conjunction with competitors, and agreeing with competitors

FIGURE 8.1   Nike Cost Structure per Pair of Shoes

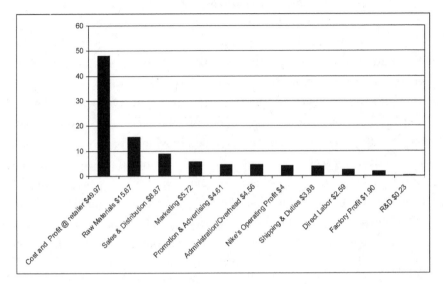

to raise wages and then prices would violate antitrust laws in the United States and the European Union. So although labor costs are a small part of what the consumer pays for a pair of Nike shoes, it is not easy to see where Nike could find the money to raise wages significantly of its subcontractors.

In addition to worrying about wages, outsourcing companies have to look carefully at working conditions of their suppliers: health and safety laws, and laws guaranteeing human rights, may be nonexistent or poorly enforced in third-world countries, and Western companies do have a responsibility to ensure that they are comfortable with working conditions of their suppliers. Checking on these facts can be difficult, as shown clearly by the discussion of outsourcing in China later in this chapter. The experience of Charles Veillon in trying to check on the conditions under which carpets are manufactured reinforces this point.

Overall, there is no conflict between responsible behavior toward poor countries and outsourcing, provided that the wages and working conditions are carefully monitored and are chosen to be as good as or better than those generally accepted in the receiving country. But ensuring this is not easy and can require a very serious monitoring effort.

What about outsourcing and the home country? Clearly, outsourcing is good for shareholders and for customers, as it lowers costs and prices and raises profits. The potentially controversial issue here is its impact on employment: as we noted, outsourcing is one of the several factors contributing to a decline in unskilled employment in the United States and Western Europe and so to a relative drop in the wages of unskilled workers. As an offset, there are industries, a majority, in which outsourcing raises profits and underwrites the expansion of domestic employment, usually in employment categories other than the unskilled. On balance the net impact of outsourcing on employment in total seems to be positive, but there are industrial sectors, such as textiles, in which this is not true. These are probably not sectors in which rich countries should seek to maintain a competitive presence as low labor costs so obviously give poor countries a competitive edge here, but nevertheless the social and economic costs of adjusting to a new world order can be very great. On balance it seems that outsourcing is good not only for poor countries, but also for the rich: it lowers prices, raises profits, and can raise employment in total.

Outsourcing in China

China is to outsourcing as Washington is to politics: it is the center, the place that everyone thinks of when the issue is raised. It is widely described, for good reasons, as the world's workshop: every industrial country now relies on China for some of its supplies of manufactured products. Yet outsourcing in China in a manner consistent with corporate responsibility is particularly difficult. The problem is that Western companies find that verifying working conditions of their Chinese subcontractors can require almost forensic skills. A recent article from the *Financial Times* sets out clearly what many companies have found.

> Factory managers in China are becoming increasingly sophisticated at falsifying worker time cards and payroll documents to disguise irregularities including underpayment, excessive hours and inadequate health and safety provision. Auditors estimate that more than half of factories they see in China are forging some of their records-meaning that many of the international companies that source from China are learning less about the actual working conditions in the factories they use, even as they step up efforts to monitor them.

The practices also mean that some western groups' assurances that they are abiding by China's labour laws and their own codes of conduct are based on faulty information. The widespread forging of records threatens to undermine the aims of the corporate social responsibility movement, a response by multinationals to the concerns of customers, non-governmental organisations and trades unions about issues including human rights and the environment.[14]

The article goes on to cite Daryl Brown, vice president for ethics and business practices at Liz Claiborne, who says

A few years ago, we were able to detect when records were altered by simply interviewing workers. Now, workers are coached. Good auditors can usually tell when the workers have been coached and we also make periodic un-announced audits to combat this. However, there are times when we need to resort to interviewing workers off premises or to surveillance to find out the truth. We also have our direct contact information posted at the factories, which allows workers to contact us confidentially, and on occasion they do.

The reporter proceeds to relate a discussion with a factory manager, who quite openly admits that records are carefully falsified, even to the point of dropping them on the ground to make them dirty and bending them to make them look real and used. Consultants employed by Western companies to help monitor working conditions in China report that possibly 90 percent of subcontractors falsify at least some of their records in this way.

Companies operating in China confirm these reports. In Nike's corporate social responsibility report for 2004,[15] the company took the unprecedented step of listing all of its subcontractors and admitting that it was unable to ensure that they all comply with its labor standards. Their motive for disclosure was the hope that others sharing the same subcontractors could join with Nike in cooperative monitoring. In an introduction to the report, the CEO Phil Knight commented:

This report taught us that to write that next chapter, we and others involved in this discussion are going to need to see common standards emerge and ways to better share knowledge and learnings created. We are *disclosing our supply chain* [emphasis added] in an effort to jump-start disclosure and collaboration throughout the industry.

I said you can't do it alone. I also know that you can't do it forever. Last November, I announced that I was stepping down as CEO (I'll still serve as Chairman of the Board). Bill Perez is the new CEO for Nike, Inc. based, in part, on Bill's track record in corporate responsibility. His philosophy is that companies must invest in and improve their communities. I'll be there to help him any way I can.

His comment about the selection of his replacement is interesting and shows the significance this issue has assumed for Nike. Acknowledging that monitoring conditions in its supply chain is too much for it to do effectively on its own, Nike goes on to talk about the role of the Fair Labor Association (FLA):

The FLA, of which Nike is a participating company, is a consortium of brands, universities and NGOs. The FLA accredits independent monitors to perform unannounced audits of five percent of our supply chain each year. This amounted to 40 independent audits of Nike factories.

They also discuss the conditions under which they drop a factory for non-compliance with labor standards:

A factory is cut from our supplier base when, over a period of time, it lacks the capacity or the will to correct serious issues of non-compliance. One supplier in China, for example, was cited for repeated violations of overtime standards and falsification of records. The compliance team established action plans, which three different Nike business units worked with the factory to implement. After six months of continuous efforts, and no improvement, the factory was dropped.

Another theme that Nike emphasizes, probably indicating the future of monitoring in countries like China, is the need for different Western companies to agree on common standards: they make the very valid point that a factory may supply four or five different Western firms, all of which can have different and potentially conflicting standards. If they really are conflicting, then the supplier is in effect being set up for noncompliance by the terms of its engagement. On this issue they comment:

> The challenge of meeting different standards can be highlighted with a simple example: Different work codes call for different placements of fire extinguishers. To stay in compliance, one factory might need to have the fire extinguisher mounted five feet high on a wall for one company's audit, four feet high for a second company's audit, or on the floor for a third one. Picking one of the standards and sticking with it means the factory is out of compliance with the other two audits. This borders on the absurd. If monitoring becomes standardized, and we can achieve consistency in the quality of audits, it should follow that it will be quicker and cheaper to acquire compliance data and to achieve broader coverage. Our first step toward harmonizing our compliance standards with those of other companies came through the American Apparel Industry Code of Conduct, established at the invitation of the Clinton administration in 1997. This effort led to the creation of the Fair Labor Association, whose membership now includes more than two dozen brands, a number of NGOs and over 175 universities with licensed apparel programs.

Nike also emphasizes the need for cooperative monitoring, so that rather than four or five Western companies separately monitoring a factory in China—to different standards—they pool their efforts and monitor more effectively. They mention the case of one factory that was audited forty times in one year, by different inspectors and with little or no coordination.

Clearly monitoring labor conditions in China is little short of a nightmare, and consumers really cannot be sure of the value of any assurances they may be given about the conditions under which goods from China were produced. Under these circumstances, is it responsible to continue to outsource to China? If few valid assurances can be given about compliance with rather basic labor codes, should Western firms still be operating in China? To show that this is not an empty question, note that Levi Strauss pulled out of China in 1993, although they subsequently reinstated some subcontracting operations there beginning in 1998. Their reason for pulling out was not so much the difficulty of monitoring, but the fact that China, in Levi's opinion, violates basic human rights, and a part of Levi's ethical code is never to operate in countries that do not respect basic human rights. Nike also mentions this as an issue of concern in its CSR report. It seems, then, that there are very real questions about outsourcing in China. Maybe the compliance problems can be resolved within a few years, by the sort of cooperative efforts that are now emerging. Even if this happens, it will not solve the human rights issues. But the contradiction there is built deeply into the international economic system: China has been allowed to become a central pillar of this in spite of being run by an authoritarian and nominally communist regime. Western countries have welcomed China into the international system in spite of this regime, perhaps in the hope that exposure to the rest of the world and growing affluence would together democratize China. Although they may well do so, they have not yet done so, and having an authoritarian regime in a central position in the international trading system has many inherent contradictions, some of which are apparent in the problems in managing working conditions in Chinese subcontractors. They will not be easily resolved. Cuba also has an authoritarian communist regime: the contrast between how we treat the two is striking.

Conclusions

Outsourcing is a really complex subject and it is easy to understand why it is controversial. Nonetheless, some important points do stand out:

- Outsourcing is good for poor people in poor countries. Even if wages appear low and working conditions poor, people there are gaining from outsourcing. This matters: outsourcing has raised living standards for some of the poorest people on earth.
- There have been instances of outrageous abuse of workers in outsourcing operations. Monitoring can prevent these, and it is important that it should do so.
- Even though there are monitoring problems in China, tens of millions of people have been pulled out of poverty in the last two decades. This is one of the most remarkable aspects of the performance of the international economy. Outsourcing was one of the main drivers.
- Outsourcing has probably not lost many jobs in the industrial countries, but it has contributed to a change in the pattern of demand for labor, away

from unskilled and toward skilled workers. This has made unskilled workers worse off, although this seems an almost unavoidable consequence of the integration of poor countries into the international economic system. Technological change drove the drop in demand for unskilled labor more than outsourcing.

On balance, then, outsourcing is good economically. It poses new management challenges—monitoring suppliers' operations for compliance with labor codes. After initially being slack at this—with the notable exception of Levi Strauss—Western companies are waking up to the need for action in this area and are acting jointly to solve the problem. But they have not done so yet. The need for collective action here is interesting. The same was true in the case of the issues to which the Equator Principles are directed—managing the social and environmental impacts of large infrastructure projects in developing countries. The need for collective action on issues of corporate responsibility seems to be an emerging theme. To emphasize this point, the toy industry, which like the apparel and footwear industries outsources much of its production to China, is also evolving a cooperative system of rating factories in China, with the ultimate aim of removing all Western toy business from factories rated as noncompliant.

The motives for trying to ensure compliance with labor codes are much the same as those for any other aspect of CSR. Most Western managers will themselves feel a need to ensure that factories run for them, if not by them, are run in a humane way. In addition, failure can lead to rejection by the consumer, loss of brand value, and even regulatory intervention. Outsourcing illustrates the second of the shortcomings of the invisible hand discussed in Chapter 1: recall that the first was the externalization of costs, and the second the failure of the market to produce a distribution of income that is compellingly fair. Fairness is clearly of the essence in the debates over outsourcing, with different conceptions of what is a fair wage in a poor country coming into play.

9

Getting Rich by Selling to the Poor

Capital Markets and Prosperity

Those of us lucky enough to live in rich countries probably do not often consider the role of capital markets in our lives. Indeed, we may even be unaware that they play any role at all. Yet they do and it is a central one. Most of us have mortgages—large loans secured against our houses and paid back from future income over periods as long as thirty years. Allowing us to borrow against future income is a major role of capital markets. When we take out a mortgage is not the only time we do this: most consumer credit, whether on credit cards or on direct lending, is of this type too. Car leases are yet another example. Educational loans, too, are paid back out of future income. In all of these cases, we make a partial payment for a good now, the seller receives full payment, and the difference is supplied by a lender. In fact, as many of these loans are packaged and securitized, the balance is supplied by many lenders, by all the purchasers of mortgage-backed securities, or of securities based on credit card debt.

Think how hard life would be without access to these loans—you would have to save for years before purchasing any expensive item. Only the children of rich parents would be able to afford houses early in their lives. But when we borrow is not the only time we use capital markets—we use them when we save too. If we save for retirement, we invest our savings in financial assets in the hope of augmenting them with interest and capital gains: at the very least, we put our savings in banks confident that when we need them in later life they will be there.

Another role for capital markets in everyday life is the provision of insurance: car insurance, homeowner's insurance, life insurance, and medical insurance. If you are reading this book, you almost surely have all of these.

They are important safeguards against life's vicissitudes. They protect you against events that will probably not happen but which could inflict massive harm on you and your family if they did. Most of us quite rightly feel naked financially without these basic insurances.

In the corporate world, too, capital markets are crucial. Starting a new business, or expanding an existing one, requires access to capital. The opening up of corporate capital markets via the formation of joint stock companies was a critical moment in economic history, as it allowed much more widespread access to capital for the formation and expansion of companies. Much of the economic growth of the United States in the last two decades has come from the growth of new companies—Microsoft, Apple, Intel, Oracle, Dell, and so on—that owe their existence to access to capital via venture capital funds, an important part of contemporary capital markets.

Capital markets, then, are important to supporting a comfortable lifestyle and important to the process of economic growth. Life without them would be limited and risky—limited because we could only buy when we had the cash to do so, and risky because we would have to bear risks ourselves rather than insuring them and in so doing passing them on to others. Yet this is exactly how people operate in most developing countries. Big firms and rich individuals there may have access to all the services of capital markets that we take for granted, but the great majority of the population do not. For example, most families whose property was destroyed in the earthquake in Pakistan in October 2005 were not insured: they had to meet all the costs of this disaster from their own meager incomes and savings. If their breadwinners were killed, there was no life insurance to compensate. The same holds for those who suffered in the Tsunami of 2004: the great majority will have no financial compensation for their losses.

Not only is there little or no access to insurance, but also the real and ever-present risks of disaster must be carried by the families themselves: there is little by way of organized loans available. In many poor communities, there are moneylenders, but the amounts they make available are small and the interest rates will often run to 10 percent or 20 percent per day—in annual rates this is in the thousands! Borrowing under these conditions is financially crippling and is a move of last resort only. Another service that is available to the poor, indeed essential to some of them, and for which they are charged grossly unreasonable rates, is the transfer of money internationally or over long distances domestically. With many poor families separated by the migration of a father or mother to find work, they face a compelling need to transfer money. Yet the rates charged are outrageous—members of the Western professional classes would never stomach them. An interesting development in this area occurred in September 2005, when Bank of America announced that all of its account holders would be able to send money free to Mexico. This move could be a boon to Mexican immigrants in the United States and a good business move for Bank of America by recruiting new clients from the immigrant population.[1]

The absence of the institutions for insuring and borrowing also makes it hard to save. A family in a remote village has no bank that it can turn to for safekeeping of its savings: these savings are often held as gold or other precious goods and kept in the house, where they are vulnerable to theft and to loss in the event of fire or earthquake or tsunami. And in some particularly cruel cases, local savings banks have been established as a home for the savings of rural communities, only to go bankrupt as a result of mismanagement or corruption, with the loss of all the savings trusted to them. (In most rich countries bank deposits are insured by the government, but in poor countries they are not.) So it is difficult and risky to make provision for old age or for emergencies in poor countries. Indeed, there is interesting evidence of the size of the problem that poor people face in saving in a recent report from India, which showed that women wanting to accumulate savings would give these into safekeeping on terms that amounted to a negative interest rate of almost -30 percent.[2] They cannot safely hold savings themselves and are willing to give up almost one-third of the amount they put aside each year if someone else will keep it safely for them, an extraordinary thought to anyone in an industrial country.

Giving the poor access to capital markets is an important step in helping them out of poverty, and it is one now being taken by some for-profit enterprises around the world. The most advanced of the developments providing access to capital markets for poor communities is the growth of microfinance or microcredit. This goes back to the 1970s, and began in Latin America. But the best-known microcredit operation is the Grameen Bank of Bangladesh, so I will use that as a model. The story behind the formation of the Grameen Bank has been told many times but still repays telling, and

I will quote from an article written about this by Columbia Business School MBA students:[3]

The story behind the first concerted effort to make financing accessible to the world's poorest is the stuff of folklore. Befitting the goal of poverty alleviation, the setting for this early experiment was a time of great tragedy in Bangladesh, one of the poorest countries in the world. A small country in the Indian subcontinent with a population of 130 million, a gross national product (GNP) per capita of about $300, and a literacy rate of only 38 percent for those over 15 years of age,[4] Bangladesh experienced drought and famine in 1974 that killed 1.5 million people. Having recently completed studies as a Fulbright scholar in the United States, Professor Mohammad Yunus was lecturing on economic theory at Chittagong University and growing increasingly frustrated at his inability to ease his neighbors' suffering. Yunus attributes the origin of his vision to a chance encounter in Jobra with Sufia Begum, a 21-year-old woman who, desperate to support herself, had borrowed about 25 cents from moneylenders charging exorbitant interest rates approaching 10 percent per day. Ms. Begum used the money to make bamboo stools that, as a condition of the loan, she sold back to the moneylenders at a price well below market value for a profit of about of 2 cents. Ms. Begum's desperate position could best be described as bonded labor. Yunus found 42 people in Jobra in the same poverty trap, and in 1976 he experimented by lending them small amounts of money at reasonable rates. Yunus lent a total of $27—about 62 cents per borrower. To his pleasant surprise, all the borrowers repaid the loans, in the process convincing him that this success could be replicated across Bangladesh....

Yunus carried his success story to traditional banks and proposed that they could also make uncollateralized loans to society's poorest. In response, the banks asserted that borrowers would never sufficiently organize themselves to repay, that proceeds from such loans were too small to cover administrative costs, and that female borrowers would simply hand over the funds to their husbands. Early critics argued that even if lenders avoided these pitfalls, the last thing the poor needed was the added burden of indebtedness.

Yunus answered these challenges by founding an institution of his own, Grameen Bank, the name of which derives from *gram,* the Bengali word for "village." He did so in the belief that capital is a friend of the poor and that its accumulation by the poor represents their best means of escaping the abject poverty that the welfare state and wasteful, corrupt, and incompetent international aid organizations have failed to combat.

Of course Yunus' venture thrived and gained global acclaim, leading to his receipt of the Nobel Peace Prize in 2006. Grameen Bank lends to very poor people, people who earn about a dollar a day. Obviously, these borrowers have no assets and, therefore, no prospect of providing collateral. Banking convention would regard lending to very poor people with no assets as highly risky, indeed foolish. Another disadvantage from a conventional banking perspective is that the loans are very small, perhaps $10, so that to make profits the bank needs to make many loans. The costs of administering many small loans to very poor people appear on the face of things to be large, again arguing against this as a sound banking strategy. As an example of this point, the ICICI Bank of India has suggested that providing $1.3 million in microloans requires forty times more staff than a single corporate loan of the same size.[5] Yet Grameen and its fellow microcredit operations have thrived, largely because they have broken out of many aspects of the conventional banking mold.

Grameen overcomes the risks posed by poverty and lack of collateral by making loans to groups of people and making each of them responsible for all of the loans made to the group. They always lend to women—they believe that women are more likely to make good use of the money than men—and lend to groups of four to ten from the same village at a time. No member of the group is eligible for a new loan until everyone in the group has paid off her loan. So if four people borrow and one defaults, the other three cannot borrow again until the defaulted loan is repaid: if they need to borrow they either pay the outstanding balance themselves or put great pressure on the defaulter. There are strong social pressures on group members not to default: by defaulting you impose great costs on your neighbors, people with whom you will have to live for the rest of your life. In addition, Grameen makes it clear that if you default on a loan, your prospects of credit in the future are poor. As this is the only credit available at reasonable rates, the threat here is real. Consequently, borrowers go to great length not to default and the default rate is very low, less than 3 percent, a figure well below the default rate on U.S. credit cards and roughly similar to default rates on personal loans in the United States, where of course borrowers are many times richer. Another way of minimizing risk is that Grameen always starts with small loans to new customers, and only makes larger loans once small loans have been paid off. So by the time a loan gets to several tens of dollars, there is a track record of successful use of a loan.

It is interesting to spend a little time thinking about what is happening in these "group loans," in which each member of the group is to some degree held responsible for the repayments of other group members. In making personal loans, typically to small-scale entrepreneurs, a bank faces two risks. One is the risk that the borrower is profligate or incompetent, and will not use the loan in a productive way, so that there is nothing to repay the loan from. Another is that the borrower is competent and effective, so that the loan is used successfully, but is dishonest, and claims not to have the resources to repay the loan even when he does. Banks in industrial countries invest effort in trying to identify borrowers who are bad risks for either of these reasons, generally from credit records and other sources of information about the borrower. This option is not available in a rural third-world village: there are no credit bureaus and most borrowers have no credit records anyway. The intriguing feature of group loans is that through them, these risks are passed from the bank to the borrowers. If a group member chooses to default on a loan when she could repay, the others, members of the same small community, will usually be able to tell this and exert real pressure on her to change. And each will have a personal interest in monitoring the activities of the others and offering advice and guidance to reduce the chances of default due to poor execution. Indeed, competent and honest people will have an incentive to seek each other out to form borrowing groups, so that they will not have to carry the burden of underperforming colleagues. Another source of power that the banks have over borrowers stems in part from their policy of lending only small amounts for relatively short times, so that many borrowers will plan to borrow again and again. If, as is often the case, there is no alternative source of capital, the borrower is dependent on the bank and knows that her access to capital can be cut off if the group does not perform. Interestingly, this source of the bank's power is undermined if there is a competing institution, as a borrower has an alternative and is less dependent on retaining the goodwill of the current lender. There is empirical evidence that this effect matters: competition between microlenders leads to higher default rates.[6]

Besides the risk of default, the administration of many small loans appears problematic to most banks. Again, Grameen and its fellows have a novel two-pronged approach. One part of this is to change very high interest rates by our standards: annual rate of 20 percent and 30 percent are common on microloans, high by our standards but far less than the alternatives available, and in keeping with the rates on credit card debt in industrial countries. The second part of the solution to the problem of high administrative costs is to have the customers do some of the work. Each loan group meets weekly to review the progress of the projects funded by the loans and to review progress in paying back the loans, and field workers from the bank attend all of these meetings. The field workers record the weekly repayments of the loans, and by attending the group meetings are well placed to anticipate difficulties that borrowers might have in making payments and can offer advice on how to overcome these. Because the default rate is so low, the process of administration of the loans is relatively simple.

A criticism leveled at Grameen Bank, and an indicator of its success, is that its original clients have become middle class so that the bank no longer serves the poor. Certainly, the bank has had remarkable success in promoting economic and social mobility among its borrowers, many of whom no longer count as the real poor. An important reason for this is related to Grameen's social ethos, which goes beyond its role as a bank: Grameen encourages all of its clients to ensure that their children attend school full time and rates them by whether they meet this goal. So an unusually large number of Grameen clients, themselves from poor circumstances, have children who have graduated from high school and in some cases college. Yunus' response to the criticism that Grameen is now serving those who are comfortably off was typically unorthodox: at the start of 2004, he required that each branch of the bank make every effort to acquire at least one client who is a beggar, beggars being clearly the poorest of the poor. As of March 2004, Grameen Bank had four thousand beggar clients—all on interest-free loans. It is hoping to turn some of them into successful entrepreneurs.

The Grameen model has now been replicated worldwide many times. Indeed, it is probably not fair to call it the Grameen model, as this type of microlending appears to have been practiced first in Latin America by

ACCION, which like Grameen made small loans to groups of people that were collectively guaranteed. Over seventeen thousand such organizations are in operation today, so in about thirty years the concept has really taken off. This has had an impact: a World Bank report on the impact of micro-credit lending concludes that:

> The results are resounding: micro-finance matters a lot for the very poor borrowers and also for the local economy. In particular, micro-finance programs matter a lot to the poor in raising per capita consumption, mainly on non-food, as well as household non-land assets. This increases the probability that the program participants may be able to lift themselves out of poverty. The welfare impact of micro-finance is also positive for all households, including non-participants, indicating that micro-finance programs are helping the poor beyond income redistribution with contribution to local income growth. Programs have spillover effects in local economies, thereby increasing local village welfare. In particular, we find that micro-finance helps reduce extreme poverty more than moderate poverty at the village level. Yet the aggregate poverty reduction effects are not quite substantial (enough) to have a large dent on national level aggregate poverty. This concern brings to the fore the effectiveness of micro-finance as an instrument to solve the problem of poverty in Bangladesh.[7]

This assessment seems accurate: as we noted at the start, access to capital markets is critical for many forms of economic activity and underpins much of our own prosperity. Grameen and similar institutions play an invaluable role in giving the poor access to loans, allowing them to start businesses and send children through school. Many of their loans are used to expand farming operations—to buy cattle or chickens, to buy seeds and fertilizers. Modest expenditures on these can make a profound difference to a poor family's life. Other loans allow clients to start small businesses making handcrafts, as in the case of Sufia Begum, one of Mohammed Yunus's original clients. Yet others, as we shall see in Chapter 10, allow women to buy cell phones and use these to provide communal telephone services to their villages.

Yet the role of Grameen and other microcredit institutions is not limited to providing loans. As we noted earlier, capital markets provide many important services—credit, savings, and insurance being perhaps the most important. Microcredit has expanded in these directions. Grameen provides life insurance—indeed, it requires that clients who have borrowed large (by their standards) amounts must pay for life insurance. And as a bank, it can take deposits and pay interest on them, encouraging savings by offering a secure and profitable home for them. In fact, it offers pensions: clients can contribute to pension plans, with the proceeds being used to buy an annuity on the life of the contributor. (Becoming a bank able to take deposits requires in most countries obtaining a banking license from the banking regulators, something that has not always been easy for microcredit firms.) Other microcredit operations have become even more sophisticated financially, offering farmers crop and drought insurance.

Although the scale of microcredit operations has expanded vastly since the early experiments of the 1970s, there are still hundreds of millions, if not a billion or more, who do not have access to what it offers. But if they did, this clearly would revolutionize the lives of the world's poor, perhaps more than almost any other reasonably foreseeable development. If the scale of microcredit is to expand to the point where most of the needy have access, there needs to be more capital available to these institutions. And for this to happen, large mainstream banks need to be convinced that this is an area in which they can make profits and can therefore reasonably deploy their capital. So we have to look at the profitability of microcredit.

Profits were not the main concern of most of the pioneers in this movement: they were happy to break even, and capital was in general available to them from international aid agencies and from nongovernmental organizations devoted to poverty alleviation. Their bottom lines were therefore not under close scrutiny, although in fact many of them could have borne scrutiny: in general, they at least broke even, and in many cases did more, though they perhaps did not match the return on capital that a commercial bank would require. So what are the prospects that this line of business can be profitable enough to attract large commercial banks with their access to deep capital markets? What are the prospects that this is a field in which banks can do well by doing good?

Fortunately, these prospects seem good. Commercial banks are increasingly interested in microcredit, often in partnership with existing players in the business. The reason, or at least a reason, is that there is money to be made there. And it opens up a completely new market, with access to hundreds of millions of "unbanked." A good example of a commercial bank that has profited from microcredit is Bank Rakyat Indonesia (BRI), a bank that was founded by Dutch colonists in 1895. For most of its life, BRI was state owned and targeted Indonesia's elite as its customers but made little money from them. In 1983, it changed strategy radically, giving loans to the poor rather than to the rich and politically connected and has never looked back financially.[8] In fact, it was able to change status and become a public company in 2003.[9]

There are no systematic studies of the profitability of microcredit companies: the nearest we have to this is data from an experiment conducted in Latin America from 1995 to 2005. A group of socially oriented investors raised $23 million to create a Latin American microcredit fund called ProFund. The leading institutions in forming the fund were ACCION International of Canada, Fundes from Switzerland, and the Dutch group Triodos. This group invested their fund for ten years and then liquidated their investments in 2005. The results from this are shown in Table 9.1.[10]

Looking across the line "return on average assets," we see that this ranged from 1.1 percent to 38.9 percent and on average worked out at 6 percent. Although not exciting as a return to a risky investment, this, as *The Economist* noted in its review,[11] is in fact good for investments in this part of the world over the decade from 1995 to 2005. The countries in which the fund invested experienced political turmoil over this period, and their currencies depreciated strongly against the dollar, in which the investments were denominated. So 6 percent is in fact a good return relative to many other hard-nosed commercial investments in the same time and place. The table shows the countries in which ProFund invested and the names of the institutions in those countries. All are providers of microloans, and ProFund took a stake of between 15 percent and 30 percent in each of them with the aim of allowing them to extend the scale of their microlending. The chairman in his report to shareholders[12] comments:

> The microfinance sector demonstrated its ability to do well in the complicated and disruptive socio-political conditions found in many of our investee countries, including Bolivia, Haiti and Venezuela. The ability to outperform the traditional commercial banks in these markets was in large measure attributable to the resilience and independent nature of the informal economy and the ability of the MFI community to respond to the market's needs.

TABLE 9.1 Returns to Components of the ProFund Microfinance Portfolio

	Visión—Paraguay	BancoSol—Bolivia	Mibanco—Peru	Solidario—Ecuador	Finamérica—Colombia	BanGente—Venezuela	Compartamos—Mexico	SOGESOL—Haiti
Portfolio								
Gross loan portfolio (000s US$)	29,523	97,123	115,784	146,537	21,236	6,602	72,510	5,808
Microclients	55,000	64,359	114,271	49,718	22,724	8,496	239,900	7,293
Number of loan officers	128	184	424	153	83	52	760	45
Average microloan (US$)	552	1,509	1,013	1,348	935	777	302	796
Arrears (>30 days) (%)	11.1	5.5	4.5	2.2	5.0	1.8	0.8	11.1
Balance sheet								
Assets (000s US$)	40,452	113,820	114,791	205,843	24,653	12,259	91,660	5,162
Equity (000s US$)	4,065	15,981	31,620	18,146	4,823	2,777	36,515	824
Net income (000s US$)	730	3,250	7,500	2,312	248	1,184	17,356	755
Performance								
Return on average equity (%)*	18.9	19.8	24.7	13.1	5.4	46.7	50.3	98.1
Return on average assets (%)*	1.9	2.8	5.5	1.2	1.1	11.3	19.7	38.9
Operating expenses/average portfolio (%)*	17.2	12.7	21.6	18.5	18.3	47.5	36.3	42.2
Open equity exposure ratio (%)	51.3	-3.1	-4.5	-1.9	9.5	-8.2	-6.5	59.7
Liabilities/equity	8.9	6.1	2.1	10.3	4.1	3.4	1.5	0.8
Growth (% US$) June 2003 to June 2004								
Gross portfolio	36.0	15.3	8.0	34.0	39.0	60.0	48.0	120.0
Equity	28	4	16	36	9	38	49	177
Net income	21.0	123.0	28.0	-18.0	306.0	-114.0	44.0	1556.0

*Annualized.

ProFund investees' success in profitably expanding and serving the regional microenterprise market, especially in difficult socio-economic conditions, led commercial lenders and financial institutions to continue to enter into the microfinance market through what is being called "downscaling". Commercial banks were already a major force delivering microfinance services in the Andean countries and their presence impacts the industry in many ways: requiring greater efficiency from traditional players, increasing the number of product and service options, lowering interest rates, etc.

There is more interesting information in Table 9.1: you can see the average size of the loans made, which ranges from $500 to $1,300, and the number where payments are overdue, which ranges from 0.8 percent to 11 percent. All but two of the companies showed rapid growth of net income, ranging from annual rates of about 20 percent to about 1,500 percent. Table 9.2 gives more information: for a sample of microfinance operations from the same part of the world, it shows how the financial performance varies with the size of the loan made. On small loans, of about $300, the banks lose money, with net income as a percent of assets being −2.1 percent, but on average and large loans in the range $1,000 to $2,000 they make better returns, of about

TABLE 9.2 Returns to Investment in ProFund by Loan Size

	Minimum	Average	Maximum
Loan portfolio			
Gross loan portfolio	$2,714	$32,078	$93,148
Number of borrowers	2,505	33,915	217,454
Average loan balance (per borrowers)—			
actual amounts	$290	$982	$2,126
Portfolio at risk/gross loan portfolio	0.7%	5.2%	14.3%
Productivity indicators			
Total operating expense/average gross portfolio	10.7%	19.7%	65.7%
Number of borrowers per credit officer	101	256	443
Number of borrowers per staff	48	102	213
Financial ratios			
Net income/average equity (ROE)	−11.5%	22.4%	52.1%
Net Income/average assets (ROA)	−2.1%	4.8%	18.0%

Except if noted otherwise figures are in thousands.

5 percent and 18 percent, respectively. This reflects the fact that the costs of administering a loan do not vary greatly with its size, so that the costs eat into profitability for small loans—they can more than outweigh the interest from the loan. Banks hope that small customers will grow over time and graduate into profitability, and indeed the evidence is that many do just this.

There are reasons other than profitability for wanting to enter this market. One, of course, is the desire to do good, to use a bank's expertise and experience to help people who really need and appreciate the help. That certainly has attracted some international banks into the microcredit business. In addition, there is a more traditional financial argument based on diversification. There are two aspects of diversification that can be associated with entry into the microcredit business. One is that the fortunes of very small businesses are thought to have little correlation with traditional business cycles and to be more resilient than those of large firms during economic downturns. The second is that a portfolio of loans to small enterprises spreads the risk over thousands of businesses in different geographical areas and lines of business throughout the economy.

A current trend is that large banks, some domestic and some international, are entering the microcredit market—this is called *downsizing*. Some are moving to sell financial products directly to poor consumers and small enterprises, but for the most part they are partnering with existing firms in the microcredit business. They make capital available to these so that they can extend their loan portfolios, and they help in designing financial products and in developing technology for delivering these products. Deutsche Bank has followed this model, raising capital on German bond markets for ProCredit.[13] Citigroup has entered into partnerships with many microfinance enterprises, and in addition to providing access to capital it provides life insurance policies. Insurance is not a business in which a really small financial institution can easily make money: successful insurance operates via the law of large numbers and pools many independent risks to arrive at a statistically valid premium. So the resources of a large bank are really needed for some products to be offered profitably. Another U.S.-based company, American Insurance Group (AIG), has also entered the market for small-scale insurance, in partnership with the Foundation for International Community Assistance (FINCA) in Uganda. FINCA-Uganda offers life and health insurance, although the coverage of the health insurance is limited to a small range of medical services and procedures. The Self-Employed Women's Association (SEWA) in Ahmedabad, India, has ventured to offer insurance against property damage by earthquakes and other catastrophes. After entering this business in 2000, it faced claims to the huge (by its standards) amount of $48,000 the year after as a result of the Gujarat earthquake of 2001.[14] This illustrates the importance of adequate capitalization of insurance operations.

Crop insurance is an insurance product that would be of immense value to poor farmers in third-world countries. With only rain-fed irrigation, they are at the mercy of erratic seasonal rains such as monsoons, many of which are becoming less predictable as one of the impacts of global climate change. In southern Africa, for example, rainfall patterns are strongly affected by El Niño events, which are becoming more frequent and extended. Crop insurance is available to many farmers in developed countries, and in the United States it is available through the U.S. Department of Agriculture. The basic idea of this contract is to provide compensation for farmers if their crops are unusually low. A real problem for those who offer the insurance is "moral hazard." The point here is that if a crop fails, it can be hard for the insurer to tell whether this is because the farmer was lazy and inefficient, or because the weather was unusually inclement or there was an unexpected pest infestation. The insurance is intended to cover eventualities such as the latter two, but not of course poor performance by the farmer. Indeed, the mere existence of insurance may make the farmer less careful in the management of his or her crops, increasing the risk of failure and the cost to the insurer. This makes it almost impossible to offer conventional crop insurance in third-world countries, as the potential for monitoring farmers to screen for moral hazard is very limited. An alternative being developed relies on some recent "high-tech" financial instruments, weather derivatives. These are securities that pay an amount that depends on the weather at a specified time and place. For example, in the United States they would payout if the temperature in a particular region of Texas exceeds 95°F for more than ten days in August 2006. Or they would pay if rainfall in a specified region falls below a certain total over one or two months. Such weather derivatives have been used in the United States for hedging weather-related risks for several years now by both farmers and utilities: the former to insure against the adverse effects of extreme weather on crops and the latter to insure against the unexpectedly high demand for power during very hot spells. An interesting feature of these contracts is that they can provide farmers with some insurance against crop failure, at least to the extent that it is correlated with unusual weather patterns. The weather being something that the farmer cannot manipulate, they are not vulnerable to moral hazard. Currently, the World Bank is working with reinsurance companies such as Swiss Re to implement this type of weather insurance on a pilot basis in some poor countries.

The entry of large commercial banks into microlending may change this business. As they have a lower cost of funds and more efficient infrastructure than the current microfinance firms, they may drive some of these out of the market. However, there will probably remain very poor clients with borrowing capacity so limited that their loans will be so small as to be unprofitable for the large banks and whose needs can only be addressed by enterprises like Grameen Bank, operating with an explicit social goal. Such enterprises will continue to raise capital from aid agencies and nongovernmental organizations, as they do today. As the volume of microcredit business grows, there will be a need for the kind of infrastructure that supports the credit business in industrial countries—credit rating and credit reporting.

When many banks are competing to lend money to small farmers or very small firms, each bank will need to know whether a potential client already has a loan from a competitor, how big that loan is, and whether anything has been offered as security. Lending to someone who already has assumed several loans is clearly much less attractive than lending to someone of the same financial stature with no debt. In poorly documented village communities this will be challenging. The pioneers like Grameen avoided this problem because their village agents knew the local village well enough to be aware of any outstanding loans, by the group lending practice (you would not want to be in a group with heavily indebted neighbors), and of course by the fact that for most of Grameen's life it had no competition— there was no one else providing loans.

What message can we take away from this discussion of microcredit? Certainly that there has been real progress in making access to capital markets a reality for millions of the poor in developing countries and for many small firms that were previously well below the radar screens of commercial banks. Clients of microcredit number in the tens of millions, which seems impressive until you compare it with the number who need these services, which is probably in the billions. But a start has been made, and, more importantly, the pioneers in this field have established a model that works and can be scaled up to address the problem on a global level. Banks have hitherto stayed away from the poor, or—even worse—exploited them. There is now a model of how they can relate to them as profitable customers, offering great growth opportunities. An important point is that this model is different from the standard banking model in high-income countries. That is the model of branch banking, advertising for customers, and packaging credit cards, consumer loans, and mortgages together as far as is possible. In microcredit, branches play a minor role, as does advertising. Potential customers do not read newspapers or watch TV: in many cases they will have no access to either and may be unable to read even if they get a newspaper. Field agents meet potential customers, gauge their interest and suitability, and develop relationships with them. This process is labor intensive, but labor is cheap in poor countries, and is light on advertising and sales. A lot depends on the agent being a good judge of character and of a potential customer's economic situation. Strangely enough, this is the way banking was in the rich countries forty or fifty years ago, when bank managers had real authority and developed relationships with customers.

Consumer Goods and the Poor

Manufacturers of basic household goods—soap, washing powder, shampoo, toilet paper, and so on—face a saturated market in the rich countries. Most families already have as much as they need of these and are unlikely to buy more. Marketing in industrial countries is therefore more or less a zero-sum game: one firm can expand its sales only at the expense of competitors. But there is one part of the world where this is certainly not true—developing countries. Most families there would gladly consume more of all of these staples. So there is a market here with great potential for growth, a market that has been called "the bottom of the pyramid."[15]

Obviously there is a catch here: there are reasons why poor people consume little of these staple consumer goods. One, of course, is that they are poor and can afford little. Another is that there are no shops or supermarkets where they live, so they have no access. And as they generally do not read and may have only limited access to radio and television, marketing campaigns may pass them by.

Hindustan Lever, the Indian subsidiary of the Unilever, has developed ways of circumventing these obstacles. They first tackled this problem with the sale of salt, which is used by almost every family for cooking. After that they, and other Indian consumer goods companies, branched out to soaps, detergents, shampoos, and a wide range of other consumer goods. And Unilever branched out to other countries, importing the new sales methods to other low-income countries, beginning with Ghana in West Africa.

The salt story is an interesting one and illustrates well most of the issues that arise in selling profitably to poor communities. A key background point is that many of the poor in India suffer from iodine deficiency, which causes a condition called goiter, an enlargement of the thyroid gland at the lower front of the neck. In bad cases, this can lead to developmental defects and seriously affect health.[16] Iodine is normally present in a balanced diet, but the minerals that provide it may be missing in a poor family's diet. A widespread way of providing iodine is by adding it to dietary staples such as salt or flour, and Hindustan Lever Limited (HLL) decided to enter the market for salt sales to the poor and to add iodine to their salt. Salt was widely available, both from some competitors of HLL's and also from salt pans that produced salt by evaporating sea water. Under these conditions, HLL would need something to differentiate their product from competitors and to justify a premium price, and they decided that this would be the purity of their salt and the addition of iodine. They would play on mothers' interests in the health of their families and emphasize the health benefits of HLL's brand of salt, which they called Kissan Annapurna.

Although this seemed a good strategy in principle, execution was not easy. They still had to overcome the obstacles of poverty in their target market, find a way of getting their message to a dispersed rural population, and then actually get the salt to them. Here, they were ingenious. To overcome the limited purchasing power of their target clientele, they packed salt in very small amounts that could be sold for only a few cents each. Larger amounts were available too, for those whose cash flow allowed them to hold a stock of salt, but in breaking into the market for the very poor, providing very inexpensive access was critical. They adopted a completely innovative marketing strategy, and instead of the usual mix of broadcast and print media, HLL sent performers to attend village fairs and markets to stage entertainments in which they lauded the value of Kissan Annapurna salt. As villagers had little access to live entertainment, these events attracted intense attention and began to get the message across. Finally, they had to address the issue of a distribution network for a population not served by regular retail outlets. Here, they used a method that had already been used in the United States to a very different demographic group.[17] They encouraged villagers to become sellers of Kissan Annapurna, holding small stocks purchased at a discount from HLL and selling these to neighbors.

Even when this well-constructed plan was in place, HLL encountered another unanticipated obstacle: villagers did not believe the claims made about the health effects of iodized salt. They thought HLL was tying to mislead them into paying for a more expensive product than they really needed, at no extra benefit to them. HLL eventually overcame this response by asking the government to endorse their claims that iodized salt could prevent goiter. When this endorsement was forthcoming (in response to a payment to the government that was used to fund medical research), everything else fell into place. HLL's marketing and distribution system finally seemed about to work as intended.

At this late stage, when HLL was ready to reap the rewards of their campaign, they encountered a final obstacle. Indians usually add salt to food while cooking it, rather than when it is served. If iodine mixed with salt is cooked with the spices often used in India, it is vaporized and leaves the food, negating the potential benefits from iodized salt. This lead to several years of research into a way of adding iodine to salt that ensured that the iodine was stable and remained in the food even after cooking with strong spices. HLL's research labs eventually resolved this problem, HLL patented the process worldwide, and they were finally able to enjoy the outcome that they had long anticipated—dominance of the very large salt market in India. It is a profitable business, and clearly one that benefits the company's customers. The parent company, Unilever, has built on this success by selling salt with stable iodine in many other poor hot countries where food is cooked under the same conditions.

HLL has now built on this success with iodized salt and is selling a range of other household staples to poor rural communities using similar techniques. To date they have been successful with soap, shampoo, and detergents. In the case of soap, there was a tie-in with health benefits, as in the case of iodine in salt, and once again HLL encountered a credibility problem and needed ingenuity to overcome it.

The health benefits of more extensive use of soap are clear: in poor rural areas, people often handle animals, defecate, and handle dirty machinery and then eat without washing their hands. A consequence is a very high rate of diarrhea, which in the case of small children is often fatal. The World Bank has identified diarrhea as one of the main killers of children and one that is in principle easily avoided. A World Bank study in India showed that about 10 percent of the population had been sick with diarrhea within the last two weeks before the survey.[18] Washing hands with soap can break this cycle and has the potential to reduce illness and death in poor communities. So promoting the use of soap is a very worthwhile humanitarian aim, and HLL went about this using many of the approaches developed for iodized salt. Traveling entertainers promoted the use of soap and its health benefits and promoted HLL's brand. Villagers were encouraged to buy discounted soap for resale to their neighbors, and soap was packaged in amounts small enough to sell for a few cents each. Yet at first the impact on sales was small. Investigation revealed that villagers did not believe that their hands were dirty unless they could actually see dirt on them. They therefore did not believe that they needed to wash after handling animals or after defecating, and HLL's message promoting the use of soap as a health measure was received with skepticism.

To overcome this skepticism, HLL teamed up with the local arm of Ogilvy and Mather, a major international advertising company, to devise a strategy. The key part of this strategy was to develop a dark powder that became invisible when wet but would nevertheless glow under ultraviolet light, even when wet. In presentations to schools and villages, two participants from the audience were asked to coat their hands with this powder and then wash them, one in water without soap and the other with soap and water. Their hands were then viewed in ultraviolet light, and the audience could see that the powder was still present on the hands washed in water only but not on those washed with soap. This persuaded the audiences that the fact that they could see no dirt on their hands did not mean that there was none, and also that dirt could be invisible, the key steps in their argument for the use of soap on a regular basis. Another element of the campaign was to introduce villagers to the idea that diseases are caused by bacteria, organisms that are too small for them to see and that washing with soap will remove these. This campaign was taken to thousands of schools and to specially organized Village Health Days, in all cases emphasizing the health benefits of frequent use of Lifebuoy, HLL's low-priced soap product. Within a year of start up, HLL expected to reach over 100,000,000 people with this message, at a cost per person in the region of a few cents.

HLL has seen its soap sales rise rapidly in the period since this campaign was started, and their success with salt and soap, and the identification of their brand with health and consumer welfare has placed them well to compete in other markets for household staples. They are using similar sales strategies with detergents and shampoos, with great success. In both cases they have followed the strategies that proved successful before, selling small units for a few cents each, recruiting village women to stock and sell the products (in the process providing an additional source of income for the more entrepreneurial women), and staging entertainment events at village fairs and markets to promote their products. With both detergents and shampoos, HLL has taken trouble to study exactly how potential buyers will use the product and modify it to suit these conditions. For example, most women wash clothes in cold water in a stream, so that the suds produced float away quickly. This is a very different environment from a washing machine, for which most of Unilever's detergents are designed, and HLL's research teams modified standard detergents to make them perform better under village conditions. Similarly for shampoos: these were often used in cold stream water rather than in a shower and needed modification for best performance. Recognizing that buying both soap and shampoo might stretch some budgets too far, HLL also developed a soap-cum-shampoo that worked well in village use.

HLL is not alone in the way it has developed a strategy for selling profitably to very poor customers, but it is perhaps the largest and most visible company to do this. Its experience shows that large multinational corporations can both do well and do good by targeting the poorest of the poor as clients, but that they need to develop strategies and products tailored to this market. Both Unilever and other companies are now doing this in India and in other poor countries. Another interesting example of the adaptation of a standard middle-market product for the very poor is provided by the sale of jeans to the poor in India by Arvind Mills, a company that is one of the world's largest denim manufacturers. Realizing that jeans priced at $40 a pair would never sell in poor communities, they developed Ruf & Tuf® jeans, which came in ready-to-make kits containing the denim, zipper, rivets and patches needed to make a pair of jeans. These were distributed through small tailors, including rural village tailors. The purchaser could make the jeans herself or pay the tailor to complete them. In the hope that the latter would be the chosen course, tailors could be relied on to promote sales of the jeans. Economically, this is an interesting example of a manufacturer replacing factory labor by the customer's own labor or by that of the village tailor, who would certainly charge less than the costs of assembly in a factory. It is not only ingenious but also good, because it helps several groups who need help—the rural consumer acquires clothes she could not otherwise afford and the rural tailor finds extra employment.[19]

10

Cell Phones and Development

Phones and Economic Growth

We are so used to using the telephone that it requires a feat of imagination to think of life without phones and the services based on them, services that include faxes, e-mail, and Internet access. Without phones you would depend for communication on the vagaries of the postal system, or on personally visiting the people to whom you want to talk. The time and effort required to communicate would be many times greater than we are used to and would surely consume much of the day. Productivity would be less, because of the time spent in communicating and the impossibility of tight coordination. Much of modern supply chain management depends on effective and timely communication. How would we manage global outsourcing without telecommunications? Timely and accurate communication greatly improves the management of economic activity. And with little in the way of communications, access to information would be less, ruling out the information-based society toward which we are evolving. We would no longer use Google to find information, but would have to go to a library, with all the frustrations of books missing or checked out and the time spent traveling to and fro.

Economic studies have confirmed this picture of the importance of telecommunications, indicating that in the rich countries of the Organization for Economic Cooperation and Development (OECD) between 1970 and 1990, one-third of the total growth of output was due to improvements in phone services and their more widespread use. This mention of widespread use introduces an important point about the economics of telephone systems—it is that the more people have phones, the more useful they are. If you have a phone and few others do, there is not much you can do with it: if, however, everyone else has one, then you can use your phone to communicate with anyone. The productivity and economic value of your phone go up as more people join the phone network. Not surprisingly, economists call this a "network effect." It holds for phones, for fax machines, and for e-mail connections. In all of these cases, your connection is more valuable if many others are also connected. This is one reason why the move to almost-universal phone access in the OECD leads to a sharp increase in productivity and caused the phone system to contribute greatly to economic growth. The study of phones and the growth of the OECD countries, by Roller and Waverman,[1] tried to determine those factors that had contributed to the growth of output in the OECD countries over the twenty years up to the mid-1990s. Possible contributors to economic growth were capital accumulation, population growth, technological change, and improvements in communications technologies. The authors concluded that about a third of the very large growth in output in the rich OECD countries over two decades was attributable to improved telecommunications, and in particular that the bulk of the benefits from telecoms came when the telecom market was close to saturation and phone service was almost universally available and adopted. Although the United States and Canada had near-universal phone service by 1970, this was not true for many other OECD countries. For example, in 1970 France, Portugal, and Italy had, respectively, only eight, six, and twelve phones per one hundred inhabitants, a standard measure of market penetration by the phone service. Not until near the end of the period did these countries reach a point where every household had a phone, and only then did they realize the economic potential of telecommunications.

In the OECD countries, phone service was almost universally available by the 1990s. Yet in the great majority of developing countries this was far from the case: in 1995, the average number of fixed-line phones per one hundred of population was a meager two in developing countries. In other words, almost no one had phone access. So the gains from good communications were almost totally unrealized. Add to this the fact that in most developing countries road and rail services are poor, as is the postal service, and you begin to see that managing large-scale organizations and managing international trade would have been very tiresome indeed. It could easily take two or three days for someone in a capital city of a poor country to send information to an agent in a rural area. And even in the capital cities, communications with the rest of the world were poor and erratic, making subcontracting for foreign firms difficult. As an illustration of this point, consider for a moment the outsourcing of software development and of call centers to poor countries such as India. Both of these developments are important sources of employment and economic growth in India, and both are absolutely dependent on good communications links with industrial countries. Software engineers in India are often working closely with system designers in the United States or the United Kingdom, with both parties having access to the same code via the Internet. Indeed, all of the outsourcing that we discussed in Chapter 8, a phenomenon that is a dominant feature of today's global economy, is dependent on high-quality communications. The increase in the quality and decrease in the cost of communications in poor countries were a precondition for much of what we think of as globalization.

Although there were only two landline phones per one hundred people in the average developing country in 1995, by 2003 there were eight mobile phones per one hundred people. Mobile phones rapidly overtook conventional phones as the main means of telecommunication. There were several reasons for this, some economic and some political. Economically, cellular phone service is more attractive as a way of providing phone services in a country where there is currently none. It requires much less capital. Rather than running fiber-optic cables all over the country, a massively expensive undertaking, it is only necessary to build signal towers every twenty miles or so, taking less capital and less time. A recent study in India suggested that the capital costs of providing fixed-line services in an area were six times those of cellular services, a dramatic difference in a country where access to capital is scarce.[2] So the economics of expanding through cellular service is more attractive than that of expanding via landline service in a country without landline coverage, the situation of most developing countries.

There is a political aspect of the landline–cellular choice. In most developing countries, and indeed in many developed, the landline system was and still is a monopoly of the state. With no competition and a bureaucratic administrative structure, landline companies moved slowly and felt little pressure to respond to consumers' needs. It was not uncommon in the 1990s to have to wait several years for a phone to be installed in most poor countries. Furthermore, phone service was restricted to the major cities: running phone lines to remote rural areas was costly and unprofitable. Cellular service, in contrast, was usually available from many competing international companies, who might operate on their own or in partnership with local operations. Each was keen to get into the marketplace and sign up subscribers as quickly as possible, as cell phone companies were generally valued by their subscriber numbers. So once a government decided to begin cellular service, its implementation moved fast.

Somalia provides an instructive example of entrepreneurial provision of phone services in a very poor country. Somalia is close to lawlessness: governments change rapidly and have little power when in place. Yet Somalia has good phone service, both landline and mobile. It takes only three days for a landline to be installed, a contrast with several years in neighboring Kenya, and landline and mobile services are good. The absence of a government has meant the absence of a government-run telecommunications monopoly to restrict competition and the absence of a telecom ministry to require licenses and delay their issuance.[3] In Kenya, the time required for the installation of a new phone only dropped from years to days when private competitors entered the phone market.[4]

Not only do cellular systems allow rapid implementation, but they also allow a quite different mode of use, which has allowed much wider access to phone service than the basic data on phone penetration would suggest. This is strikingly illustrated by the fact that in a recent survey, 97 percent of the population of Tanzania, a very poor country, reported that if they needed to they could have access to a mobile phone.[5] Only 28 percent reported that they could have access to a landline.

Such widespread access to mobile phones suggest that these should be having an impact on the economic development in poor countries, just as landlines did for rich countries in the 1970s and 1980s and 1990s. A recent study of the impact of mobile phones in poor countries confirms that this is the case. The authors, Waverman, Meschi, and Fuss,[6] find that access to cell phones did indeed make a significant difference to economic growth in poor countries. They summarize their conclusions on the impact by saying that an increase of ten mobile phones per one hundred people over the period from 1996 to 2003 would have increased economic growth by about 0.59 percent per annum. An increase of twenty mobile phones per one hundred people would have had doubled this impact, and in many countries the mobile phone penetration rate did in fact rise by in the region of ten to twenty per one hundred people. So the growth of cell phone usage may have raised economic growth by between 0.5 and 1 percent per year in many poor countries. With growth rates in many of these countries in the region of 1.5–3 percent, this would have been an important increase. Our earlier remarks about the critical role of communications in outsourcing, one of the main drivers of foreign direct investment in poor countries, make these numbers seem intuitively reasonable. Next, we turn to a discussion of how exactly phones, mobile phones in particular, are used in poor countries and what business opportunities they offer.

Mobile Phones in Poor Countries

We have already noted that rich country business models do not carry over to doing business in mass markets in poor countries. Banking is different, selling household goods is different, and we will now see that selling phone services is different too.

In poor countries, cell phones are too expensive for individuals to buy for their own use. They cost at a minimum $50, generally more, and for people earning a few dollars a day this is clearly not affordable. Nor are the Western-style charges, which could amount to a day's wages for a single phone call. A different usage model has evolved, one more appropriate to the financial circumstances in developing countries. Typically, there is a community phone, used by many. It is rather like a public phone in a Western community in the days before everyone had their own line. Often these phones are not communally owned, but rather are bought or rented by a member of the community with entrepreneurial tendencies, for the purpose of selling time on them to others. Local mobile phone companies structure their billing procedures to support this type of usage, charging by the second and making it easy for the owner to know exactly how much each call has cost.

The Grameen Bank again is in the forefront. They have a subsidiary called GrameenPhone, which in 2005 had about 2.5 million subscribers, many of them poor. The evolution of this venture actually started in New York, with Iqbal Quadir, a Pakistani who in 1993 worked for a New York investment bank. Quadir had the idea that the lives of the poor in Bangladesh would be greatly improved by access to communications: he recalled how he as a boy in Bangladesh had once wasted a day walking miles to a pharmacy to collect medicines, only to find that they were not in stock. Many poor people must waste their time in this way, he thought, and time is the only asset the poor have as much of as anyone else. In 1994, when Bangladesh had only one landline phone per three hundred people, one of the lowest levels of connectedness in the world, Quadir took his idea to the Bangladeshi government. He was greeted with incredulity, but persevered and eventually found a business partner in Telenor, the largest Norwegian phone company, then state-owned. The chief executive backed the idea and was willing to put resources into it.

Telenor could provide money and technology, but the idea still needed a partner who could distribute phones to rural communities, and for this Quadir went to Grameen Bank. They had the idea of issuing loans to existing reliable customers who could use them to buy phones and sell time on them, paying off the loan and generating income for their families. The customer would be given a discount on the airtime so that she could retail it at a profit. This discount would be possible because Grameen would buy airtime in bulk and handle the administration of charges and collecting money for calls made.

GrameenPhone has proven profitable for its owners and also for the "telephone ladies" who own phones and rent time on them to their fellow villagers. But over time, new companies have copied the idea, providing competition and driving prices down—all good for the villagers, for whom communications are becoming cheaper and cheaper.[7] This has real economic value to villagers, who typically use the phones for access to economically important information. Often they use the phones to check prices: they could be searching for the lowest price for something they need to buy, like fuel or components for machines, or for the best prices for their products. There are many examples of farmers increasing their incomes by one-third or more as a result of better information about market prices for their products. In the past, with no way of shopping around, they had to take the prices they were offered: now they can break the monopolies of the local dealers and improve the terms on which they do business.

The keys to extending phone services to the villages in Bangladesh were microfinance and mobile telephone technology, and both are now available in most countries, so there is no reason why this model cannot be used in most developing countries.

The way people use mobile phones in poor countries is very different from the way we use them, and understanding this is important to seeing how mobile phones have made a difference. Mobile phones are, as we have noted, rarely bought for the owner's own use, but are bought to resell the time on them. Everyone in a village who might expect a call will give out the village phone number, and when they are called the owner will bring the phone to their house. Mobile phones are also widely used to send and receive text messages, and as most villagers cannot read or write there is now a class of interpreters and writers who will translate or write text messages. In Zambia, text messages on mobile phones are used to give payment instructions to banks: this avoids the need for merchants to carry cash, reducing the risk of theft.[8] In communities where migrant labor is the norm, access to phones allows families to stay in touch even when one, typically the father, is far away. Social workers suggest that the contact this provides with the father can be important to children, greatly enhancing their sense of being part of a complete family.

Another socially important role for mobile phones is to provide access to medical services or medical advice. Poor communities in developing countries rarely have doctors or clinics, and usually the sick get little or no medical treatment. With phone services, people can call for advice, and even summon an ambulance in some cases. There is an interesting medical application of cell phones in Rwanda, one of the poorest countries in Africa and the site of the terrible genocide of the 1990s. Genocide is over but AIDS has arrived and an impoverished health system is trying to cope with the rapid spread of the disease. One of the obstacles has been the difficulty in communicating: it has sometimes taken several months for test results to reach a patient or his doctor, and access to medical records has been similarly slow. Now all this information is kept on a Web site that can be accessed from mobile phones, through a system called TRACnet: the same Web site gives information about treatment regimes for rural health workers, who have little or no access to medical literature.

In South Africa, rather richer than other African countries, Vodacom, the subsidiary of the British company Vodafone, has established a network of "phone shops," shops that sell phone services over cellular networks. Vodacom houses these phone shops in shipping containers, which are stationed in poor neighborhoods without landline service. Typically, they are joint ventures between Vodacom and an entrepreneur, with Vodacom providing technology and some capital and their partner providing the management and also some capital. They operate as a franchise system. Phone shops allow customers to make calls and will take messages for them as well, providing an answering service. They can also send and receive faxes and e-mail messages. They have proven so successful that by 2001 there were 2,335 in operation. Estimates suggest that each phone shop generates five jobs directly, and typically small local businesses grow up nearby to take advantage of the communications with suppliers and customers.[9] Cellular phones are acting as catalysts for small-scale entrepreneurial development.

Another model of the use of modern communications in poor rural communities is provided by the introduction of "e-choupals" in India. "Choupal" is Hindi for a traditional village gathering place, and an e-choupal is in effect an electronic village marketplace. The system of e-choupals was established by ITC, a large Indian company with a presence in many fields, including agribusiness. Its original aim was to streamline the procurement of soybeans, although it has now been extended to a wide range of other important applications. ITC buys and processes soybeans for export, and so needs access to a steady stream of high-quality produce at predictable prices. The original procurement system did not deliver this, leading instead to supplies of variable quality and leaving ITC in the dark about the factors affecting the yields of the small farmers who were their ultimate suppliers. Farmers traditionally sold their beans at auctions called mandis. Typically, they had to transport their produce many miles to a mandi, with no advanced knowledge of the price it would realize. If they felt the price was low, they really had no redress: the option of returning home with their produce and then going elsewhere was not a real one. The absence of prior price indicators was a major irritant: a typical farmer could choose to go to one of several mandis that were within traveling distance, and with no access to information about their prices he had to trust luck or gossip. Equally irritating was the treatment meted out at the mandi, where he would be made to wait for payment, sometimes even return again another day, and where some of the crop was often stolen by the employees of the auction.

It was not only the farmers who felt poorly treated in the original system: it had real drawbacks for ITC too. They bought from brokers who purchased at the auctions and who often marked prices up unreasonably before selling to ITC. And the presence of the brokers between farmers and ITC made quality control difficult and also blocked the flow of information between suppliers (farmers) and ITC, who needed to know how the supply of their input was evolving—whether farmers were planning to plant more or less acreage under soy, and what factors were affecting quality. Given their dependence on farmers as the starting point of their supply chain, ITC could benefit from closer relationships with the growers.

To resolve these problems, ITC set up computers with Internet access in farming villages. They were located in the house of a villager who was chosen carefully as the manager of the new electronic village marketplace—someone entrepreneurial, well respected, and with a good understanding of the dynamics of village life. These people were called Sanchalaks. A Sanchalak had access to the prices that ITC was willing to pay for beans of different qualities and was authorized to appraise a farmer's beans and offer a price for them on ITC's behalf. If the farmer accepted this, then the Sanchalak would give him a contract for payment and the farmer had to deliver his beans to the nearest ITC collection center and receive payment there. In addition to quoting a price on behalf of ITC, the Sanchalak could quote the most recent prices at all the nearby auctions or mandis, so that the farmer could make an informed decision about the sale of his produce. Furthermore, the computer could be used to access more general price information via the Internet, including prices on the Chicago Board of Trade and futures prices. From this, farmers could get an idea of price trends and decide to postpone harvesting in the hope of price gains.

Both farmers and ITC gained greatly from ITC's investment in rural information technology. Farmers sold produce for better prices and felt that the sale process was more transparent and more under their control. ITC eliminated the middlemen and so saved their commissions: they could afford to pay more to farmers and still save money. They could control the quality of what they bought. And more importantly in the long run, they were able to establish working relationships with their suppliers. This gave them the opportunity to work with farmers to improve the quality of the produce bought, by offering advice about seed varieties, fertilizers, pesticides, and soil management to farmers. They made information about all of these available over the computer and also offered services such as soil testing, which enabled farmers to tailor seeds and fertilizers to their local soil conditions. Local weather forecasts were also broadcast over the e-choupals. In effect, the e-choupals became a sophisticated agricultural advice system.

Over time, their uses have been extended in other ways. ITC is now using the same system for buying wheat. And it is making the channel two-way, allowing other firms to use the e-choupal to offer goods to farmers. Seeds, pesticides, and fertilizers are all on sale over the network, with ITC taking a commission on the sales. Poor rural farmers have access to a greatly enhanced range of products, with advice on how to use them. Beyond this, the computer gives the whole village a window on the outside world that it never had before. Children can use it as a part of school lessons and have a chance to learn how to use a computer. Adults can access not only agricultural advice, but also medical information and advice on many other important issues. An innovation that began as a mechanism for a large corporation to manage better its supply chain has become a mechanism for rural empowerment and education.[10]

Conclusions

All the phone services discussed here are profitable for the phone companies providing them: all of them are making money. The businesses are growing fast, too. But they are not only profitable: they make an immense difference to the quality of life in the communities that they serve, overcoming decades of isolation and the costs that come with that. They bring economic benefits, with better access to buyers and suppliers, and social gains, through access to distant family members and to medical services. The latest communications technologies are helping some of the poorest people on Earth, and making profits for their owners as well. But a prerequisite for successful operation in poor communities is a change of business model, something that we have already seen with banking and with the sale of consumer goods. The poor in developing countries will buy some western-style goods and services and benefit from them, but obviously are seriously constrained by their low incomes. The goods often have to be made available on a per-use basis rather than sold outright, and distribution systems have to be different because these markets cannot support the cost of Western-style distribution networks. Ingenuity can overcome these obstacles, and we will surely see the spread of mobile phones in poor communities around the world. In some areas of Africa, mobile-phone networks are providing Internet access for remote communities, again of course on a community basis as no one family could afford the cost on its own. This is raising new challenges and providing new business opportunities. For example, the Internet is text-based and most inhabitants of rural areas in poor countries cannot read or write, so someone has to set up the business of reading Internet sites and e-mail messages and writing responses.

11

Measuring Corporate Responsibility

There are people who measure corporate social and environmental performance for a living. I emphasize this because it might seem a rather intangible concept, interesting and intellectually important but nonetheless unquantifiable. This is not so: we encountered measures in Chapter 2, in reviewing empirical studies of the effect of corporate responsibility on corporate financial performance. Each of the studies reviewed there used a quantitative measure, more often than not of the environmental dimension. We also encountered there the work of companies like KLD Research and Analytics of Boston and Innovest Strategic Value Advisors of New York. Both sell comprehensive social and environmental ratings as their main product—their employees are some of the people who measure corporate social and environmental performance for a living. But there are others: other companies who sell corporate responsibility ratings, as well as the managers of indices such as FTSE4GOOD and the Dow Jones Sustainability Index. They manage indices of the share prices companies that are highly rated and in doing so have to rank companies by their social and environmental performances.

Increasingly, companies are trying to assess and report on their own social and environmental performance. They do this in reports, often known as CSR or sustainability reports, which are published annually alongside their more formal annual reports to shareholders. There is a searchable database of some of these reports maintained by the U.S group CSRwire at http://www.csrwire.com/reports and another supported by the U.K. group CorporateRegister.com. There is of course no general legal obligation to publish such reports, no standard format, and no standard set of contents. There are some exceptions to this statement: in France the publication of a CSR report is mandated by the New Economic Regulation Act of 2001, and in the United States certain elements that would be an important part of a CSR report are required of industries that use or make toxic chemicals and also are required of the banking industry. We have already encountered the U.S. EPA's Toxics Release Inventory (TRI) in Chapter 2. Under the 1984 Emergency Planning and Community Right to Know Act, companies above a certain size are required to disclose the amounts of a list of about 650 toxic chemicals that are stored or that are released into air, water, ground, and to waste disposal sites. This information is to be made available for each operating site, so it is available at a much more disaggregated level than that of the corporation as a whole. The banking industry in the United States is affected by the Home Mortgage Disclosure Act, which was passed along with the Community Reinvestment Act to prevent racial discrimination in lending. Under this and subsequent legislation, banks must provide data on income levels and racial mix of their lending on single-family and multi-family housing. Both of these required disclosures provide exactly the type of information that one would wish to see in a CSR report.

In the United Kingdom, the government considered moving toward a requirement that some aspects of CSR reporting be contained in the corporation's annual report, within a section called the Operating and Financial Report (OFR). A recent report by the U.K. Department of Trade and Industry (DTI) had the following to say about the government's intentions:[1]

4.30 The Government agrees that companies should provide more qualitative and forward looking reporting, in addition to information that is quantitative (e.g. the balance sheet), historical (e.g. the financial results in the past year) or about internal company matters (e.g. the size of the workforce). It recognises that companies are increasingly reliant on intangible assets such as the skills and knowledge of their employees, their business relationships and their reputation. Information about future plans, opportunities, risks and strategies is just as important to users of financial reports as a historical review of performance.

4.31 It also recognises that, in deciding in good faith what would be most likely to promote the success of the company, directors need to take account—as in the proposed statutory statement of directors' duties (see paragraph 3.2 et seq)—of a wide range of factors within and outside the company which are relevant to achieving its objectives. These include relationships with employees, customers and suppliers and the company's impact on the wider community. They also include the company's impact on the environment which the

Government believes every director needs to consider as first among equals. The OFR proposals would require information on all these factors, where relevant to an assessment of the company's business, to be covered in the narrative report. This will help give members the information they require to hold directors to account.

4.32 A reporting requirement in these terms would also be a major benefit for a wider cross-section of a company's stakeholders. The new requirement to report, for example, on material environmental issues would be a major contribution to both corporate social responsibility and sustainable development initiatives. The Government has long recognised, and promoted, the business case for these and sees the OFR as the opportunity for directors to demonstrate their response to this business case.

4.40 The company's auditors will be required to report on the OFR. The auditors' review of the OFR will differ from that for the financial statements in that it will essentially concern the adequacy of the process of preparation, focusing on how the report was prepared, not its detailed content. However, there will also be a requirement for auditors to report on compliance with applicable rules and if the OFR is inconsistent with the financial statements or other information they are aware of as a result of the audit.

This is an interesting statement in several ways—it recognizes explicitly the interest that shareholders have in information about aspects of a company's social and environmental performance, and proposes that reporting this be made compulsory for companies above a certain size. It also proposes that these statements be reviewed by the company's auditors, implying that there must be substance to them. But there is no prescribed format for the presentation of this information. Furthermore, this statement refers to a proposal for legislation that was modified significantly in response to opposition from the business community. The 2006 Companies Act contains a requirement for an annual Business Review that covers a corporation's social and environmental impacts, but in less detail than was originally proposed.[2] Several other countries have already taken steps in this direction: in Australia, Belgium, Denmark, France, and Sweden companies are required to report on some aspects of their social and environmental performance.[3] The precise requirements vary and typically there is no requirement that these reports be audited, so reports are not readily comparable across companies and represent the company's unchecked self-assessment. Nevertheless, these requirements are beginning the habit of collecting and presenting some information about corporate social and environmental performance.

It is informative to see what current CSR reports are saying and how they present information. We have already spoken at length about the garment industry in the context of outsourcing, so we start with two garment firms, GAP and Nike. GAP's report has a nice statement in it—"We believe that 'what gets measured gets managed.'"[4] This is their rationale for trying to quantify their social and environmental goals and achievements, and it is one that seems reasonable. If we want managers and shareholders to take more notice of social and environmental goals, these have to be measured and performance relative to them recorded. The greater part of the GAP report, not surprisingly, is taken up with labor conditions in the factories that supply their products. As is standard in textiles and footwear, these are not owned by the brand owner but are independent firms, often quite large in their own right. GAP, like most companies in its position, tries to ensure proper treatment of workers in the factories that are a part of its supply chain and sets out in the report what is involved in this process and what it sees as the unsolved problems. Subsequent sections of the report address employee satisfaction within the GAP chain and the environmental impact of GAP (through energy use in stores and the use of water in dying clothing). At the end, the report has a short section summarizing the information in the report in the format required by the Global Reporting Initiative (GRI), about which more is given later in this chapter. An interesting feature is the presence of two independent evaluations of GAP's factory inspection program by the NGOs Social Accountability International and Verite. This is a little like having an outside audit, as suggested in the U.K. government report quoted earlier, although of course neither of these NGOs has any professional training in the skills that go into an audit.

Nike's report follows a similar structure. The greatest part is again about workers in contract factories, with data on the rate of inspection and the rate of compliance, and lengthy (and interesting) discussions of the difficulties in ensuring compliance in certain parts of the world. We quoted from this in Chapter 8. Like GAP, Nike has a form of audit of its report contained in the report: they use a Report Review Committee composed of people from KLD, academia, and other large corporations and NGOs. Nike asked the committee to work with the AA1000 Assurance Standard and provide an opinion on how well Nike's report

(a) covers Nike's key business impacts and includes information on the issues of greatest concern to Nike's stakeholders (materiality);

(b) indicates Nike's awareness of and ability to understand and address its impacts (completeness);

(c) provides evidence that the company engages and listens to its stakeholders (responsiveness).

The Review Committee comments that

Our task was to look at various sources of information that could be used to evaluate Nike's performance, rather than comment on performance. The Committee would like to commend Nike's announcement in this report that it will disclose the names and locations of its supplier factory base. This is a groundbreaking step in transparency and should help remove barriers to the collaboration needed to improve labor standards throughout the global apparel and footwear industry. Our assessment of this report is as follows:

Materiality

(a) Nike's report covers the key impacts of the "Nike brand" business activities and appropriately places most emphasis on the labor and social impacts on workers in its supply chain. The report further describes how Nike is beginning to integrate corporate responsibility into its fundamental business practices, through incorporation of CR compliance, price, quality and delivery into the Balanced Scorecard used for its purchasing process. The environment section appropriately focuses on innovative and sustainable product design, manufacturing impacts, climate change and toxics elimination.

Completeness

(b) The report lacks consistent provision of multiple years of performance data for its key indicators, which would permit improved evaluation of impacts over time. Nike indicates in the report that this is one of its challenges and notes its intention to develop the improved metrics and management systems needed for better reporting in future years. While the report may seem to provide excessive information on Nike's process of setting up diagnostic and compliance tools and systems related to workers and factories, we feel that this information will be important for future reference.

Responsiveness

(c) The report documents Nike's progress since the last report in engaging varied stakeholders on issues and impacts, through efforts such as the Stakeholder Forum held in 2004, numerous stakeholder partnerships and the formation of this Report Review Committee. In response to stakeholder interest in seeing targets reported as well as past performance, Nike's report does contain some targets for future improvement, and indicates where it will be developing additional targets and more specific timelines for meeting these. Nike's decision to disclose the names and locations of its suppliers indicates a notable level of responsiveness to stakeholders concerned about labor practices.

As with the GAP report, this is not a real audit, but provides at least some indication that Nike is not pulling the wool over the reader's eyes. After the lengthy section on "Workers in Contract Factories," there are briefer chapters on "Employees and Diversity" and on "Environment," and then sections on "Community and Public Policy" (engaging with governments). A final section on "Challenges and Opportunities" deals mainly with doing business in China and with the end of the Multi-Fiber Agreement. Then there is an appendix in the format of the Global Reporting Initiative, as in the GAP report.

Two rather different reports are those of Exxon Mobil and BP, the world's two largest oil companies. Exxon has sections on transparency and the Extractive Industries Transparency Initiative (EITI), on Exxon and the environment, on health and safety, and on corporate citizenship with many illustrative cases dealing with CSR. There is no outside evaluation and no presentation in the GRI format. For a major oil company, Exxon's report is light on climate change, containing the statement that "we recognize that, although scientific evidence remains inconclusive, the potential impact of greenhouse gas (GHG) emissions on society and ecosystems may prove to be significant." Most scientists familiar with the field of climate change would disagree strongly with the statement that "scientific evidence remains inconclusive" and would also argue that "may prove to be significant" is a considerable understatement. Climate change is an area where Exxon has been in a state of aggressive denial, and its sustainability report continues this tradition, albeit in muted form. BP's report is more open on climate change, seeing this as a major issue in its section on BP and the environment. Like the other reports, BP also devotes space to its social impact and the welfare of its employees. It does contain a limited evaluation by BP's auditors, Ernst and Young, and an appendix indicating how it meets GRI recommendations.

Even within this small sample of sustainability reports, there is a lot of variation in what is covered and how it is covered. The Global Reporting Initiative (GRI http://www.globalreporting.org) is an attempt to bring some standardization to this process, to ensure that there are common features to all reports. In its own words, "The GRI *Guidelines* organise 'sustainability reporting' in terms of economic, environmental, and social performance (also known as the 'triple bottom line')." Of course, using the GRI format is strictly voluntary, but the idea of bringing some order to the potential chaos of thousands of reports in different formats and addressing different questions seems a worthy goal and, as we have already seen, a number of influential companies have agreed to follow the GRI guidelines. The core of the GRI guidelines lies in the performance indicators that it suggests, covering economic, environmental and social performance, the "triple bottom line" to use GRI's own phrase. Here is GRI's description of these indicators:

Economic Indicators. Economic indicators concern an organization's impacts, both direct and indirect, on the economic resources of its stakeholders and on economic systems at the local, national, and global levels. Included within economic indicators are the reporting organization's wages, pensions, and other benefits paid to employees; monies received from customers and paid to suppliers; and taxes paid and subsidies received. In a few instances, economic performance information overlaps with that in conventional financial statements. In general, however, the two are complementary.

Environmental Indicators. Environmental indicators concern an organization's impacts on living and nonliving natural systems, including ecosystems, land, air, and water. Included within environmental indicators are the environmental impacts of products and services; energy, material, and water use; greenhouse gas and other emissions; effluents and waste generation; impacts on biodiversity; use of hazardous materials; recycling, pollution, waste reduction, and other environmental programs; environmental expenditures; and fines and penalties for noncompliance.

Social Indicators. Social indicators concern an organization's impacts on the social systems within which it operates. GRI social indicators are grouped into three clusters: labour practices (e.g., diversity, employee health, and safety), human rights (e.g., child labour, compliance issues), and broader social issues affecting consumers, communities, and other stakeholders (e.g., bribery and corruption, community relations). Because many social issues are not easily quantifiable, GRI requests qualitative information where appropriate.

For each of these categories, the GRI indicates some core data that will always be needed and then gives additional sector-specific guidelines. A company operating only in the European Union will not need to worry about its impact on indigenous peoples, whereas an oil company probably will as it is likely to have drilling or production operations where they could affect indigenous groups. Sector-specific guidelines add this type of sectoral detail. Figure 11.1, taken from GRI's guidelines, indicates the core topics on which data should be provided under each of the three main headings, economic, environmental, and social.

GRI guidelines also touch on the issue of audits of CSR reports, though they do not use the word "audit": they refer rather to the desirability of "assurance" of the report by independent parties, though they have little to add above this basic observation.

We have spent some time reviewing what is available by way of corporate social and environmental reports. Many companies now produce these, though many still do not. Some are perfunctory in the extreme, some are pure public relations, and some are a serious attempt to inform outside constituencies about the firm's position in society. There are almost as many formats are there are reports, although a handful of companies are using the format suggested by the Global Reporting Initiative. There is some

FIGURE 11.1 GRI classifications

	Category	Aspect
Economic	Direct economic impacts	Customers
		Suppliers
		Employees
		Providers of capital
		Public sector
Environmental	Environmental	Materials
		Energy
		Water
		Biodiversity
		Emissions, effluent, waste
		Suppliers
		Products and services
		Compliance
		Transport
		Overall
Social	Labor practices & decent work	Employment
		Labor/management relations
		Health & safety
		Training & education
		Diversity & opportunity
	Human rights	Strategy & management
		Non-discrimination
		Freedom of association
		Collective bargaining
		Child labor
		Forced & compulsory labor
		Disciplinary practices
		Security practices
		Indigenous rights
	Society	Community
		Bribery & corruption
		Political contributions
		Competition & pricing
	Product responsibility	Consumer health & safety
		Products & services
		Advertising
		Respect for privacy

Source: Global Reporting Initiative Web site (www.globalreporting.org).

government involvement: in the United States, banks are required to disclose demographic information about the recipients of home loans, and all companies have to disclose data on the emission of toxic chemicals. The U.K. government is considering a requirement that corporations disclose certain types of information relevant to an appraisal of their CSR performance, and in France there is a general requirement to disclose information about the social and environmental impacts of a business.

How does this match up to what we would like to see? Is any of what we have a good model of where we should be going? To answer this, we first have to decide on the audience for these reports. Are these for shareholders or for employees? Are these for outside stakeholders such as NGOs, or for regulators and the government? Or are these perhaps for the firm's customers? Certainly the corporation owes its shareholders as owners a duty to make available any information that could affect their appraisal of the company's performance. From a business perspective, it makes sense to keep employees well informed about the company's performance, as ultimately their behavior can make or break the firm. It also makes business sense to inform NGOs and keep them in a discussion, as they can influence the public's perception of the company for the worse. Customers are critical, particularly if they are retail customers: their perception of the company and what it stands for can make a difference to their buying decisions and that is where the money ultimately comes from. So the answer is that a social and environmental report needs to be aimed at all of these groups.

To develop some ideas about how this could be achieved, we need to go back to our original discussions of corporate responsibilities and the tentative definition put forward in Chapter 1. Recall that there we spoke of a set of policies designed to reduce conflicts between the corporation and society by aligning corporate and social goals, and in particular by internalizing external costs and by paying attention to potentially controversial distributional issues. All of the examples of responsible corporate behavior that we have considered since that definition fit within its scope, from reducing the emissions of greenhouse gases to broadening the access to medical products. And almost all of the conflicts between companies and regulators or NGOs come from ignoring one of these sources of conflict. So a good way of measuring the effectiveness of a company's social and environmental policies is to measure the extent to which it has addressed these two issues and aligned its interests with those of the broader community. How could this be measured, and how might a report go about presenting such measures?

There is a well-established precedent for measuring these issues and reporting them in an accounting framework: this is in the field of social cost–benefit analysis. Social cost–benefit analysis is the analysis we conduct to decide whether a government project is worth carrying out. Should we build a new road between two cities, or enlarge an airport, or a dock? Whenever governments invest in large infrastructure projects they should (and usually do) carry out this type of analysis, researching and quantifying the impact of the proposed project on all the groups who are likely to be affected by it. The principles of social cost–benefit analysis were developed by international agencies in the late 1960s and early 1970s, with the World Bank, the Organization for Economic Cooperation and Development (OECD), and the United Nations all playing central roles, with inputs from some very distinguished economists.[5] As a result, it is a well-developed, well-tried, and well-documented set of techniques for valuing the economic, environmental, and social impacts of economic activity. This is precisely what a thorough social and environmental report requires—an analysis of the impact of the company's operations on all of those who are affected by it. And the key issues in this will be those central to our definition of CSR, namely the extent to which the company created external costs (or benefits) and the extent to which it creates or undoes injustices through its operations.

What this suggests in operational terms is that one of the tasks of a company's social and environmental report should be to attempt to quantify the external costs or benefits of the company's operations. This requires measuring the impacts of its operations on third parties and then valuing these. In many cases, this will be straightforward. Take as an example the emission of the greenhouse gas carbon dioxide: this is an external cost imposed by any entity using fossil fuels on the rest of the world. The amount of carbon dioxide released can be measured directly from the amounts of fossil fuels used, as we know how much CO_2 is released by burning a ton of any fossil fuel. We can put a price on this CO_2 in several ways, but the most obvious is to look at the price paid for a permit to emit CO_2 on the European Union's Emission Trading Market, which is currently in the region of $25 per ton of CO_2. If we happen to feel that this price is temporarily nonrepresentative, then there are many academic studies of the external costs of CO_2 emissions that could be used to value the external effects of CO_2 release. A similar method could be used for most gaseous pollutants: we can readily estimate the amount of sulfur dioxide released from burning sulfur-containing fuels and then find a price for the emission of SO_2 from the United States' SO_2 market, established by Bush1 as a part of the 1990 Amendments to the Clean Air Act. Certainly, there are some pollutants for which there is no market and so no market price, but there are many methods for valuing nonmarket goods and services and they could be readily applied to emissions of pollutants for which there is no market price. These methods were used by the World Bank in its recent study *Where is the Wealth of Nations?,* in which it evaluates the total capital stocks and investments flows of rich and poor countries. Total capital stocks means that it measures not only conventional physical capital, but also stocks of human capital and of natural or environmental capital. In doing this, it has to place values on external effects such as pollution that detract from the value of the natural environment, just as is required in a comprehensive environmental report.

Valuing external costs in this way brings them into comparability with the company's production and sales operations, whose outputs are also stated in dollar terms. The value of the external costs can be compared directly to the incomes paid to employees and to the company's profits. With this data we can ask questions like "If this company were required to pay for the external costs it imposes on others, would it still be profitable?" In the extreme case that the answer is no, this tells us that, taking into account its external costs, the company does not add value for society as a whole: if external costs exceed profits, its operations reduce rather than increase value for the economy overall.

There are cases in which external effects do not take the form of the emission of pollutants. Suppose for example that a lumber company cuts a forest, producing income from the sale of the timber. The local community may feel a loss from this and there may be some real external costs associated with cutting the forest, but these are not from the emission of pollutants. The key issues here will generally be that the forest provides a range of amenities to the local community and when it is cut they will lose these amenity values and the birds and mammals that lived in it. There are many studies of the values of such amenities, and the methods developed for these studies can readily be applied to the external costs of a corporation's activities. In particular, they could readily be applied to value the loss to the local community from the cutting of a forest. So placing a value on the external effects associated with a company's operations is relatively straightforward.

Valuing the external costs or benefits is probably easier than valuing the impact of corporate activity on injustices. These are more subjective, more a matter of opinion, and harder to measure and to assign a widely agreed value. Nevertheless, there are options available to a company that wants to try to report quantitatively its impact in such a controversial area as outsourcing. Take as an example a company whose goods are produced in China by subcontractors. There are several ways in which we could measure the effort the company makes to protect those making its goods. We could compare the wages paid to them with the legal minimum wage or with the going market wage in that region for similar work. If wages paid exceed either of these, then we have a partial measure of the extent to which workers' interests are being protected. Similarly, we can look for data on health and safety in the workplace and compare subcontracting factories with a more general population. Of course this presumes that we have access to reliable data on wages paid and conditions at work, and as we saw in Chapter 8 this may not be the case in China, though it is likely to be true in most other countries.

Many studies have gone further than this, by assigning value to generating income for poor people. These studies start from the premise that a dollar paid to someone earning $2 per day is far more important socially than the same amount paid to someone earning $100 per day, for the obvious reason that this makes far more difference to the living standard of the poor person than to that of the richer, and they (somewhat arbitrarily, it must be admitted[6]) assign a value in excess of one dollar to $1 paid to a really poor person. Perhaps this is $3, saying that a dollar to the $2-a-day person is three times more important to society than the same amount to the $100-a-day person. With such a valuation, if the company pays $1 million annually to people earning $2 per day, it can then say that the social value of this payment is $3 million and that it is creating social value in excess of what it pays out to the tune of $2 million. Obviously, such an approach is potentially controversial and would probably not appeal to a lot of corporations, but is nevertheless an option that is available for quantifying the positive distributional impacts of a company's actions, an option that has many respectable precedents.

It may be helpful in making these ideas more concrete to illustrate how they would work for some companies that we have already encountered. The two tables show income statements for 2004 for both Exxon Mobil and BP Amoco, with additions following the principles suggested here (Tables 11.1 and 11.2).

The first three lines on each statement are copied from the company's income statement in its annual report, in both cases available on the Web site www.exxon.com or www.bp.com. These three lines give the company's

TABLE 11.1 Exxon Mobil Modified Income Statement—2004 (US$, Millions)

Total revenues and other income	298,035
Total costs and other deductions	256,794
Net income	25,330
Value of external benefits	100
External cost of direct GHG emissions	3,025
Profits after direct GHG emissions	22,405
External costs of indirect GHG emissions	14,000
Profits after all GHG emissions and external benefits	8,405

TABLE 11.2 BP Modified Income Statement—2004 (US$, Millions)

Group turnover	285,059
Replacement cost of sales	248,714
Profit after taxation	15,961
Value of external benefits	200
External cost of direct GHG emissions	2,000
Profits after direct GHG emissions	14,161
External costs of indirect GHG emissions	13,000
Profits after all GHG emissions and external benefits	1,161

top line, its total revenue, then the cost of goods sold, and finally the conventional bottom line, profits after tax. Both companies were very profitable in 2004 by conventional accounting measures, with net incomes of $25 billion and $16 billion, respectively. I have added the last five lines of each income statement to reflect the suggestion made earlier of including as costs on the income statement the external costs that companies impose on others. The first of these lines, "Value of external benefits," captures any external benefits the company may generate for others. The numbers here— $100 million for Exxon Mobil and $200 million for BP—are arbitrary and purely illustrative. Both companies give money to charitable operations in the countries in which they operate and help provide schools, hospitals, and other social goods. In addition, BP spends heavily on research and development for renewable energy sources, expenditure which may have a social value in excess of its cost to BP. "Value of external benefits" credits the company with the social value added by these nonmarket activities.

Next is the line "External costs of direct GHG emissions." This captures the external costs of the carbon dioxide emitted by the company as a part of its operations. In the case of Exxon, this is slightly over 120 million tons in 2004, and for BP it was about 80 million. The emission of CO_2 is charged at $25 per ton, which at time of writing is the price to be paid for the right to emit a ton of CO_2 in the European Union's Emission Trading Scheme. So the two companies are charged with roughly $3 billion and $2 billion, respectively, as the cost of the CO_2 emitted by their operations. In each case, this amounts to more that 10 percent of their net profits, a significant charge. Immediately after the cost of direct GHG emissions is a new profit total reflecting the credits for external benefits and the charges for GHG emissions.

I have used the European Union's CO_2 emissions price because it is the only price we have for CO_2 emissions that is established by market forces in a reasonably liquid market: there are other markets and prices, such as the prices implied by the Clean Development Mechanism[7] and that of the Chicago Climate Exchange, but both of these see only sporadic transactions and do not reflect supply and demand in an active and liquid market. Academic estimates of the price of the right to emit a ton of CO_2 when the Kyoto Protocol is fully implemented are generally considerably in excess of the current $25 price in the EU's trading scheme.

The final adjustment reflects the cost of what I have called indirect greenhouse gas emissions. Behind this lies the fact that Exxon and BP produce and sell oil and gas, major sources of greenhouse gases. In the lines "External costs of indirect GHG emissions," I calculate the external costs imposed by the use of the fossil fuels that they sell. These are not used by Exxon or BP: they are used by their customers, who generate the emissions of greenhouse gases. So it may not be appropriate to charge these to Exxon and BP, as they are not directly responsible for them as they are for their own direct emissions. But it is clear that someone has to be charged for these and Exxon and BP play a major role in their production, although they could no doubt argue that if they did not produce this oil and gas then someone else would and in that sense they are not contributing to its combustion. Anyway, it is clear that the logic behind this adjustment is weaker than that behind the others, which is why I have placed it last. I have calculated these indirect emissions by taking the total production of oil and gas measured in barrels of oil equivalent from the two companies' annual reports,[8] and then calculating how much CO_2 would be released by burning this much oil. The conversion factors I used to calculate CO_2 emissions come from the Oak Ridge National Laboratory.[9] The external costs associated with the use of the fuels produced by Exxon and BP are huge: about $14 billion and $13 billion, respectively. These are enough to reduce Exxon's profits by about two-thirds and BP's by about 80 percent, which are dramatic changes.

These examples illustrate how easy it is to make quantitative dollar-based estimated of the value of prominent external costs associated with a corporation's operations, showing that we could easily quantify at least this part of a corporation's CSR report and integrate it with the financial reports, merging it into the income statement.

Another option available for providing a quantitative basis for CSR reports is to use the ratings provided by the various CSR rating agencies such as Innovest and KLD, particularly in the areas—such as impacts on underprivileged populations—where it is difficult to provide any alternative firm quantitative assessments of a company's operations. The rating agencies usually provide an arm's-length and impartial evaluation of the firm's performance, not necessarily completely accurate but probably more so than the firm's self-evaluation, which is almost inevitably self-serving to some degree. Providing not just the company's own rating but also the average ratings of other comparable corporations would allow the reader to make comparisons and place the ratings in perspective.

Summarizing this discussion, it appears that there are many quite accessible ways in which a company's CSR report could quantify its performance on social and environmental grounds as well as on economic grounds. There are ways, in other words, to quantify the triple bottom line and make the information in CSR reports far more quantitative and comparable across companies than it is at the moment. This would move such reports in the direction of financial reports, which are of course both quantitative and also in a standardized format, which makes cross-company comparison relatively straightforward.

The Global Reporting Initiative, the most widely followed proposal for standardization of CSR reports, sadly makes no move toward quantification. Indeed, it is completely lacking in this respect: although there is reference in its guidelines to the "triple bottom line," there is nothing in its proposals that would actually measure this in a single bottom line number that represents all three fields in which a company may have impacts—economic, environmental, and social—as would be possible by importing ideas and techniques from social cost–benefit analysis.

12

Social and Environmental Policies and Corporate Strategy

How a company behaves on social and environmental issues can affect its financial performance. Senior executives responsible for financial performance therefore need to concern themselves with these matters. In this chapter, I present a framework for thinking about corporate responsibility from the executive's perspective, tying together material from the earlier chapters to focus it on executive decisions, and ultimately on the place of social and environmental policies in a corporation's overall business strategy.

I want to start by emphasizing what social and environmental policies are *not*. They are not philanthropy, not public relations, and not marketing. All of these have legitimate places in business strategy, but those places are different from the place occupied by social and environmental policies. Companies often make charitable donations: tobacco companies support the arts, other companies support medical treatment for children, yet others provide donations and material support in disasters. Wal-Mart, for example, provided financial and logistical support for the victims of Hurricane Katrina in 2005. All of these may be legitimate and appropriate uses of corporate resources, but they are in general not exercises in social or environmental responsibility. Companies also engage in public relations as a way of promulgating their perspectives on current issues and of ensuring the recognition they think they deserve for their achievements. They use PR as a form of damage control when things go against them. Again all of these are very legitimate and appropriate but are not doing what social and environmental policies can do. And, of course, all companies engage in marketing for obvious reasons, and of the trio of philanthropy, public relations, and marketing, marketing is probably the closest to what we are talking about. Yet it is different: there are goals that social and environmental policies can reach that are beyond any marketing campaign and vice versa.

How, then, can we best characterize social and environmental policies from the perspective of corporate strategy choices? These are a focused response to social and environmental issues arising directly from a company's operations. Articulating a social and environmental strategy requires that the company identify the social and environmental problems that are associated with its operations and then devise ways of reducing these. The policies have to fit a firm's business circumstances. This explains why when a tobacco company gives to the New York Metropolitan Opera, this is not what we are talking about. It is philanthropy and possibly PR, but it is not a response to the social or environmental issues raised by the operation of a tobacco company. Inventing harmless cigarettes would count as a responsible response to the tobacco company's circumstance, as would finding a cure for lung cancer and the other diseases associated with the use of cigarettes. I am not aware of tobacco companies investing in these activities. Corporate social and environmental policies are responsive to a firm's circumstances, and giving to the opera or other fine arts is not responsive to the circumstances of tobacco companies.

Cutting back on greenhouse gas emissions and developing renewable energy sources are responsive to the circumstances of an oil company, which is why these actions by BP do count as a corporate response to its environmental impacts. Making drugs available to those who are otherwise priced out of the market is responsive to the issues associated with producing pharmaceuticals, and also counts. So the programs run by pharmaceutical companies to make their drugs available at reduced prices to those on low incomes do count as socially responsible. Reducing the environmental impact of catching fish is a response to the issues raised by being a major vendor of fish, which is why Wal-Mart's decision to supply only fish from fisheries designated as sustainable by the Marine Stewardship Council again counts. Likewise, Wal-Mart's recent decision to improve the fuel efficiency of its vehicle fleet significantly is a response to the pollution generated by its very extensive shipping operations and counts as an environmentally responsive policy.

The strategic purpose of these responses, as I emphasized in earlier chapters, is to avoid conflicts with governments or civil society. It is to align to a greater degree than would otherwise be the case the interests of the corporation and the wider society. When corporate and social interests are aligned, the corporation can do well by doing good. But this only happens when interests are aligned. This matters because doing well by doing things that are not good is often not sustainable. It can bring punitive responses. Key here are the issues of external costs and of distributional equity. There are therefore two classes of corporate social and environmental responsibility, based, respectively, on internalizing the external costs associated with a company's operations and on modifying the way in which the company's activities would, if left to market forces, impinge on its poorest employees or customers. We have seen plenty of examples of both types. BP cutting greenhouse gas emissions, Wal-Mart purchasing sustainably harvested fish, Interface cutting back on waste in carpet production are all examples of the first type. As to examples of the second type, think of Starbucks sourcing coffee from fair trade dealers, or paying more than needed for coffee that meets its environmental and quality criteria. In the same vein, another example is Starbucks paying its "baristas" more than is typical in retail food operations. Of course, all the efforts made by Western companies to monitor wages and employment conditions in their Asian subcontractors are also in this camp: the aim there is to mitigate the inequality that would result from a completely free play of market forces.

The main payoff to this type of corporate responsibility comes because most conflicts between corporations and governments or civil society come from either external costs or distributional disagreements. We have seen clear evidence that capital markets appreciate the fact that external costs are a liability, something reflected in the way capital markets mark down the share prices of companies with bad pollution records. It is clear that in many cases, the imposition of external costs on others can lead to liabilities, so that in the long run it may be less costly to cut these external effects back right from the outset. It is also clear that being seen to cause or perpetuate poverty among employees or customers is socially unacceptable: the boycott of Nike as a result of sweatshop allegations is an illustration, as is the political pressure on pharmaceutical companies to provide access to essential medicines for people who clearly could not afford the retail prices. Corporate social and environmental responsibility, then, is a management tool for preempting conflicts of either sort—over environmental impacts or over the exploitation of the poor. On both issues, governments and civil society can take actions that can be costly to the corporation if the conflict is left to develop and fester.

This suggests that from a management perspective, this has to be seen to a significant degree as a risk-management tool, and this is indeed how several large corporations structure their social and environmental operations. Citigroup, for example, links these operations to risk-management overall. There are several dimensions to the risks being managed here. Most obvious are the financial risks of lawsuits or decreases in share prices. Additionally, there is risk to a company's brand, which in many cases is one of its principal assets, and which it may have spent many years and billions of dollars building up. There are also of course political risks associated with confrontations with governments or regulators, on whose good will a company will subsequently be dependent.

An interesting point to emerge from our review is that corporate social and environmental policies are not homogeneous. There are the two basic types that we have already noted, addressing external costs or distributional conflicts. There are also further ways of differentiating, between policies that are primarily directed at environmental issues, usually concerned with internalizing external costs, those that are related to labor issues (such as Starbucks' treatment of its employees, or for that matter Wal-Mart's), and those related to the community in which a firm operates. As an example here one could think of support for education or infrastructure in the community in which a company operates. Empirical evidence suggests that companies are rarely highly rated on all these fronts, and indeed if social and environmental policies are a response to specific business conditions we would not expect this. BP has a case for internalizing external costs and therefore might rank highly in the environmental area, but it has no reason to pay particular attention to distributional issues. Textile manufacturers, on the other hand, have every reason to be concerned about the wages and working conditions of those who make their products, but far less reason to worry about environmental issues.

Corporate Responsibility and Risk Management

It is easy to give a list of companies that have suffered from neglecting social and environmental issues, and to use this to illustrate the risks to which poor policies can expose a company. Many have already been mentioned.

Nike suffered a loss of revenues and market share in 1997 and 1998 at the height of the sweatshop allegations against it. It has recovered, but since then has made a real point of emphasizing its commitment to and concern about the treatment of workers in the factories to which it subcontracts. Shell suffered in northern Europe in 1995 when Greenpeace alleged, wrongly it subsequently emerged, that Shell's proposal for disposing the Brent Spar oil buoy was environmentally irresponsible. The extent of public concern over this issue was substantial and quite surprising. Heinz, another well-established blue chip, faced a consumer boycott as a result of revelations that many dolphins were killed by the fishing boats that provided it with tuna. Again, the response was widespread and strong, to the point that children in movies were shown criticizing their parents for serving tuna. Wal-Mart has faced persistent and active criticism because of allegations that it exploits its employees. As we have seen, this is a complex issue and it is far from clear that Wal-Mart's critics have right on their side, but this has nevertheless been a continuing thorn in the company's flesh and has led to restrictions on its ability to expand. Citigroup was the target of a very aggressive campaign because of its alleged funding of environmental despoliation in developing countries and was forced to respond. It had anyway been considering the issues and the eventual outcome was the Equator Principles, a step forward with respect to the financial industry's position on social and environmental matters in poor countries. Perhaps the most dramatic of all is the story of Monsanto, which was in effect sent into bankruptcy by unanticipated environmental opposition to its products. In its new incarnation, the company has grown fast, though there are still uncertainties about its sustainability.

All these examples illustrate the same point: failure to think about the social and environmental impacts of a firm's activities can lead to exposure to some very damaging risks, even for companies as large and well established as Nike and Citigroup.

Corporate Responsibility and Brand Value

Corporate responsibility can have a positive dimension too: that is to say, it need not be only a defensive move, protecting against damaging surprises.

Several companies have used their social and environmental strategies as a tool in building their brand images. Starbucks has featured in the analysis several times, and it has certainly pursued this strategy. In Starbucks' business, image is critical, and the company's widely publicized positions on shade-grown coffee and fair trade coffee, together with its relatively generous treatment of its in-store employees, have certainly contributed to building its brand and conveying the image of a place where its target customers would feel comfortable spending time. Patagonia has followed a similar route. Selling to an environmentally oriented outdoor crowd, it has emphasized its environmental credentials. It has sponsored environmental activists, and its latest move was to begin using only organic cotton in its products. Organic cotton was significantly more expensive than regular cotton when this move was made, but its production was vastly less damaging to the environment. Cotton is very vulnerable to pests, which means that cotton production by conventional agriculture involves the application of sufficient pesticide to be damaging to the local environment. Organic cotton farming of course avoids this damage, but produces lower yields. Patagonia advised its customers well in advance that it would replace regular by organic cotton in its products and raise prices to cover the increase in costs and found that there was no drop in sales when the new prices went into effect.

In a very different field, Toyota has burnished its green credentials to great advantage. The first to produce a hybrid gas–electric car, and with many small and fuel-efficient vehicles, Toyota has promoted itself as the green automaker par excellence, and it is the only major vehicle brand to have achieved almost cult status among those who are environmentally concerned, largely because of the success of its Prius hybrid and the risks it took in producing that long before it was obvious to other manufacturers that there would be a demand for such a vehicle.

In the apparel field, both Levis and American Apparel have established reputations for avoiding the sweatshop-related issues that have plagued many of their competitors. In the case of Levis, this was due to their careful strategy for monitoring conditions of the subcontractors right from the time that they first started to outsource to low-wage countries: they recognized from the start that there was potential for conflict with their own ethical standards without careful control of labor conditions of the subcontractors.

American Apparel followed a different path: their products are made entirely in the United States and they claim to pay "the highest wages in the garment industry." Here is their statement in detail:

> Clothing manufacturing is a very tough job, but we've always tried to do things differently. In the early days we talked about "sweatshop free"; now we talk less, however we continue to provide the same benefits (and more) to our workers.
>
> For us "sweatshop free" was never about criticizing other business models; it was about attempting something new. It comes down to this: not blindly outsourcing, but rather knowing the faces of our workers and providing them the opportunity to make a fair wage.
>
> The average sewer with experience at American Apparel is making about $25,000/yr (i.e. $12/hr, well over twice the federal minimum). This can be higher in some cases. We also offer parking, subsidized public transport, subsidized lunches, free onsite massages, a bike lending program, a program of paid days off, ESL classes and much more. Most importantly we guarantee job security and full-time employment; this is an anomaly in the garment industry, which has historically been dominated by seasonal work.
>
> We also continue to provide all of our employees and their families with company-subsidized, affordable health insurance ($8/week, $1–3/week for children). And we just made everyone's lives a little easier by opening an onsite medical clinic. This facility, which is the first of its kind, offers primary care services along with pediatric, urgent and preventative health care.
>
> As our company continues to grow, we will make further improvements to the work environment. In fact we're already devising some exciting new ways to make things better for our workers, so stay tuned.[1]

Clearly, to be successful they have to produce clothes that people want, and their social strategy will not ensure this, but their position on looking after workers has created a buzz about the company that has earned them huge press exposure and a great deal of good will in some consumer segments. So if their clothes have potential, their treatment of their employees may help them realize it.

The idea that corporate responsibility can contribute to brand image is supported by some statistical studies by my colleagues Ray Fisman and Vinay Nair and me. We tried to understand the characteristics of companies that take social responsibilities seriously, at least in the sense of having high ratings from the agencies like Innovest and KLD. A striking finding was that companies that rate highly are typically companies that spend heavily on advertising: this suggests that social responsibility matters to businesses to which image matters. Another finding of ours was that social responsibility has most impact on profitability for companies for which advertising expenditures are large, so that they appear to gain most from responsible behavior.

Corporate Responsibility is Often Collective

An interesting point to emerge from a number of the cases we have reviewed is that action on social or environmental issues is often best taken by a group of firms all in the same business and facing the same problem. The two notable examples that follow this format are the Equator Principles agreement and the Fair Labor Association. Recall that the Equator Principles were agreed initially by a small group of banks prominent in the area of international project finance, and that others subsequently joined the group, and still more follow the group's principles even though they have not formally joined. The Fair Labor Association also emerged as an agreement between firms, in this case in the textile and footwear business. There are good strategic reasons why firms may want to move collectively on CSR issues, although this also raises some problems.

The reason for wanting to move collectively is to avoid the loss of competitive position that might come with being the first and only mover. Take the Equator Principles case: if one bank alone had announced that it was going to implement these principles, there would have been a real risk that borrowers who were not inclined to meet the standards set in the Equator Principles would just have moved to competitors. The first mover would have lost business and the problem of adverse environmental impacts would not have been solved. In short, we would have had a truly negative outcome:

a loss for the bank trying to do good and no social gains. By ensuring that the Equator Principles were adopted by most of the major players in the project finance business, the banks avoided both problems. Exactly the same argument applies to the Fair Labor Association: if one firm had moved alone, it would have faced higher costs than all of its competitors and could just have lost market share to them. Again a loss for the firm trying to solve the problem, with the underlying problem unsolved.

The downside to acting collectively is that it can look like action in restraint of competition and so appear to violate laws intended to promote competition. It does have some of the characteristics of cartel action. In the Equator Principles case, this risk was avoided because the banks did not all sign an agreement to adopt the principles: instead each bank individually chose to make them a part of its own internal operating procedures. Technically, there was no agreement between the banks. Actually there is little doubt that if this procedure were followed to set interest rates or some other business terms, it would be seen as a violation of antitrust laws and would lead to prompt investigation by the competition authorities. It appears that the authorities cut the banks some slack because of their obviously good intentions in this case.

How Do Social and Environmental Strategies Work?

First and foremost, good social and environmental policies reduce conflicts and the liabilities, legal and otherwise, that arise from them. Pollution, as we have seen several times, is a liability or at least a potential liability, and indeed capital markets treat it as such. Environmental damage can lead, and in the past often has led, to lawsuits with massive damages. It can also lead to regulatory intervention that can be costly to the company. So reducing environmental damage can avoid lawsuits, avoid regulatory actions, and avoid consumer boycotts. All of this makes good business sense. A key to success here is to recognize what a company's negative environmental impacts are and investigate how to minimize these. As we have emphasized, social and environmental policies should be a response to the situation of the corporation and not a generic form of public relations or of philanthropy.

It is not just environmental damages that can lead to a range of liabilities that are better avoided: the same goes for a range of actions that are socially unacceptable. Low wages, poor working conditions, abuse of employees, and abuse of customers all come into this category. Nike, GAP, and WalMart all illustrate this point: all have been accused—rightly or wrongly—of socially unacceptable actions and have seen a costly response from consumers or from civil society. Good social and environmental policies avoid these situations.

Do Social and Environmental Policies Work?

Finally, let us review the evidence that appropriate social and environmental policies do indeed have the beneficial effects that the last section summarizes. There is a growing amount of evidence and taken as a whole it is compelling.

One noteworthy fact is that every fall U.S. Environmental Protection Agency announces Toxics Release Inventory (TRI) data and that the shares in companies featuring prominently in the TRI drop immediately. The bottom line here—pollution hurts your share price. It raises the cost of capital. This was well illustrated by the discussion in Chapter 3 of "sin stocks"—stocks in companies providing alcohol, tobacco, and gambling— which are undervalued relative to the rest of the stock market and face a higher cost of equity capital. In addition, a wide range of studies show that superior environmental performance is correlated with a stock-market valuation premium. These studies also suggest that environmental performance relative to peers is what affects valuations. It is not enough to have a good environmental performance: you have to be better than your competitors. And the more competition a company faces, the more its social and environmental performance matters to its financial performance. As we noted earlier in this chapter, the beneficial effects on financial performance are strongest for companies that advertise heavily and for which image is therefore presumably important.

Consumers' willingness to pay extra for products from companies that have a good social and environmental profile gives another angle on how responsible behavior can affect profits. There are certainly cases in which some consumers will pay more for goods with unimpeachable social or environmental credentials. Starbucks' experience with fair trade and shade-grown coffee illustrates this, as does Patagonia's experience in converting from regular to organic cotton. The success of cause-related marketing also speaks to this point. Consumers have often proven willing to purchase preferentially goods that generate donations to a cause they value, as the discussion of Whirlpool's experience in Chapter 2 illustrates. There are many other cases of successful cause-related marketing, and they all make the same point: knowing that buying a product will aid a good cause will affect consumers' buying decisions, particularly the decisions of those sympathetic to the cause. There is also another side to this: even when consumers are not willing to pay more for a good that has good social or environmental credentials, it may still be the case that if they have a choice of two similar products at similar prices, one with good credentials and one without, they will choose the former. In other words, even if having good social or environmental credentials will not earn a price premium, not having them may lose a sale to a competitor with good credentials. This is consistent with the Fisman-Heal-Nair finding that social and environmental policies matter more in competitive markets.

Summary

Social and environmental policies are an important aspect of how a company presents itself to the world. They can affect how consumers react to its products and how it is valued by the stock market. They can be an important part of a brand's image, and so matter more in businesses where image is important. There are many examples of companies whose images have been enhanced by their social or environmental stands, just as there are examples where the opposite has happened.

But to work in this way, social and environmental policies must be related to the specific situation of the company's business, of the potentials for conflict that this situation contains. They must address these potential conflicts. In this sense, they are not marketing, not public relations, and not corporate philanthropy. They are a focused response to the way in which a company's activities are embedded in the wider economy and polity, and an attempt to respond to issues raised by this embedding.

13

Conclusions

Doing Well by Doing Good?

We saw in Chapter 1 that divergences between corporate and social interests can occur naturally when external costs are associated with a firm's activities, as in the case of pollution or greenhouse gas emission, or when the outcome of the activity is controversial because of its distributional implications, the classic example here being the use of low-wage labor in poor countries. In these cases, what is most profitable is not always most desirable from a social perspective. Companies will want to use polluting activities more than can be justified from a social perspective, or to pay wages that in spite of seeming unfair suffice to attract all the labor they need.

Subsequent chapters revealed that there are ways in which the conflicts between profits and social well-being can be reconciled. Lawsuits based on the damages generated by externalized costs can make it smart for a company to reduce pollution even when there is no regulation requiring this. As we noted in Chapter 2, the stock markets react to information about a company's pollution record and tend to mark down the shares of polluters. There is a capital market penalty for the most hardened of sin stocks, as we also remarked in Chapter 3. Some analysts have even proposed that companies record pollution as a contingent liability on their balance statements, precisely because it can become a source of financial liabilities to the company through legal actions.

There are other factors that tend to reduce the gap between what is good for the corporation and what is in the common good. Actions by consumer groups or nongovernmental organizations, often acting together, can change the incentives facing the corporation. Boycotts and campaigns aimed at damaging a company's reputation pose a real threat to companies that are in the public eye or under regulatory scrutiny. They have done harm to several, and these examples have made many others sufficiently concerned to take the possibility seriously.

To summarize, for a significant part of the corporate world, perhaps the most visible part, powerful forces, generated by civil society, act to align corporate and social interests. Although it may not be true for such companies that "what's good for General Motors is good for America," there is certainly a lot of overlap.

Is there a set of conclusions that we can take away from this, a set of ideas about when the corporate world can be a trusted partner for society as a whole and when it cannot? Or a set of ideas about how policymakers or corporate leaders can react to the issues raised by our discussions? In assessing this, it is important to understand the limitations to the idea that corporations do well by doing good and to understand that relying on non-market institutions to bring social and corporate goals into alignment is not a panacea. There are, sadly, firms that appear to do well by doing harm to society.

Many firms have found it in their interest to be environmentally or socially more benign than is legally mandated. We have just rehearsed the persuasive reasons why they should do this, stemming from society's reaction to the externalization of costs or to what is seen as unfair treatment of the underprivileged. Yet many firms do not find it in their interests to behave well: they do well financially while doing harm from a social perspective. We talked in Chapter 3 about sin stocks, the stocks of companies making alcohol or tobacco or organizing gambling. These companies illustrate the point: they do not find it profitable to minimize their negative social impacts, in spite of the fact that these provoke a clear reaction from capital markets and indeed more generally from the legal and political systems. How is this consistent with the paradigm we have set out? How can the factors that make Starbucks worry about the environmental impact of coffee growing, or Toyota worry about the environmental impact of automobile use, also lead tobacco companies to promote cigarettes to the young? Or lead gun makers to lobby for fewer controls on gun ownership? Or lead timber companies to log virgin rainforest, often illegally?[1]

There are several components to an answer. The incentives for good behavior discussed in Chapters 2 and 3 work partly through the behavior of consumers and NGOs, as in the case of Nike and sweatshops or Citibank and the Equator Principles. Consumers, alone or organized by NGOs, put pressure on Nike and on Citibank to change their ways. The incentives for good behavior also operate in part through capital markets and the socially responsible investment movement. Shareholders put pressure on executives to change behavior. But there is a limitation: some companies are immune to these forces and are outside the range of mechanisms we referred to above. They may not sell to consumers, and so are not vulnerable to consumer boycotts or for other reasons operate in markets where they are not subject to NGO pressure. Some companies not yet there could be brought within the reach of these mechanisms. A company may not sell to the public, but it probably sells to others who sell to the public, or to the public sector. If its behavior is unacceptable, civil society can pressure its customers not to deal with it. To some degree, this already happens, with consumer-product companies being held responsible for labor conditions and environmental impacts all along their supply chains, as in the case of firms like Nike being held responsible for conditions of their suppliers. The limitation here is that if a consumer-oriented company is only one of many clients of a misbehaving manufacturer of intermediate goods, then its leverage over that manufacturer is probably limited. Companies may also escape the pressures to behave well because they may be privately owned, increasingly common with the growth of private equity groups, or they may be a part of a large conglomerate, and so in either case not susceptible to pressure from capital markets.

There are also companies that do sell to consumers, but for reasons specific to their products, the possibilities of boycotts and of damage to their reputations are irrelevant. Tobacco is a good illustration of such a case: because their product is addictive, consumers cannot boycott tobacco companies. Many would surely love to, by giving up smoking, but it is close to a physiological impossibility for them to do so. If a corporation's consumers are addicted to and dependent upon its product, it doesn't have to worry about repeat purchases, which are more or less guaranteed. It's the consumers who have to worry about repeat purchases!

The self-interested arguments for responsible corporate behavior are weakened when the corporation does not sell to consumers, or is private and not dependent on the capital market, or is not subject to the pressures of NGOs. In such cases, firms may generate significant external costs, but short of direct government regulation there are no mechanisms through which these can be brought back to the firm, no mechanisms via which it can be held responsible for them.

There is another category: firms for which social irresponsibility is of the essence of their product. Without irresponsibility, they would have no product. Tobacco companies are again probably the most obvious examples of companies that are profitable yet socially harmful and illustrate well some of these points. The only way to reduce the social harm from smoking is to reduce the extent of smoking, which of course would reduce the profits of tobacco companies. There is a direct conflict here between what is profitable and what is good for society: profitability has to be at the expense of responsibility. But as noted above, the tobacco companies will never be boycotted by their customers, because the customers are addicted, quite literally, to their products. The obvious response of consumers to a harmful product is ruled out. Tobacco companies have of course been punished by governments: their products generally carry high retail taxes, and in the United States the companies have been subject to many law suits brought by various state governments seeking compensation for the costs of treating victims of smoking. As we noted in the discussion of "sin stocks" in Chapter 3, tobacco companies also pay a price for their antisocial activities in terms of their stock-market valuations. But because of the strength of their basic economic position, the tobacco companies nonetheless continue to be profitable. Because of its addictive nature, demand for their product is almost totally insensitive to price, allowing them to set highly profitable prices. In the developing world, tobacco companies face no restrictions on their activities and are able to promote smoking aggressively to the youth of the third world as a desirable and sophisticated lifestyle. The payoff here is potentially vast: teenagers who take up smoking are likely to remain smokers until their (probably early) deaths. The bottom line here is that for a variety of reasons, tobacco companies are immune to the pressures that society can exercise in response to antisocial behavior.

Gun companies in the United States provide another example of this immunity, although for different reasons. Handguns are extensively used as accessories to crimes, and there is a clear social interest in restricting their availability. This would conflict with the profitability of their manufacturers and sellers. As with tobacco, there is a direct and unavoidable conflict between profits and principles. In this case, the immunity from sanctions comes again in part because the buyers of handguns are not likely to boycott their makers or sellers—it is the nonpurchasers who feel threatened by the abundance of handguns. An additional part of the immunity comes from the political power of the gun lobby.

International Dimensions

Leaving the United States gives us a wide range of companies that can do well and do harm at the same time. Rimbunan Hijau is a Malaysian timber company operating in many forested developing countries. It is widely accused of illegal logging, obtaining logging permits by bribery, and violating the human rights of its employees in logging camps.[2] I have worked extensively with the government of Papua New Guinea, the site of much of Rimbunan Hijau's alleged illegal logging and bribery and have little doubt that there is some merit in the allegations against the company. Citibank, one of the company's bankers, was sufficiently concerned about the allegations against it that in 2005 it required Rimbunan Hijau to comply with the requirements similar to the Equator Principles,[3] then recently adopted by Citibank. There is no news on the results of this requirement. There is no doubt that if Rimbunan Hijau were based in the United States or Europe, they would be subject to boycotts, law suits, and a range of other actions by NGOs. But as a Malaysian company operating mainly in third-world countries, they are immune to these sanctions. They don't sell directly to European or U.S. consumers, and although they have a banking relationship with Citibank, they do not depend on this: there are banks in Malaysia and China that will provide finance without the safeguard of standards such as the Equator Principles.

The same issues appear very clearly in the case of companies doing business with the Government of Sudan, which according to many is sponsoring or at least permitting genocide in the Darfur region. The United States has a complete trade embargo on Sudan,[4] many European countries have partial embargos, and most socially responsible investment groups avoid the shares of companies doing business with the Sudanese government. The Sudanese government's financial support comes from the country's oil reserves, which are being developed by a group of Asian oil companies, largely state owned or at least state controlled. Prominent among these are CNPC (the Chinese National Petroleum Corporation), Petronas (the Malaysian national oil company, wholly owned by the Malaysian government), Oil and Natural Gas Corporation (ONGC, a publicly trade Indian oil company) and TAFTNET, a Russian oil company. All these companies are immune to the pressures that we have discussed in earlier chapters. They sell in markets where NGOs are banned (China, Russia, and Malaysia) or where there are no concerns about social or environmental issues in foreign countries, and they do not depend on Western capital markets for access to finance.

There is one informative exception to this lack of dependence on Western capital: in April 1999, CNPC announced plans to raise $10 billion in share capital on the New York Stock Exchange. Human rights groups and others objected to this initial public offering, contending that the deal would be tantamount to U.S. support for genocide in Sudan. In response, CNPC restructured the transaction. It created a new subsidiary, PetroChina, which would operate only inside China, to be owned 90 percent by CNPC and 10 percent by private investors. On April 6, 2000, $2.9 billion of shares in PetroChina were sold on the New York Stock Exchange to private investors. At that time, CNPC's investment bankers, Goldman Sachs, asserted to investors that none of the money raised in the IPO would be used to fund CNPC's projects in Sudan.[5] What this reveals is that in a capital-intensive field such as oil exploration and development, access to Western capital markets may be essential even for companies operating in China, with its vast internal pools of savings and extensive banking system. This will give socially responsible investors some leverage over such companies, albeit limited.

There is a clear bottom line here: when the social interest conflicts with the profit motive, the incentives for behaving well are not all-powerful. They are at their best with companies that are in the public eye, mainly though not exclusively because they sell to the public, and in countries where consumers are aware of social and environmental issues and have the right and the ability to form groups to express their concerns. In such cases, the incentives to behave well are powerful, as social and environmental behavior can affect a brand's image and its success in the market.

Companies that are in the public eye because they sell to the public are also typically subject to pressures from capital markets, which can add to the incentives for environmentally or socially benign behavior. But there are companies that are immune to all these pressures, and for these companies there is absolutely no incentive to behave responsibly if this conflicts with profitability.

Another fundamental limitation stems from the lack of nongovernmental organizations in some major economies, such as China, Russia, and several other third-world countries. It is hard, if not impossible, to put pressure on Russian or Chinese companies to do less social or environmental harm. Only the development of free speech in those countries, coupled with an increase in awareness of social and environmental issues, will lead to changes.

In situations where corporate and social interests are not naturally aligned and civil society cannot realign the corporate interests to coincide with the social, the only other measure available is government regulation. By taxing activities whose social costs exceed their private, governments can bring about this realignment. This is the basic stuff of any textbook on economic policy. There are, however, real limitations here too. Take the case of the Equator Principles, one we have discussed often. Could action by the U.S. government have achieved the same outcome as the Equator Principles, if the Equator Banks had not put these in place? Probably they could not. The main reason is that the Equator Principles concern the actions of U.S. and European banks in third-world countries. A government such as that of the United States rarely legislates about the behavior of its corporations in other countries. The international convention is that behavior in, for example, Nigeria should be governed by Nigerian laws, not American laws. There is an exception to this, the U.S. Foreign Corrupt Practices Act passed in 1977 and amended in 1998 to implement the antibribery conventions of the Organization for Economic Cooperation and Development, "the FCPA prohibits corrupt payments to foreign officials for the purpose of obtaining or keeping business."[6] This then is an attempt by the U.S. government to regulate how U.S. companies behave in foreign markets. It is conceivable that similar legislation could be passed to regulate environmental behavior outside the United States. One could imagine, for example, the U.S. government requiring that U.S. corporations meet U.S. environmental standards any where in the world. But as soon as you think of this, you begin to see the difficulties. How can the U.S. government enforce environmental legislation in Azerbaijan or Nigeria? At home, it enforces it primarily through the Environmental Protection Agency, which of course has no jurisdiction outside of the United States. And at best the U.S. government could regulate the behavior of U.S. corporations in the third world, but never that of German or French companies. Yet the Equator Principles, as a voluntary code agreed by the banks, has a chance of doing all of these things.

In the field of social rather than environmental impacts, matters are even more complex. Could the U.S. government instruct a U.S. bank not to provide funds for a Chinese dam whose construction involves displacing villagers without compensation? The Chinese government could legitimately complain that this is interference in its own domestic affairs. We may not approve of their internal policies, but we have no standing to complain about and alter these, except perhaps in extreme cases involving clear violations of human rights.

This example highlights another aspect of the international dimension of our problem. A lot of the difficulties we are facing arise from inadequacies in the performance of governments in poor countries. Implementing effective social and environmental policies requires substantial legal and bureaucratic infrastructure. You need agencies like the U.S. Environmental Protection Agency (EPA) or the U.S. Occupational Safety and Health Administration (OSHA), together with courts in which they can prosecute violators of the protective legislation. These are all expensive and demand abundant high-level professional expertise. In most poor counties, there are no equivalents, or the equivalents when they exist are grossly underfunded and lack the necessary expertise. A consequence is that a Western company operating in such a country faces little or no local regulation on social or environmental matters. In effect it has to regulate itself. It has to do some of the government's job. This is true even in a relatively prosperous country like China. The State Environmental Protection Agency exists but has very limited powers and cannot enforce the limited regulations that exist. Minimum wage legislation also exists, but again is not enforced, and the minimum wages indicated under this legislation would anyway not satisfy most Western NGOs concerned about the welfare of workers at Chinese subcontractors.

244 WHEN PRINCIPLES PAY

In the absence of regulations, or in a context where they exist and are not enforced, or are just too lax to do their intended job, a corporation has to decide what standards it should adopt. Should it observe local standards, or use higher ones, perhaps those current in is home country? These are complex issues that a corporation operating in industrial countries does not normally need to address. It seems that there are few general answers. A number of prominent U.S. companies have chosen to adopt U.S. environmental standards wherever in the world they operate. Others have set their own standards at levels higher than those required in the United States. And yet others choose to take advantage of relatively lax local standards in developing countries. We noted in Chapter 2 that, according to a study by Dowell, Hart, and Yeung, the companies with the highest standards—the second category—have the highest stock-market valuations, whereas those with the lowest standards have the lowest valuations.

It is interesting that precisely this issue of which standards a U.S. company should choose in a third-world country is now the central issue in a lawsuit brought against the U.S. oil company ChevronTexaco in Ecuador. The lawsuit is complex and not all of the details are relevant, but at the core of one part of it is the allegation that a subsidiary of Texaco, operating in conjunction with the government of Ecuador, endangered the lives of people in the Amazonian forests where it was extracting oil by using water remediation technologies that were legal at the time in Ecuador, but had been illegal in the United States for almost half a century. The central point here is that producing oil in the conditions of Amazonia almost inevitably leads to the production of polluted waste water, and at issue is how this was disposed of and whether Texaco made a serious effort to clean it before disposing of it. Texaco's claim is that it used techniques that were legal at the time in Ecuador and were approved by the government. Representatives of people who were harmed by the polluted water claim that Texaco had a responsibility to use the best available techniques and argue that the fact that the methods used were outlawed in the United States shows that they were an inappropriate choice. This seems to be a clear example of a situation where using U.S. standards even when they were not legally required would have saved a lot of ill will and damage to the company's reputation, whatever the eventual outcome of the trial.

Although it may well make sense to use environmental standards that are higher than those mandated by the local laws, and indeed to use home-country standards, this argument does not carry over to wages. If a U.S.-based company paid U.S. wages in Southeast Asia, then it would negate the entire reason for being there in the first place, namely to benefit from labor costs that are lower than those in the United States. Without a significant wage differential, the company would be better off producing near its final markets in the United States and Europe.

Conclusions

Adam Smith's invisible hand was a powerful and prescient concept, but as a description of how today's economy works it has shortcomings. Two that are central to this book are the failure to wrestle with external effects, with differences between private and social costs, and its neutrality with respect to the distribution of income and wealth. The market does not care if some people are very poor and others very rich: society in general does. These shortcomings have their images in two common problems—pollution that damages the environment and wage differentials between the rich and poor that are truly dramatic.

Karl Marx famously commented that capitalism contains the seeds of its own destruction. To the contrary, these problems of the capitalist system have in part generated their own solutions. Capital-market activism, legal systems, and political activism, often going hand in hand, have in many cases found a way of reconciling social and corporate interests. Not fully and not always, but they seem to have indicated a direction in which our social and economic systems should evolve if we want them to deal with these issues. If people worry about pollution, climate change, and inequality and are willing to let their purchasing decisions be guided to some degree by their concerns—to put their money where their mouths are, to put it crudely—then they can generate incentives to which the corporate world will respond. In the process, corporations will make the world a better place.

1. Introduction

1. David P. Baron, *Business and Its Environment,* 5th ed. (Upper Saddle River, NJ: Prentice Hall, 2005), 666.

2. Milton Friedman, "The Social Responsibility of Business Is to Increase its Profits," *The New York Times,* September 13, 1970.

3. There are actually some more conditions that have to be met for the invisible hand to be exemplary—See Chapter 2 of my book *Nature and the Marketplace* (Washington, D.C.: Island Press, 2000).

4. That is to say, people value and are willing to pay for the existence of forests even if they personally make no use of them. Existence value is a major category of value for threatened species and for many wild places.

5. Forest Reinhardt, "Global Climate Change and BP Amoco," *Harvard Business School Cases,* April 7, 2000.

6. Geoffrey Heal, "Environmental Disaster—Not All Bad News," *Financial Times,* October 30, 2000.

7. The opportunity cost of an activity is a source of revenue foregone by carrying out that activity. It is not a cash cost—there is no bill associated with it. A commonly encountered opportunity cost is that associated with the internal use of a company's earnings, which could be invested outside the company to earn a return. The external return is the opportunity cost of the internal use of the funds.

8. Richard H. K. Vietor, Forest Reinhardt, and Peggy Duxburym, "StarKist (A)," *Harvard Business School Cases,* April 22, 1994.

9. For more details, see J. Gary Taylor and Patricia J. Scharlin, *Smart Alliance: How a Global Corporation and Environmental Activists Transformed a Tarnished Brand* (New Haven, CT: Yale University Press, 2004).

10. For background on Monsanto, see Ulrich Steger et al., "Monsanto's Genetically Modified Organisms: The Battle for Hearts and Shopping Aisles," *Harvard Business School Cases,* January 1, 2001; Michael D. Watkins and Ann Leamon, "Robert Shapiro and Monsanto," *Harvard Business School Cases,* April 10, 2001. The investment advisory group Innovest has an interesting analyst's

report on Monsanto: "Monsanto & Genetic Engineering: Risks for Investors," Innovest, http://www.innovestgroup.com/pdfs/2005-01-01_Monsanto_GeneticEngineering.pdf (accessed November 22, 2007).

11. See Joan Magretta, "Growth Through Global Sustainability: An Interview with Monsanto's CEO Robert B. Shapiro," in *Harvard Business Review on Business and the Environment,* ed. Amory Lovins and L. Hunter Lovins (Harvard Business Review Press Book, 2002).

12. See Dale Russakoff, "Human Toll of a Pension Default," *The Washington Post,* June 13, 2005, A01, http://www.washingtonpost.com/wp-dyn/content/article/2005/06/12/AR2005061201367.html (accessed November 22, 2007).

13. See http://www.lapres.net/dodge.html (accessed November 22, 2007).

14. See Einar R. Elahuge, "Corporate Managers' Operational Discretion to Sacrifice Corporate Profits in the Public Interest," in *Environmental Protection and the Social Responsibility of Firms: Perspectives from Law, Economics, and Business,* ed. Bruce L. Hay et al. (Washington, DC: RFF Press, 2005), 30.

15. Ibid.

16. Quoted in Elahuge, "Corporate Managers' Operational Discretion to Sacrifice Corporate Profits in the Public Interest," 24.

17. Sumantra Ghoshal, "Bad Management Theories Are Destroying Good Management Practices," *Academy of Management Learning & Education* 4, no. 1 (2005): 75–91.

2. Social, Environmental, and Financial Performance

1. Over the last few years, there has been a glut of coffee and world market prices have fallen, reducing the living standards of coffee farmers in poor countries. Fair Trade seeks to ensure that a larger-than-normal fraction of the sale price of the coffee beans goes to the farmers.

2. For details, see James E. Austin and Cate Reavis, "Starbucks and Conservation International," *Harvard Business School Cases,* October 2, 2002.

3. Freshfields Bruckhaus Deringer, "Corporate Social Responsibility," April 2004, http://www.freshfields.com/practice/disputeresolution/publications/pdfs/ 8221.pdf (accessed November 29, 2007).

4. See Richard H. K. Vietor, Forest Reinhardt, and Jackie P. Roberts, "Note on Contingent Environmental Liabilities," *Harvard Business School Cases,* February 11, 1994.

5. Julie Hudson, "Why Try to Quantify the Unquantifiable?" UBS Investment Research—Q-Series®: Corporate Social Responsibilities, April 11, 2005, http://www.gppi.net/fileadmin/gppi/UBS_Why_try_to_quantify_report_4-2005.pdf (accessed November 29, 2007).

6. For details, see Geoffrey Heal, "Environmental Disaster—Not All Bad News," *Financial Times,* October 30, 2000.

7. There is evidence that the president of Merck and Co. was given credit for Merck's sterling reputation as a responsible company (see note 9) at recent U.S. Congressional hearings on the withdrawal of Vioxx.

8. See David B. Montgomery and Catherine A. Ramus, "Corporate Social Responsibility Reputation Effects on MBA Job Choice" (working paper, Stanford Graduate School of Business, May 2003), http://papers.ssrn.com/sol3/papers.cfm?abstract_id=412124 (accessed November 29, 2007).

9. See The Business Enterprise Trust, "Merck & Co., Inc A, B, C and D," 1991, Case 9-99-021. This discussion also draws on personal communications with Dr. Vagelos and remarks made by him at Columbia Business School on August 25, 2004. See also P. Roy Vagelos and Louis Galambos, *Medicine, Science, and Merck* (New York: Cambridge University Press, 2004).

10. "Doing Well by Doing Good," *The Economist,* December 12, 2002.

11. He used share prices rather than the market-to-book ratio, but as the book value of the companies studied would not have changed in the few days around the release of the TRI data, the denominator of this ratio would not have changed while the numerator is proportional to share price.

12. See Susmita Dasgupta, Benoit Laplante, and Nlandu Mamingi, "Pollution and Capital Markets in Developing Countries," *Journal of Environmental Economics and Management* 42, no. 3 (2001): 310–35.

13. See Susmita Dasgupta et al., "Disclosure of Environmental Violations and the Stock Market in the Republic of Korea" (working paper 3344, World Bank Policy Research, June 2004).

14. Glen Dowell, Stuart Hart, and Bernard Yeung, "Do Corporate Global Environmental Standards Create or Destroy Market Value?" *Management Science* 46, no. 8 (August 2000): 1059–74.

15. Middle-income developing countries are a category defined by the World Bank and consist of those countries with gross national income (GNI) per capita between $906 and $11,115.

16. Interestingly, this is exactly how financial analysts assessed the appropriateness of the drop in Merck's share price after the withdrawal of Vioxx—they calculated the loss of profits and then also the legal liability to which Merck was exposed because of the costs possibly imposed on the users of its product Vioxx.

17. Andrew A. King and Michael J. Lenox, "Does It Really Pay to Be Green? An Empirical Study of Firm Environmental and Financial Performance," *Journal of Industrial Ecology* 5, no. 1 (2001): 105–116, http://www.greeneconomics.net/DoesItPayToBeGreen.pdf (accessed November 29, 2007).

18. They add together the emissions of different chemicals, weighted by an index of how harmful they are.

19. There are many other influential studies on this topic. See Shameek Konar and Mark A. Cohen, "Does the Market Value Environmental Performance?" *The Review of Economics and Statistics* 83, no. 2 (May 2001): 281–89.

20. Gary Silverman, "Bono Sees Red as Means to Fight AIDS in Africa," *Financial Times,* January 26, 2006, p. 1.

21. For details, see Ramon Casadesus-Masanell et al., "Households' Willingness to Pay for Public Goods: Evidence from Patagonia's Introduction of Organic Cotton Sportswear" (working paper, Harvard Business School, presented at the Allied Social Science Associations Annual Meetings, January 2005); Forest Reinhardt, Ramon Casadesus-Masanell, and Debbie Freier, "Patagonia," *Harvard Business School Cases,* March 18, 2003.

3. Socially Responsible Investment

1. See the Calvert Web site (http://www.calvert.com/).

2. There are issues related to the use of poisonous chemicals in chip-making and to the disposal of unused electronic equipment, but these are so far small relative to the environmental impacts of many other industries.

3. Christopher Geczy, Robert F. Stambaugh, and David Levin, "Investing in Socially Responsible Mutual Funds," Social Science Research Network, October 2005, http://ssrn.com/abstract=416380 (accessed December 4, 2007).

4. "Corporate Storytelling," *The Economist,* November 4, 2004.

5. www.innovestgroup.com.

6. Rob Bauer, Kees C. G. Koedijk, and Rogér Otten, "International Evidence on Ethical Mutual Fund Performance and Investment Style" (working paper, Maastricht University and Erasmus University Rotterdam, November 2002), http://www. socialinvest.org/pdf/research/Moskowitz/2002%20Winning%20Paper%20-%20Moskowitz.pdf (accessed December 4, 2007).

7. Harrison G. Hong and Marcin T. Kacperczyk, "The Price of Sin: The Effects of Social Norms on Markets" (working paper, Sauder School of Business, The University of British Columbia, Vancouver, British Columbia, March 15, 2006), http://ssrn.com/abstract=766465 (accessed December 4, 2007).

8. See Bernard S. Black, "Shareholder Activism and Corporate Governance in the United States," in *The New Palgrave Dictionary of Economics and the Law,* vol. 3, ed. Peter Newman (New York: Palgrave Macmillan, 1998), 459–65; Stuart Gillan and Laura T. Starks, "A Survey of Shareholder Activism: Motivation and Empirical Evidence," *Contemporary Finance Digest* 2, no. 3 (Autumn 1998): 10–34.

9. ISS recently purchased IRRC.

10. Claudia Cattaneo, "Lingering 'Sudan Effect' Likely to Tarnish Talisman," *Financial Post, Calgary,* February 24, 2000.

11. Talisman Energy, "Talisman to Sell Sudan Assets for C1.2 Billion," *News Releases*, October 30, 2002, http://www2.ccnmatthews.com/scripts/ccn-release.pl?/2002/10/30/1030131n.html?cp=tlm (accessed October 2005).

12. EarthRights International, "Defending the Alien Tort Claims Act," September 15, 2004, http://www.earthrights.org/site_blurbs/help_defend_atca.html (accessed October 2005).

13. Ibid.

14. Talisman Energy, "Talisman Corporate Social Responsibility Report 2004," http://www.talisman-energy.com/responsibility/cr_report/?disclaimer=1 (accessed October 2005).

4. Financial Institutions and Social and Environmental Performance

1. For a list, see http://www.equator-principles.com/.

2. Paul West, "Banking on the Environment: A Model Campaign Against Financing Eco-Destruction," *Peacework*, April 2004, http://www.peaceworkmagazine.org/pwork/0404/040416.htm (accessed December 4, 2007).

3. ABN AMRO, Barclays, BNP Paribas, Citigroup, Deutsche Bank, Royal Bank of Scotland, Sumitomo Mitsui Banking Corp., and WestLB.

4. The banks attending were ABN AMRO, ANZ Bank, Bank of Scotland, Barclays, BNP Paribas, Citigroup, Credit Agricole Indosuez, Credit Lyonnais, HypoVereinsbank, ING Bank, KBC Bank, Mizuho Corporate Bank, NORD/LB, Rabobank, Royal Bank of Scotland, and WestLB.

5. The bankers were Chris Beale, Pam Flaherty (senior vice president, head of Citigroup's Environmental and Social Policy Review Committee), Madeleine Jacobs (senior vice president, head of Reputation Risk Management at ABN AMRO), and Andre Abadie (vice president, head of Environmental and Social Risk Management at ABN AMRO). The NGOs included Conservation International, Environmental Defense, Friends of the Earth, World Wildlife Fund, and World Resources Institute.

6. On April 8, 2003, the banks met with European-based NGOs to review the current draft of the EP. The bankers attending included, from ABN, Madeleine Jacobs, Paul Mudde (senior vice president, head of Reputation Management and Sustainable Development) and Andrew Abadie; from Citigroup, Elliston and Flaherty; from Barclays, Chris Bray; and from WestLB, Hans Hoeveler and two members of a staff unit representing the WestLB Board, Frank Borstelman and Martina Neuber. Glen Armstrong from IFC also attended. The NGOs included World Wildlife Federation UK, Aid Environment, Milieu Defensie (Friends of the Earth) of France, Italian Campaign for World Bank Reform, and Urgewald of Germany.

7. This criticism, however, is limited to projects reliant on IFC funding; clearly, the Equator Principles have far wider application and are not confined to IFC-funded projects.

8. A Rumanian gold deal was turned down by ICF and by some non-EP banks.

9. ERM Report, Credit Risk Management, "Banking Industry Integrating Environmental and Social Issues: How Much and How Fast?" 2004, quoted in Freshfields Bruckhaus Deringer, "Banking on Responsibility," http://www.freshfields.com/practice/environment/publications/pdfs/12057.pdf (accessed December 30, 2007).

10. FSC Principles cover the impacts on affected societies, such as land title and land use rights; the rights of indigenous people; community relations and workers' rights; and economic benefits from forestland use.

11. Bank of America reaffirmed its commitment in April 2004 to the Ceres Principles, a ten-point code of corporate environmental conduct.

12. Reviewed by Foley Hoag LLP (www.foleyhoag.com).

13. See, by way of comparison, Tangguh Independent Advisory Panel Reports of 2002, 2003, and 2005 and *Insight Investment Investor Responsibility Bulletin,* Spring 2004. Panel reports at http://www.bp.com/liveassets/bp_internet/ globalbp/STAGING/global_assets/downloads/I/Indonesia_Tangguh_ Independent_Advisory_Panel_BP_response_2002.pdf.

14. "Caspian Development Advisory Panel Releases Report on Turkey and Project-Related Security and Human Rights Issues in Azerbaijan, Georgia and Turkey," December 17, 2003, www.prnewswire.co.uk.

15. In its report, "Principles, Profits or Just PR—Triple P Investments under the Principles," June 2004, Banktrack, for example, suggested that the project continued "virtually unaltered" despite the adoption of principles. Furthermore, in June 2003, seventy-two human rights and environment groups from twenty-nine countries called for a moratorium on the BTC pipeline, arguing that it would worsen the human rights situation along the pipeline route and that a background of lack of freedom of speech in the region made proper consultation impossible (www.bakuceyhan.org.uk/press_releases/news08. htm).

16. For a copy of ABN AMRO's press release of December 10, 2003, explaining the reasons for its participation in the project, see www.abnamro.com/ com/about/data/abnamro_btcpipeline.pdf. The BTC legal documents can be accessed on www.bakuceyhan.org.uk/links.htm.

17. Société Générale, "Sustainable Development," 2003, http://www. ir.socgen.com/en/download_a/Societe-Generale_2003-Annual-Report_ 4-sustainability.pdf (accessed December 4, 2007).

18. "Can Chuck Prince Clean Up Citi," *Business Week,* October 4, 2004.

19. Charles Prince, chairman and chief executive, Global Corporate and Investment Bank, Citigroup; "10 Global Banks Endorse Socially Responsible 'Equator Principles,'" *Agence France Presse,* June 5, 2003, http://www.equator-principles.com/afp1.shtml (accessed December 4, 2007).

20. See note 9.

21. Alison Maitland, "Barclays Banks on a Good Name," *Financial Times,* February 19, 2004.

22. See note 9.

23. Quoted from Z. Greenfield, "The Equator Principles: A New Industry Framework for Environmental and Social Standards in Global Project Finance

Lending" (paper based on an internship at Citigroup as Columbia Business School's Social Enterprise Program, MBA05 Columbia Business School, 2004), http://www2.gsb.columbia.edu/socialenterprise/downloads/EquatorPrinciplesZevGreenfield.pdf (accessed December 4, 2007).

5. Pharmaceuticals and Corporate Responsibility

1. All data refer to the quarter ending June 30, 2005, and were taken from the Web site of the Smith Barney group (www.smithbarney.com).

2. Frank R. Lichtenberg, "Sources of U.S. Longevity Increase, 1960–1997" (NBER Working Paper No. W8755, Columbia Business School, New York, February 2002).

3. To increase the life expectancy of one person by one year.

4. Cited in "Prescription for Change," *The Economist,* June 16, 2005, http://www.economist.com/background/displaystory.cfm?story_id=4053970 (accessed November 30, 2007).

5. For details, see The Business Enterprise Trust, Cases 9-991-021, 9-991-022, 9-991-023, and 9-991-024 and also P. Roy Vagelos and Louis Galambos, "The Moral Corporation," *Medicine, Science, and Merck* (New York: Cambridge University Press, 2004).

6. Vagelos and Galambos, "The Moral Corporation," 254.

7. "Drug Companies in the Dock," *Economist (London)* 359, no. 8218 (2001): 65.

8. Nonsteroidal anti-inflammatory drugs—a class that included aspirin, ibuprofen (Advil), and most over-the-counter painkillers.

9. For more details, see David P. Baron, *Business and Its Environment,* 5th ed. (Upper Saddle River, NJ: Prentice Hall, 2005), 727–28.

10. The companies are Abbot Laboratories, Astra Zeneca, Bristol Meyers Squibb, GlaxoSmithKline, Janssen, LifeScan, Novartis, OrthoMcNeil, Pfizer, Sanofi Aventis, Takeda, and TAP Pharmaceutical.

11. For details, see John Luke Gallup and Jeffrey D. Sachs, "The Economic Burden of Malaria," *American Journal of Tropical Medicine and Hygiene* 64, Suppl. no. 1 (2001): 85–96, http://www.ajtmh.org/cgi/reprint/64/1_suppl/85 (accessed November 30, 2007).

12. "Vaccinating The World's Poor," *Business Week,* April 26, 2004, http://www. businessweek.com/magazine/content/04_17/b3880098.htm (accessed November 30, 2007).

13. For more details, see www.clintonfoundation.org/programs.

6. Wal-Mart and Starbucks

1. See Robert S. Pindyck and Daniel L. Rubinfeld, *Microeconomics,* 6th ed. (Upper Saddle River, NJ: Prentice Hall, 2005), 495–96.

2. See Pankaj Ghemawat, "Wal-Mart Stores' Discount Operations," *Harvard Business School Cases,* August 19, 1986.

3. Ibid.

4. "Is Wal-Mart Unstoppable?" *The Economist,* December 6, 2001.

5. Ibid.

6. The numbers refer to 2004: see "Wal-Mart: How Big Can It Grow?" *The Economist,* April 15, 2004.

7. Ghemawat, "Wal-Mart Stores' Discount Operations."

8. Ibid.

9. Wal-Mart retained Global Insight to conduct this study, that is, Global Insight did not have an arm's-length relationship with Wal-Mart. The Global Insight study is entitled "The Economic Impact of Wal-Mart" and dated November 2 2005.

10. The figures for the United States as a whole are not conventional averages but weighted averages, with the weights reflecting the percentage of Wal-Mart employees in a particular position in a particular MSA.

11. Greg Hughes et al., "U.S. Productivity Growth, 1995–2000," McKinsey Global Institute, October 2001, cited in Pankaj Ghemawat, Ken A. Mary, and Stephen P. Bradley, "Wal-Mart Stores in 2003," *Harvard Business School Cases,* revised January 30, 2004.

12. Jerry Hausman and Ephraim Leibtag, "Consumer Benefits from Increased Competition in Shopping Outlets: Measuring the Effect of Wal-Mart," *Journal of Applied Econometrics* 22, no. 7 (2007): 1157–77.

13. Emek Basker, "Job Creation or Destruction? Labor-Market Effects of Wal-Mart Expansion," *Review of Economics and Statistics* 87, no. 1 (February 2005), http://ssrn.com/abstract=371102 (accessed December 30, 2007).

14. David Neumark, Junfu Zhang, and Stephen Ciccarella, "The Effects of Wal-Mart on Local Labor Markets" (working paper 11782, National Bureau of Economic Research, Cambridge, MA, November 2005).

15. Thomas A. Hemphill, "Rejuvenating Wal-Mart's Reputation," *Business Horizons* 48, no. 1 (January-February 2005): 11–21, 13.

16. Ibid.; cites a figure of 38 percent without giving a source.

17. Michael Barbaro, "Putting on the Brakes," *Washington Post,* May 23, 2005, E01.

18. Ransom A. Myers and Boris Worm, "Rapid Worldwide Depletion of Predatory Fish Communities," *Nature* 423 (2003): 280–83.

19. Michael Grunwald, "Warming to the Inconvenient Facts," *Washington Post,* July 23, 2006, B01.

20. John M. Broder, "Voters in Los Angeles Suburb Say No to a Big Wal-Mart," *The New York Times,* April 8, 2004.

21. Barbaro, "Putting on the Brakes."

22. Market capitalization as of June 21, 2006.

23. Quoted from http://www.starbucks.com/aboutus/default.asp (accessed June 23, 2006).

24. Available at http://www.starbucks.com/aboutus/FY05_CSR_Total.pdf (accessed December 1, 2007).

25. James E. Austin and Cate Reavis, "Starbucks and Conservation International," *Harvard Business School Cases*, October 2, 2002, p. 3.

26. Details are given in Austin and Reavis, "Starbucks and Conservation International." Most of the details of the collaboration between Starbucks and Conservation International are taken from this source.

7. Interface and Monsanto

1. For more background on Interface, see Rogelio Oliva and James Quinn, "Interface's Evergreen Services Agreement," *Harvard Business School Cases,* February 25, 2003.

2. Quoted from Oliva and Quinn.

3. For background on Monsanto, see Ulrich Steger et al., "Monsanto's Genetically Modified Organisms: The Battle for Hearts and Shopping Aisles," International Institute for Management Development, March 20, 2003; Michael D.

Watkins and Ann Leamon, "Robert Shapiro and Monsanto," *Harvard Business School Cases,* April 10, 2001. The investment advisory group Innovest has an interesting analyst's report on Monsanto: "Monsanto & Genetic Engineering: Risks for Investors," Innovest, http://www.innovestgroup.com/pdfs/2005-01-01_Monsanto_GeneticEngineering.pdf (accessed November 22, 2007).

4. See Joan Magretta, "Growth Through Global Sustainability: An Interview with Monsanto's CEO Robert B. Shapiro," in *Harvard Business Review on Business and the Environment,* ed. Amory Lovins and L. Hunter Lovins (Harvard Business Review Press Book, 2002).

5. For more information, see Stephen L. Buchmann and Gary Paul Nabhan, *The Forgotten Pollinators* (Washington, DC: Island Press, 1997) and Gretchen Daily, ed., *Nature's Services: Societal Dependence on Natural Ecosystems* (Washington, DC: Island Press, 1997), esp. Chapter 8, "Services Provided by Pollinators," by Stephen L. Buchmann and Gary Paul Nabhan .

6. Watkins and Leamon, "Robert Shapiro and Monsanto," 12.

7. "Monsanto & Genetic Engineering: Risks for Investors," 19, 20.

8. Ibid., 36.

8. Outsourcing

1. Ann Harrison and Jason Scorse, "The Nike Effect: Anti-Sweatshop Activists and Labor Market Outcomes in Indonesia" (working paper, University of California—Berkeley, Department of Agricultural and Resource Economics, March 2004), http://www.econ.yale.edu/seminars/trade/tdw04/Harrison_032204.pdf (accessed December 5, 2007).

2. "Nike CEO Phil Knight Announces New Labor Initiatives," *PR Newswire,* May 12, 1998, cited in Jennifer Burns and Debora L. Spar, "Hitting the Wall: Nike and International Labor Practices," *Harvard Business School Cases,* January 19, 2000.

3. Quoted in David P. Baron, *Business and Its Environment,* 5th ed. (Upper Saddle River, NJ: Prentice Hall, 2005), 122.

4. Ibid., 121.

5. Ibid.

6. For details see Forest Reinhardt, Charles Veillon, Harvard Business School Cases 2006.

7. Harrison and Scorse, "The Nike Effect."

8. Ibid.

9. Jagdish Bhagwati, *In Defense of Globalization* (New York: Oxford University Press, 2004).

10. Eric Edmonds and Nina Pavcnik, "Does Globalization Increase Child Labor? Evidence from Vietnam" (working paper, National Bureau of Economic Research, Cambridge, MA, February 2002), http://www.nber.org/papers/w8760 (accessed December 5, 2007), cited in Bhagwati, *In Defense of Globalization.*

11. For more details, see the InsightNewsTV video clip on this available at http://video.google.com/videoplay?docid=4786079244183070132.

12. Olivier Cadot and Daniel Traça, "Soccer Balls Made for Children by Children? Child Labor in Pakistan (A B)," NSEAD, 2001.

13. Usman Khan, founder of Sudhaar, quoted in "Soccer Balls Made for Children by Children: Child Labor in Pakistan (A)," INSEAD case 300-004-1, 1999. All the information about soccer-ball manufacture is taken from this case and its companion "Soccer Balls Made for Children by Children: Child Labor in Pakistan (B)," INSEAD case 301-144-1, 2001.

14. Lauren Foster and Alexandra Harvey, "Why Ethical Sourcing Means Show and Tell," *Financial Times,* April 22, 2005.

15. Available at http://www.nike.com/nikebiz/nikebiz.jhtml?page=29&item=fy04.13. Available at http://www.nike.com/nikebiz/nikebiz.jhtml?page=29&item=fy04.

9. Getting Rich by Selling to the Poor

1. "A Survey of Microfinance," *The Economist,* November 5–11, 2005, p. 12.

2. See Beatriz Armendáriz and Jonathan Morduch, *The Economics of Microfinance* (Cambridge, MA: MIT Press, 2005), 161.

3. Evaristus Mainsah et al., "Grameen Bank: Taking Capitalism to the Poor," *Chazen Web Journal of International Business,* Spring 2004, http://www2.gsb.columbia.edu/journals/files/chazen/Grameen_Bank_v04.pdf (accessed December 5, 2007).

4. CIA, *The World Factbook 2003*, s.v. "Bangladesh," https://www.cia.gov/library/publications/the-world-factbook/geos/bg.html (accessed December 5, 2007).

5. "A Survey of Microfinance," 10.

6. See Beatriz Armendáriz and Jonathan Morduch, "Beyond Group Lending," in *The Economics of Microfinance* (Cambridge, MA: MIT Press, 2005).

7. Shahidur R. Khandker, *Fighting Poverty with Microcredit: Experience in Bangladesh* (New York: Oxford University Press, 1998); Shahidur R. Khandker, "Micro-Finance and Poverty: Evidence from Bangladesh," *Grameen Dialogue*, no. 54 (April 2003), http://www.grameen-info.org/dialogue/dialogue54/coverstory.html (accessed December 5, 2007).

8. "A Survey of Microfinance," 10.

9. See http://www.bwtp.org/arcm/indonesia/II_Organisations/MF_Providers/BRI.htm (accessed December 5, 2007).

10. Taken from http://www.profundinternacional.com/htm/invest_perf_sum.htm (accessed December 5, 2007).

11. "A Survey of Microfinance," 12–13.

12. See "Letter of the Chairman," http://www.profundinternacional.com/htm/letter.htm (accessed December 5, 2007).

13. "A Survey of Microfinance," 11.

14. See Armendáriz and Morduch, "Beyond Group Lending."

15. A phrase introduced by C. K. Prahalad in his book *The Fortune at the Bottom of the Pyramid: Eradicating Poverty through Profits* (Philadelphia, PA: Wharton School Publishing, 2005).

16. Goiter is an "enlargement of the thyroid gland, causing a prominent swelling at the throat. The thyroid can grow to 50 times its normal weight, interfere with breathing and swallowing, and cause a choking feeling. Simple (endemic) goitre, the most common, is due to low iodine intake. It and related conditions result from various defects in thyroid hormone synthesis (hypothyroidism)," http://www.britannica.com/ebc/article-9365772?query=hyperthyroidism&ct= (accessed November 13, 2005).

17. There is a similarity to the "Tupperware parties" and "Avon Ladies," who used to sell these products to the middle classes in the United States in the 1950s and 1960s.

18. For details on this and other points relating to HHL's experiences in India, see Prahalad, *The Fortune at the Bottom of the Pyramid*, Part II, Section II.

19. See C. K. Prahalad and Stuart L. Hart, "The Fortune at the Bottom of the Pyramid," *Strategy + Business,* First Quarter (2002): 2–14, http://www.

strategy-business.com/press/16635507/11518 (accessed December 5, 2007). See also http://en.wikipedia.org/wiki/Arvind_Mills.

10. Cell phones and Development

1. Lars-Hendrik Roller and Leonard Waverman, "Telecommunications Infrastructure and Economic Development: A Simultaneous Approach," *The American Economic Review* 91, no. 4 (September 2001): 909–23.

2. Diane Coyle, "Overview," in *Africa: The Impact of Mobile Phones* (The Vodafone Policy Paper Series, Number 3, March 2005), http://www.vodafone. com/etc/medialib/attachments/cr_downloads.Par.78351.File.dat/GPP_SIM_ paper_3.pdf (accessed December 6, 2007).

3. Joseph Winter, "Telecoms Thriving in Lawless Somalia," BBC News, November 19, 2004, http://news.bbc.co.uk/2/hi/africa/4020259.stm (accessed December 6, 2007).

4. Peter Baumgartner, *Tages-Anzeiger,* Zurich, Switzerland, November 26, 2003.

5. Jonathan Samuel, Niraj Shah, and Wenona Hadingham, "Mobile Communications in South Africa, Tanzania and Egypt: Results from Community and Business Surveys," in *Africa: The Impact of Mobile Phones* (The Vodafone Policy Paper Series, Number 3, March 2005), http://www.vodafone.com/etc/ medialib/attachments/cr_downloads.Par.78351.File.dat/GPP_SIM_paper_ 3.pdf (accessed December 6, 2007).

6. Leonard Waverman, Meloria Meschi, and Melvyn Fuss, "The Impact of Telecoms on Economic Growth in Developing Countries," in *Africa: The Impact of Mobile Phones* (The Vodafone Policy Paper Series, Number 3, March 2005), http://www.vodafone.com/etc/medialib/attachments/cr_downloads.Par.78351. File.dat/GPP_SIM_paper_3.pdf (accessed December 6, 2007).

7. For more details on this case, Marco Visscher, "How One New Company Brought Hope to One of the World's Poorest Countries," *ODE,* January/ February 2005.

8. "Mobile Phones and Development," *The Economist,* March 10, 2005.

9. See "Vodacom: Extending Telecom Services to South Africa's Poor," World Business Council for Sustainable Development, http://www.wbcsd.org/

web/publications/case/vodafone_full_case_final_web.pdf (accessed December 6, 2007).

10. For more information, see C. K. Prahalad, *The Fortune at the Bottom of the Pyramid: Eradicating Poverty through Profits* (Philadelphia, PA: Wharton School Publishing, 2005), Part II, Section IV; and also World Bank, "India—The Indian Oilseed Complex: Capturing Market Opportunities," July 31, 1997, http://www-wds.worldbank.org/external/default/WDSContentServer/WDSP/IB/1997/07/31/000009265_3971104184215/Rendered/PDF/multi_page.pdf (accessed December 6, 2007).

11. Measuring Responsibility

1. The U.K. government has removed the original proposal from its Web site: a summary can be found at http://www.sustainability.com/insight/issue-brief.asp?id=283.

2. For more information, see http://www.intrinsec.co.uk/docs/Business%20Review.pdf and also Wikipedia at http://en.wikipedia.org/wiki/Companies_Act_2006#General_provisions.

3. For details, see Maef Woods, "The Global Reporting Initiative," *The CPA Journal* June (2003): 7, cited in David Vogel, *The Market For Virtue: The Potential and Limits of Corporate Social Responsibility* (Washington, DC: Brookings Institution Press, 2005). There is also a compilation of data about different countries' rules in "KPMG International Survey of Corporate Responsibility Reporting 2005," KPMG International, June 2005, http://www.kpmg.com/Industries/IM/Other/CRSurvey.htm (accessed December 2007).

4. "What is a Company's Role in Society? Gap Inc. 2005–2006 Social Responsibility Report," Gap Inc., http://www.gapinc.com/public/documents/CSR_Report_05_06.pdf (accessed December 7, 2007).

5. Some classic references on this are P. S. Dasgupta, S. Marglin, and A. K. Sen, *Guidelines for Project Evaluation* (New York: United Nations, 1972) and Ian D. Little and James A. Mirrlees, *Manual of Industrial Project Analysis for Developing Countries* (Paris: OECD, 1969).

6. The valuation of $1 to a poor person need not be completely subjective. Most advanced countries levy taxes to provide money to raise the incomes of

their poorest members, and from the tax rates and the amount of redistribution it is possible to infer the value placed on raising the incomes of the poorest.

7. The Clean Development Mechanism is a provision of the Kyoto Protocol that allows firms in advanced countries to pay developing countries to reduce emissions instead of doing so themselves.

8. In BP, the output of oil and gas includes that produced by its Russian subsidiary TNK.

9. Available at http://cdiac.esd.ornl.gov/pns/convert.html.

12. Social and Environmental Policies and Corporate Strategy

1. See their mission statement at http://www.americanapparel.net/contact/ourworkers.html.

13. Conclusions

1. These are not usually U.S. or European timber companies.

2. Factual information on the company and a summary of the allegations against it can be found in Wikipedia at http://en.wikipedia.org/wiki/Rimbunan_Hijau. This site also has links to the company's home page and the home pages of various environmental groups.

3. For details, see http://www.commondreams.org/news2005/0303-16.htm.

4. Details are on the U.S. Treasury's Web site at http://www.ustreas.gov/offices/enforcement/ofac/programs/sudan/sudan.pdf.

5. David B. Ottaway, "Chinese Fought on NYSE Listing," *Washington Post,* January 27, 2000; "China's Involvement in Sudan: Arms and Oil," *Human Rights Watch,* November 2003, http://www.hrw.org/reports/2003/sudan1103/26.htm#_Toc54492754 (accessed December 19, 2007).

6. http://www.usdoj.gov/criminal/fraud/docs/dojdocb.html (accessed December 7, 2007).

Note: Page numbers in italics indicate tables and figures.

Department of Trade and Industry
(DTI) report, 209–10
Deutsche Bank, 188
Dodge v. *Ford,* 15–16
domestic firms, wages in, 161, 162
Dow Chemical, 11, 25
Dowell, Glen, 33–34, 249n. 14
downscaling, 187
downsizing, 188
drug companies: critical position
of, 106; market economy, 109
Du Pont, 25

e-choupals, 204
Ecology of Commerce, The,
137–38
efficiency wage theory, 26–27
Elliston, Simon, 73, 252n. 6
employee productivity, 26–27
endogeneity, 123
Environmental Assessment (EA),
77, 78
environmental management plan
(EMP), 77, 78
Environmental Protection Agency
(EPA), 23, 243
EP Lite, 82–83
Equator banks, 86–87, 92
Equator Principles (EP), 73;
background of, 68–70; in BP,
85; business case for, 87–91;
in Citigroup, 82–83; collective
corporate responsibility and,
232–33; consequences of,
83–86; development of, 70–72;

drafting, 72–73; elements of,
76–79; evaluation of, 91–95;
evolution of, 86–87; implications
of, 83–86; launch of, 81; lending
banks and, 93–94; lessons from,
94–95; limitations of, 92–93;
marketing and, 80; reactions
to, 81–82; test-marketing and,
79–80; web site of, 80
Evergreen Services Agreement
(ESA), 138, 139–40, 256n. 1
Evian Natural Spring Water, 38
exclusionary screens, 56, 57
exporting firms, wages in, 161, 162
external cost: BP and, 10–11;
defined, 9; Dow Chemical
and, 11; Heinz and, 11–12;
Monsanto and, 12; Starbucks
and, 12; valuing, 219, 220
Extractive Industries Transparency
Initiative (EITI), 213
Exxon Mobil, 63; CSR report of,
213–14; direct GHG emission
and, 222; external benefits value
and, 222; income statement of,
221; indirect GHG emission
and, 223

Fair Labor Association (FLA), 172,
232–33
Financial Accounting Standard
Boards (FASB), 139–40
Financial Times, 53, 74–75, 170
First Theorem of Welfare
Economics, The, 9, 17